FROM THE LIBRARY OF

# CHARLES
# SPURGEON

SELECTIONS FROM WRITERS
WHO INFLUENCED HIS
*Spiritual Journey*

COMPILED BY

## JAMES STUART BELL

INCLUDING THE WRITINGS *of* JONATHAN EDWARDS
MATTHEW HENRY • COTTON MATHER • JOHN BUNYAN

BETHANY HOUSE PUBLISHERS
*a division of Baker Publishing Group*
Minneapolis, Minnesota

© 2012 by James Stuart Bell

Published by Bethany House Publishers
11400 Hampshire Avenue South
Bloomington, Minnesota 55438
www.bethanyhouse.com

Bethany House Publishers is a division of
Baker Publishing Group, Grand Rapids, Michigan

Printed in the United States of America

All rights reserved. No part of this publication may be reproduced, stored in a retrieval system, or transmitted in any form or by any means—for example, electronic, photocopy, recording—without the prior written permission of the publisher. The only exception is brief quotations in printed reviews.

Library of Congress Cataloging-in-Publication Data
From the library of Charles Spurgeon : selections from writers who influenced his spiritual journey / compiled by James Stuart Bell.
    p.  cm.
    Summary: "A collection of more than 200 readings drawn from authors who influenced Charles Spurgeon. Includes an in-depth introduction to Spurgeon and his work"—Provided by publisher.
    Includes bibliographical references and index.
    ISBN 978-0-7642-0861-4 (hardcover : alk. paper)
    1. Spurgeon, C. H. (Charles Haddon), 1834–1892—Miscellanea. 2. Christianity—Miscellanea. 3. Christian life—Miscellanea. 4. Spiritual life—Christianity—Miscellanea. I. Bell, James S.
    BX6495.S7F76 2012
    286′.1092—dc23                                           2011044570

Scripture quotations are from the King James Version of the Bible.

Other versions are used in the excerpts but not identified.

Cover design by John Hamilton Design

Author is represented by Whitestone Communications, Inc.

12  13  14  15  16  17  18      7  6  5  4  3  2  1

I dedicate this book to Greg Shaw, friend and neighbor, who has a passion for the writings of the spiritual giants who've gone before us.

# CONTENTS

# ACKNOWLEDGMENTS

I WOULD LIKE TO THANK THE STAFF at Bethany House, especially Kyle Duncan, for supporting the value of exploring the libraries of great Christians and sharing those contributions to the spiritual formation of these men used powerfully by God. This volume follows *From the Library of A. W. Tozer,* and it is my hope that Spurgeon's library will be just as edifying to the reader. I also want to thank my colleague Sam O'Neal for his invaluable assistance.

# INTRODUCTION

A FIFTEEN-YEAR-OLD BOY was sitting in the Primitive Methodist Chapel in Colchester, England, when the preacher turned his way and said: "Young man, you look very miserable. You always will be miserable—miserable in life and miserable in death—if you don't obey my text. But if you obey now, this moment you will be saved."

The young man on the receiving end of this admonition was Charles Haddon Spurgeon. The text in question was Isaiah 45:22, where God says, "Look unto me, and be ye saved, all the ends of the earth: for I am God, and there is none else."

Spurgeon did look unto God in that moment, and what he saw made an immediate and profound impact. "I had this vision," he later recalled in his autobiography, "not a vision to my eyes, but to my heart. I saw what a Savior Christ was. . . . Now I can never tell you how it was, but I no sooner saw whom I was to believe than I also understood what it was to believe, and I did believe in one moment."

One moment changed the course of Spurgeon's life forever. More, it changed the course of the church he served more than forty years, eventually establishing himself as one of the finest preachers the world has ever known.

# A Short Biography

Born in 1834, C. H. Spurgeon was raised alternately in the homes of his father and grandfather, both of whom were nonconformist (non-Anglican) ministers in the Calvinist mode. Even so, the man later called "the Prince of Preachers" didn't mesh well with the family faith in his early years. In his autobiography, he described his formative years as spiritually depressing: "I was years and years upon the brink of hell—I mean in my own feeling. I was unhappy, I was desponding, I was despairing. I dreamed of hell. My life was full of sorrow and wretchedness, believing that I was lost."

When Spurgeon's spiritual situation changed in 1850 at the Primitive Methodist Church, his attitudes quickly changed with it. In 1851 he broke from the denomination of his father and grandfather, choosing instead a rare hybridization and functioning as a Calvinist Baptist. He began distributing tracts and visiting the poor, and soon he joined the lay preachers' association.

Herein Spurgeon found his calling. He preached his first sermon at Teversham in Cambridgeshire and accepted his first pastorate, as a teenager, in the village of Waterbeach. He was an immediate success; within two years he accepted a call to fulfill a six-month preaching engagement at New Park Street Chapel in London. He moved to the city and never moved out.

Throughout the course of his ministry Spurgeon preached all over London—including the halls at Exeter and Surrey Gardens—and other parts of England. In 1861 his congregation moved into the newly completed Metropolitan Tabernacle, which could hold nearly six thousand per service.

In 1856 Spurgeon founded a pastor's college that moved to the Tabernacle in 1861. It subsequently was renamed Spurgeon's College in 1923 and still exists today. He also presided over an orphanage, which he founded in 1867, and a publishing arm that distributed books and pamphlets.

This latter endeavor quickly became an influential ministry wing. In 1865 Spurgeon began editing a monthly magazine called *The Sword and the Trowel*, and he continued for twenty-eight years until his death. All told, he wrote and edited more than two hundred books, albums, and pamphlets—the most famous being *The Treasury of David* (a commentary on Psalms) and a daily devotional called *Morning by Morning; Evening by Evening*. Most impressive, his sermons were published weekly in various periodicals, a practice that started the year after he arrived in London. Today his collected sermons fill sixty-three volumes, each holding more than fifty sermons.

There's no doubt Spurgeon was a beloved and popular preacher—the most heard of his time, in fact. But his ministry was not without criticism and controversy. He was regularly lampooned by the secular press, most notably a publication called the *Saturday Review*. And he received regular criticism from fellow Protestants for his dramatic style and affinity for sentimental stories. Spurgeon's response to these latter reproaches is telling: "I am perhaps vulgar, but it is not intentional, save that I must and will make people listen. My firm conviction is that we have had enough polite preachers."

The most notable controversy connected with his ministry is known historically as the "Down-Grade Controversy," which began in 1887. In several *Sword and the Trowel* articles, Spurgeon criticized members of his denomination (and the broader Protestant church) for "down-grading" biblical doctrine and theology through liberal interpretations. Specifically, he felt three essential doctrines were being abandoned: biblical infallibility, substitutionary atonement, and the finality of judgment for those who die outside of Christ.

Spurgeon's claims were met with intense opposition and an

increasing furor, which he attempted to diffuse by resigning from the Baptist Union. This did not work, and the debate that raged on more than a year ultimately resulted in Spurgeon's being censured by the Council of the Baptist Union, the denomination suffering a damaging schism, and Spurgeon's own health taking a turn for the worse.

C. H. Spurgeon preached his final sermon in June of 1891. He died six months later and was survived by his wife and twin sons. More than sixty thousand came to pay homage during the three days his body was displayed at the Metropolitan Tabernacle; more than a hundred thousand lined London's streets to watch the funeral parade that officially announced the Prince of Preachers had finished his earthly work and had been faithful.

## WHY YOU SHOULD READ THIS BOOK

C. H. Spurgeon was an extraordinary man, but one of the most remarkable elements of his story is his lack of formal education. His schooling as a youth was spotty at best, and he accepted his first pastorate without having earned a degree.

So how did this relatively uneducated man rise to take his place among the most influential preachers the world has ever seen?

The primary answer is that Spurgeon was a ferocious learner despite his lack of formal training—a characteristic driven by his voracious capacity for reading. At the time of his death, his library held more than twelve thousand volumes, many of which bore his handwritten comments and notations.

Much of Spurgeon's intellectual and spiritual formation was contained in those volumes. He committed himself to learning from the spiritual giants who'd gone before him, and in part because of his devoted study he took his place among them.

Thus this book's value. These pages contain more than 150

excerpted readings from those whose writings were instrumental in Spurgeon's development. The highlighted writers are some of the most famous and influential minds in the history of Christianity, and the excerpts provided below represent the pinnacle of their achievements.

Why should you read this material? Because C. H. Spurgeon did, and it played a significant role in his spiritual growth. These served as his textbooks and professors combined, and they can serve you as well.

## How to Read This Book

Each of this book's eight chapters emphasizes a major theme from Spurgeon's life and writings—from the power of prayer, to evangelism, to God's Word and Christian doctrine. The short readings themselves focus on subjects that are important to your life and your connection with God.

One approach could be to make this book a part of your daily devotional experience. Consider reading one excerpt each day, along with a passage of Scripture. As you do, be sure to allow yourself times of silent reflection in order to think deeply about what each author is communicating. You may even want to read this book in concert with *Morning by Morning; Evening by Evening* (current editions are titled *Morning and Evening*) or another of Spurgeon's written works, thereby gaining a real-time understanding of how these writers influenced and guided him.

This book can also serve as an excellent educational resource. A broader look at each chapter will impart a great deal about the essential doctrines and practices of our faith; it will also help you find wisdom for developing transformative habits and for overcoming many obstacles.

If you aren't familiar with all the authors represented in the following pages, learning a bit about their stories in the Biographies, near book's end, can yield appreciation for what they have to say. In addition, as you identify certain passages and writers you find especially impactful, consider reading the complete volumes from which the excerpts were taken. You'll find the source of each excerpt listed on the same page; you can identify all the books excerpted by each author in the Excerpts Taken From . . . section.

## MOVING FORWARD

Charles Haddon Spurgeon was a man who desired to be used greatly by God—to bring to light the power of God's Word and to harvest souls for His kingdom. He's known as a spiritual giant because he poured all of himself into this desire, and it is well for the church that he succeeded.

A significant reason for that success was Spurgeon's willingness to be continually discipled by the great men and women of God—the Puritans, evangelists, writers, and teachers—who'd preceded him through centuries of church history. His mentors had one thing in common: in service to Jesus Christ they sought to become physicians working to diagnose and heal the souls of men and women in their care. The Word of God was their medicine, and they delivered it through both word and deed.

Take advantage of the opportunity you now have to be similarly discipled. Listen carefully and prayerfully to these teachings of God's Word. Allow that Word to continue transforming your life. You—and those under *your* care—will never be the same.

# WORSHIP:

## THE CHIEF END OF MAN

"My soul, bow down under a sense of thy natural sinfulness, and worship thy God. Admire the grace which saves thee—the mercy which spares thee—the love which pardons thee!"

—*Morning and Evening*

# WILLIAM BATES

## The Great Duty of Resignation

And what is man? A little breathing dust. God is infinitely above
us, and so strangely condescends, in having a tender care of us,
that the psalmist was swallowed up in ecstasy and amazement at
the thought of it: "What is mankind that You are mindful of them,
human beings that You care for them?" (Psalm 8:4). No, we are
beneath His anger, as a worm is not worthy of the indignation of
an angel.

Now the more we magnify God and exalt His authority in our
judgments, the more our wills are prepared to yield to Him. His
excellency will make us afraid to oppose His providence. When
the Son of God appeared to Saul in His glory and commanded in
person, he presently let fall his arms of defiance and said, "Lord,
what will You have me to do?" His resignation was absolute; nothing was so hard to do, nothing so formidable to suffer; but he was
ready to accomplish and endure in obedience to Christ.

The more we debase and vilify ourselves, the more easy it will
be to bear what God inflicts; humility disposes to submission. Our
passions are not excited at the breaking of an ordinary glass; but
if a vessel of crystal is broken, it moves us. The lower esteem we
have of ourselves, the less we shall be transported for any breach
that is made upon us.

We read in the history of Job many heavy complaints uttered
by him of his sufferings, all the sad figures of passionate eloquence

made use of to represent them, and the fruitless essays of his friends, which did rather exasperate than appease his spirit. And it is very observable that when the Lord interposed Himself to justify the ways of His providence, He did not charge upon him the guilt of his sins that deserved the severest judgments, but appeared in glory and reminded him of his original nothing. "Where were you when I laid the earth's foundation? Tell me, if you understand" (Job 38:4). He opens to him some of the excellencies of the Deity in the works of creation and providence, and the present effect was that Job adored with humble reverence the divine majesty and acknowledged his own unworthiness: "I am unworthy—how can I reply to You? I put my hand over my mouth. I spoke once, but I have no answer—twice, but I will say no more" (Job 40:4–5).

The thickest smoke, by ascending, dissipates and vanishes. If the troubled soul did ascend to heaven and consider that even the worst evils are either from the operation or permission of the divine providence, the cloudy disturbing thoughts and passions would be presently scattered. . . .

When any impatient thoughts arise, we should presently chain them up, for there are folly and fury in them. What am I, that my sullen spirit should dispute against the orders of heaven? That my passions should resist the will of the highest Lord? That my desires should depose Him from His throne? For that is what they do by implication and consequence—those who are vexed at His providence. A holy soul will tremble at the thought of it. Methinks God speaks to the afflicted and disturbed soul, in the words of the psalm, "Be still, and know that I am God." The actual consideration of His supremacy will be powerful to lay the growing storm of passions.

Impatience arises from the ignorance of God and ourselves.

# RICHARD SIBBES

## Divine Meditations

The whole life of a Christian should be nothing but praises and thanks to God; we should neither eat nor drink nor sleep, but eat to God and sleep to God and work to God and talk to God, do all to His glory and praise.

We glorify God when we exalt Him in our souls above all creatures in the world, when we give Him the highest places in our love and in our joy, when all our affections are set upon Him as our greatest good. This is seen also by opposition, when we will not offend God for any creature; when we can ask our affections, "Whom have I in heaven but You?" (Psalm 73:25).

In the covenant of grace God intends the glory of His grace above all. Now faith is fit for it, because it has a uniting virtue to knit us to the Mediator and to lay hold of a thing out of ourselves; it empties the soul of all idea of worth or strength or excellence in the creature, and so it gives all the glory to God and Christ.

To glory in any creature whatsoever is idolatry, first, because the mind sets up something to glory in which is not God. Secondly, it must be spiritual adultery to cleave to anything more than to God. Thirdly, it is bearing false witness to ascribe excellency where there is none. We have a prohibition: "Let not the wise man glory in his wisdom, nor the strong man in his strength, nor the rich man in his riches" (Jeremiah 9:23). God will not give His glory to another, and therefore when men will be meddling with that glory which belongs to God alone He blasts them aside as broken vessels and even disdains to use them.

All things out of God are only like the grass. When we rejoice in anything out of God, it is a childish joy as if we rejoiced only in flowers; after we have drawn out their sweetness we cast them away. All outward things are common to sinners as well as to saints, and without grace they will surely prove snares. At the hour of death what comfort can we have in them any further than with humility and love to God we have used them well? Therefore if we would have our hearts seasoned with true joy, let us labor to be faithful in our several places, and endeavor according to the gifts we have to glorify God.

This life is not a life for the body but for the soul, and therefore the soul should speak to the body: "If you move me to fulfill your desires now, you will lose me and yourself hereafter." But if the body be given up to Christ, then the soul will speak a good word for it in heaven: "Lord, there is a body of mine in the grave in yonder world that did fast for me and pray with me." It will speak for it as Pharaoh's butler to the king for Joseph.

It is rebellion against God for a man to make away with himself; the very heathens could say that we must not go out of our station till we be called. It is the voice of Satan, "Cast yourself down," but what says Paul to the jailer, "Do yourself no harm, for we are all here." We should so carry ourselves that we may be content to stay here till God has done that work He has to do in us and by us, and then He will call us hence in the best time.

# MATTHEW HENRY

## A Scripture Catechism in the Method
## of the Assembly's

**Question:** What is the chief end of man?

**Answer:** Man's chief end is to glorify God, and enjoy Him forever.

Is man a reasonable creature? Yes: for there is a spirit in man, and the inspiration of the Almighty gives him understanding (Job 32:8). Has he greater capacities than the brutes? Yes: God teaches us more than the beasts of the earth, and makes us wiser than the fowls of heaven (Job 35:11).

Is man his own maker? No: it is God that has made us, and not we ourselves (Psalm 100:3). Is he then his own master? No: there is a Lord over us (Psalm 12:4). Is he his own carver? No: should it be according to your mind? (Job 34:33). Is he his own end? No: for none of us lives to himself, or dies to himself (Romans 14:7).

Is it your business in the world to serve the flesh? No: for we are not debtors to the flesh, that we should live after the flesh (Romans 8:12). Is it to pursue the world? No: for we are not of the world (John 17:16).

Is your happiness bound up in the creature? No: for all is vanity and vexation of spirit (Ecclesiastes 1:14). Will the riches of the world make you happy? No: for a man's life consists not in the abundance of the things he possesses (Luke 12:15). Will the praise and applause of men make you happy? No: for it is vain glory (Galatians 5:26). Will sport and pleasure make you happy? No: for the wise man said of laughter, It is mad, and of mirth, What does it do? (Ecclesiastes 2:2). Can the gain of the world make you happy? No: for what is a man profited, if he gains the whole world and loses his own soul? (Matthew 16:26).

Is God then your chief end? Yes: for of Him, and through Him, and to Him are all things (Romans 11:36). Were you made for Him? Yes: this people have I formed for myself (Isaiah 43:21). Were you redeemed for Him? Yes: you are not your own, for you are bought with a price (1 Corinthians 6:19–20).

Is it your chief business to glorify God? Yes: we must glorify God in our body and in our spirit, which are God's (1 Corinthians 6:20). Must this be ultimately designed in all our actions? Yes: do all to the glory of God (1 Corinthians 10:31). Is God glorified by our praises? Yes: he that offers praise, glorifies me (Psalm 50:23). And is He glorified by our works? Yes: herein is my Father glorified, that you bear much fruit (John 15:8).

Is God your chief good? Yes: for happy are the people whose God is the Lord (Psalm 144:15). Does all good come from Him? Yes: for with Him is the fountain of life (Psalm 36:9). And is all good enjoyed in Him? Yes: the Lord is the portion of my inheritance, and of my cup (Psalm 16:5).

Is it your chief happiness then to have God's favor? Yes: for in His favor is life (Psalm 30:5). Is that the most desirable good? Yes: for His loving-kindness is better than life (Psalm 63:3). Do you desire it above any good? Yes: Lord, lift up the light of Your countenance upon us (Psalm 4:6–7). And should you give all diligence to make it sure? Yes: herein we labor, that whether present or absent, we may be accepted of the Lord (2 Corinthians 5:9).

Is communion with God in grace here the best pleasure? Yes: it is good for me to draw near to God (Psalm 73:28). Is the vision and fruition of God in glory hereafter the best portion? Yes: for in His presence there is fullness of joy (Psalm 16:11). Will you therefore set your heart upon this chief good? Yes: Lord, whom have I in heaven but You? And there is none upon earth that I desire besides You; when my flesh and my heart fail, God is the strength of my heart and my portion forever (Psalm 73:25–26).

# THOMAS GOUGE

## Christian Directions

At your first awakening in the morning, consecrate unto God the freshest of your thoughts by lifting up your heart to Him in praise and thanksgiving for the comfortable rest and refreshment He vouchsafed unto you last night. For, had not the Lord been the more gracious unto you, you might have slept the sleep of death; yes, you might have awoken with hell-chimes about your ears. What cause have you, therefore, to bless God for the mercies of the night—and the same for the renewing of His mercies with the day! Then heartily beg of God to keep you from all dangers that day, and especially from sinning against Him; also to direct, assist, and bless you in all your lawful undertakings.

Having thus consecrated your first waking moments unto God, then let out your heart in a serious meditation of God through some or other of His glorious attributes:

- **Of His infinite purity,** who is of purer eyes than to behold iniquity with the least approbation, but hates all sin with a perfect hatred, it being contrary to His nature. A serious consideration of this will, through God's blessing, prove very effectual for the suppressing of those worldly and impure thoughts that are apt to arise from your corrupt heart.

- **Of the almighty power of God,** whereby He is able to

supply all your wants, to support you under all your trials and temptations, and to carry you through all your undertakings.

- **Of God's continual presence about you,** and with you, wherever you are, and whatever you do. For He is about your bed and your path; He takes notice of all your actions, and when no man sees you, yet He sees you—the One before whose tribunal you must one day stand to give an account of all your actions.

- **Of the omniscience of God,** how he knows all things—even the secret thoughts of your heart and the inward intentions of your mind. Before God all things are naked and open. There is not an ambitious, worldly, or lustful thought in your heart that God is not privy to; yes, and He will bring every secret thing into judgment (Ecclesiastes 12:14). This, if it were seriously considered, would make you watchful over your very heart!

# THOMAS GOUGE

## Christian Directions

As you are rising out of your bed, take every occasion for holy and heavenly meditations. To give you some hints:

- When you see the nakedness of your body, let that mind you of your sins, which caused you first to be ashamed of it. For our first parents, before they had sinned, were not ashamed of their nakedness (Genesis 2:25). And the consideration thereof should stir you up earnestly to long after the robe of Christ's righteousness, and to be clothed with that which will make you lovely and amiable in the sight of God.

- Let your rising out of bed remind you of the resurrection from the death of sin unto the life of grace; likewise the resurrection of your body out of the grave into eternal life at the last day, when you and every one of us must appear before the great Judge to give an account of whatsoever we have done here.

- Let the light of the day mind you of Jesus Christ, who is often in Scripture described as light—yes, the true Light.

- When you are putting on your apparel, let out your heart in a serious meditation of the robe of Christ's righteousness. And by faith, apply Christ and His righteousness unto yourself, resting and relying upon it for the pardon and forgiveness of your sins here on earth, and for eternal salvation hereafter.

This will be a special means to keep worldly, wanton, and impure thoughts out of your heart, so that either they will not dare to come in or they shall more easily be kept out. This way your heart will be exceedingly fenced and guarded against the strategies of Satan, who wants to cast his hellish firebrands into your soul.

I say again: good and holy thoughts first let into the heart of a Christian will keep it in better tune all the day after.

But some will object to this, saying that to put in practice these rules and directions will take up too much time—more than their callings and employments will allow. True it is that some men's callings and employments do not allow them so much time as others do; yet there are none who cannot find some time for spiritual and heavenly meditations if it be no more than rising out of their beds and putting on their clothes.

If you have not time to put in practice all of these directions, at least you may go over some few of them. Yes, I shall give you this as my special advice: if you are strained for time, fix upon one or two of these directions rather than attempting to perform all of them in a perfunctory manner; do not ramble over them all every morning.

In addition to these morning meditations, as soon as you get up, go into your closet, or into some private place, and there offer up to God a morning sacrifice of praise and thanksgiving. Let anything be omitted rather than this. If your business be urgent and great, rise sooner. Do not attempt anything until you have commended yourself and your affairs to God by prayer. And indeed, how can you with any confidence expect God's blessing upon your pains and endeavors without it, this being the means sanctified by God for the obtaining of His blessing?

If you take any liberty to omit this duty, the devil will so work upon you that, little by little, you will wax weary of it if God's grace is not the more powerful in you.

# STEPHEN CHARNOCK

## Discourse on the Power of God

Wisdom and power are the grounds of the respect we give to men. And since they are both infinite in God, they create the foundation of a solemn honor to be returned to Him by His creatures.

If a man makes an ingenious machine, we honor him for his skill. If another man vanquishes a vigorous enemy, we admire him for his strength. Just so, shall not the efficacy of God's power in creation, government, and redemption enflame us with a sense of the honor of His name and perfections? We admire those princes that have vast empires, numerous armies, and the power to conquer their enemies and preserve their own people in peace. How much more ground have we to pay a mighty reverence to God, who, without trouble and weariness, made and manages this vast empire of the world by a word and gesture! What sensible thoughts have we of the power of the sun, the storms of the sea! These things that have no understanding have struck men with such a reverence that many have adored them as gods. Just so, what reverence and adoration does this mighty power, joined with an infinite wisdom in God, demand at our hands!

All religion and worship stands especially upon two pillars: goodness and power in God. If either of these were defective, all religion would faint away. We can expect no entertainment with Him without goodness, nor any benefit from Him without power. . . .

Because this attribute is a main foundation of prayer, the Lord's

Prayer is concluded with a doxology of it: "For Yours is the kingdom, the power, and the glory." As God is rich, possessing all blessings, so He is powerful and able to confer all blessings on us, and to make them efficacious to us. We could not, without consideration of it, pray in faith of success—nay, we could not pray at all—if His power were defective to help us, and His mercy too weak to relieve us. Who would humbly beg, or lie as a prostrate suppliant, to a feeble arm? It was upon this ability of God that our Savior built His petitions: "He offered up strong cries unto Him that was able to save him from death" (Hebrews 5:7). Abraham's faith hung upon the same string (Romans 4:21), and the church supplicates God to act according to the greatness of His power (Psalm 79).

In all our addresses this is to be eyed and considered: that God is able to help, to relieve, to ease me, to let my misery be never so great and my strength never so vigorous. "If You will, You can make me clean" (Matthew 8:2) was the consideration the leper had when he came to worship Christ. He was clear in His power, and therefore worshiped Him, though he was not equally clear in His will.

All worship is shot wrong that is not directed to, and conducted by, the thoughts of this attribute (whose assistance we need). When we beg the pardon of our sins, we should eye mercy and power. When we beg His righting us in any case where we are unjustly oppressed, we do not eye righteousness without power. When we plead the performance of His promise, we do not regard His faithfulness only without the prop of His power. As power ushers in all the attributes of God in their exercise and manifestation in the world, so should it be the target our eyes are fixed upon in all our acts of worship.

Without God's power, all His other attributes would be useless. In the same way, without due apprehensions of His power, our prayers will be faithless and comfortless.

31

# OCTAVIUS WINSLOW

## Words of Divine Comfort

"The Lord says, 'Those who honor Me I will honor'" (1 Samuel 2:30).

How necessary for our instruction and God's glory that we should accept His Word just as we find it, and not as interpreted by a fallible church or as reflected from a human standard. It is perilous to study the Bible in any other light than its own, or to recognize any other interpreter than its Divine Author. Guided by this precept, let us consider the words of God which suggest our present meditation: "Those who honor Me I will honor." They were originally spoken to Eli on the occasion of his preferring the sinful indulgence of his sons to the command and glory of God. By retaining them in the priests' offices, polluted by their iniquity and scandalized by their sacrilege, Eli had greatly dishonored God. It was on this solemn occasion that He spoke these words: "Those who honor Me I will honor, and those who despise Me shall be lightly esteemed."

The subject is solemn, searching, and instructive. God keep us from Eli's sin! May His glory be our first and supreme object. God is justly jealous of His honor. He would not be God, righteous and pure, were He to part with one scintillation of His glory. "My glory will I not give to another" (Isaiah 42:8). How, then, may I—trusting that, through electing love and sovereign grace, I am His adopted child, His chosen servant—best honor Him?

32

First, by fully believing in the divinity of His revealed Word. In magnifying His Word above His Name, God has demonstrated how closely entwined are His honor and His truth. To cast, then, a doubt upon the truth of God's Word is to cast the highest dishonor upon God Himself. My soul, beware of low views of inspiration, of tampering with the Bible, of caviling at any revealed truth; but, stand in awe of its divinity, adore its majesty, and bow unquestioningly to its authority. Then will God honor you, by making His Word your light in darkness, your joy in grief, your strength in service, your hope in despondency and despair. Thus, the gospel you do implicitly and fully accept will soothe you in life, support you in death, and be your glory and song through eternity. Thus honoring God in His Word, God will honor you by making that Word the joy and rejoicing of your soul.

Second, I honor God by trusting Him. As there is not a more God-dishonoring principle than unbelief, so there is not a more God-glorifying grace than the faith that reposes in Him, with a childlike and unquestioning confidence—a faith that trusts His veracity to fulfill, and His power to perform, all that He is pledged in His covenant and Word to do. My soul, you are tried, burdened, and in need. Have faith in God! Now is the time to bring honor and glory to His great Name by a simple, unhesitating trust in His power, faithfulness, and love. And this to comfort your sorrow, to counsel your perplexity, and to bring you out of trouble with the richest blessing springing therefrom. Then will your God honor you. . . .

Let me honor Christ by fully accepting His salvation. Oh, my soul, beware of placing your sin and guilt and unworthiness beyond the limit of Christ's ability and willingness to save. Oh! What dishonor to the Savior—a dishonor with which even devils are not chargeable—to doubt the efficacy of His blood to pardon and the merit of His righteousness to justify the very chief of sinners.

Lord! What honor have You put upon me, to ask me to believe, to accept, and to be saved! What marvelous condescension and grace that, in doing this, You should receive it as an honor done to You at my worthless hands. Blessed Lord! I will trample my own honor in the dust, if Yours be but reared upon its utter ruin. My self shall be uncrowned, that upon Your head the crown may flourish!

# RICHARD BAXTER

## The Reformed Pastor

When man was made perfect and placed in a perfect world, where all things were in perfect order, the whole creation was then man's book in which he was to read the nature and will of his great Creator. Every creature had the name of God so legibly engraved on it that man might run and read it. He could not open his eyes but he might see some image of God; but nowhere so fully and lively as in himself.

It was, therefore, his work to study the whole volume of nature, but first and most to study himself. And if man had held on in this course, he would have continued and increased in the knowledge of God and himself. But when he needed to know and love the creature and himself in a way of separation from God, he lost the knowledge both of the creature and of the Creator, so far as it could beatify and was worth the name of knowledge. And instead of it, he has got the unhappy knowledge that he affected even the empty notions and fantastic knowledge of the creature and himself, as thus separated. And thus, he that lived to the Creator, and upon him, now lives to and upon the other creatures, and on himself. And thus, "Every man at his best estate" (the learned as well as the illiterate) "is altogether vanity. Surely every man walks in a vain show; surely they are disquieted in vain" (Psalm 39:5–6).

And it must be well observed that as God did not lay aside the relation of a Creator by becoming our Redeemer, the work of redemption stands, in some respect, in subordination to that of creation, and the law of the Redeemer to the law of the Creator. So also the duties which we owed to God as Creator have not ceased, but the duties that we owe to the Redeemer, as such, are subordinate as well. It is the work of Christ to bring us back to God, and to restore us to the perfection of holiness and obedience; and as He is the way to the Father, so faith in Him is the way to our former employment and enjoyment of God.

I hope you perceive what I aim at in all this—namely, that to see God in His creatures, and to love Him, and converse with Him, was the employment of man in his upright state; that this is so far from ceasing to be our duty that it is the work of Christ to bring us, by faith, back to it; and therefore the most holy men are the most excellent students of God's works, and none but the holy can rightly study them or know them.

His works are great when they are sought out by those who take pleasure in them—not for themselves, but for Him that made them. Your study of physics and other sciences is not worth a rush if it be not God that you seek after in them. To see and admire, to reverence and adore, to love and delight in God, as exhibited in His works—this is the true and only philosophy. The contrary is mere foolery, and is so called again and again by God Himself. This is the sanctification of your studies when they are devoted to God, and when He is the end, the object, and the life of them all.

# WILLIAM AMES

## The Manner of Worship

Before the public and solemn hearing of the word and prayer, private prayer is required. And before private prayer, if it be solemn, there is required some meditation on those things with which our prayers have to do—whether about God, to whom we pray, or about ourselves, who are about to pray, or about the things which are to be prayed for.

The concomitant circumstances are reverence and devotion. A certain general reverence for God is part of any obedience that respects the commanding authority of God. But this particular reverence properly has to do with those acts of religion that stress the holiness of the things we do. Such reverence contains, first, a due prizing of the worth of such things; second, a fear of too much familiarity by which such things might be desecrated.

Devotion also contains two parts. First, a certain special readiness to perform those things which belong to the worship of God (Psalm 108:1–3). Second, a proper delight in performing them (Isaiah 58:13). Hence a greater and different concern is called for in hearing the word of God than in receiving the edicts of princes—and in calling upon the name of God than in making supplication to any man.

The consequent circumstances are two: first, to retain the force and, as it were, the taste of the worship in our minds; second, to fulfill its purpose and put it to use with full effort. The outward circumstances are those which belong to order and decency

(1 Corinthians 14:40). The general rule is that these be ordered in a way to make for the most edification (1 Corinthians 14:26). Such circumstances are place, time, and the like, which are adjuncts common to religious and civil acts.

These circumstances are likely to be called by some religious and ecclesiastical rites and ceremonies, but they have nothing proper to religion in their nature. Religious worship is not found in them, but the holiness of religious worship is in some way violated by their neglect and contempt. The common matter of order and decency which is equally necessary to religious and civil actions cannot be severed from religious worship without some loss of dignity and majesty.

# THOMAS MANTON

## A Treatise on Self-Denial

That self which we must hate or deny is that self which stands in opposition to God, or in competition with Him, and so jostles with Him for the throne. Lay aside God, and self steps in as the next heir—it is the great idol of the world ever since the fall, when men took the boldness to depose and lay aside God, as it were, and self succeeded in the throne. Fallen man, like Reuben, went up to his father's bed. Self intercepted all those respects and embraces which were due to God Himself, and so man became both his own idol and idolater.

If we would know when self is sinfully respected, we must consider what are the rights and the undoubted flowers of the crown of heaven; I mean, what are those special privileges and respects that are so appropriated to the godhead that they cannot without treason to the King of all the earth be alienated from Him or communicated to any creature? Now these are four:

First, as God is the first cause, so He would keep up the respects of the world to His majesty by dependence and trust. It is the ambition of man to affect an independency, to be a god to himself, sufficient for his own happiness. Our first parents greedily caught at that bait: "You shall be as gods" (Genesis 3:5). The devil meant it not in a blessed conformity, but a cursed self-sufficiency. And we are all apt to be taken in the same snare, which certainly is a very grievous sin. Nothing can be more hateful to God. This therefore is a great part of self-denial—to work us off from other dependences, and to trust in God alone.

Second, as God is the chief good, so He must have the highest esteem. Valuing other things above God is the ground of all miscarriage in the business of religion. When anything is honored above God, or made equal with God, or indulged against the will of God, then Dagon is set up, and the ark is made to fall.

Third, as God is the highest lord and most absolute sovereign, it is His peculiar prerogative to give laws to the creature; therefore self is not to interpose and give laws to us, but only God. His will must stand. The great contest indeed between God and the creature is just so: whose will shall stand, God's will or ours? Who shall prescribe to us, self or God? Fleshly nature sets up laws against laws, and our fleshly wills set up providence against providence. Self-will is betrayed by murmuring against God's providence, by rebellion against His laws, and when we are obstinate in our homage and obedience to self (Jeremiah 18:12). So James (1:14) the apostle makes it to be the root of all sin when a man is drawn away by his own lusts and his own will, which is set up against the laws of God.

Fourth, as God is the last end of our beings and actions, the supreme cause is to be the utmost end. "God made all things for Himself" (Proverbs 16:4). But now, in all that we do, we look to ourselves; vain man sets up self at the end of every action, and so he jostles out God. All the actions of life are but a kind of homage to the idol of self; if they eat and drink, it is to nourish self, a meat-offering and drink-offering to appetite. If they pray or praise, it is but to worship self, to advance the repute of self. The crown is taken from God's head; He is not made the utmost end. If they give alms, they are a sacrifice offered to the idol of self-estimation. "They give alms to be seen of men," says Christ; and in this self is set up, and God is deposed and laid aside.

# RICHARD SIBBES

## Divine Meditations

There are four things observable in the nature of love: first, an esteem of the party beloved; second, a desire to be joined to him; third, a settled contentment; fourth, a desire to please the party in all things. So there is first in every Christian a high estimation of God and of Christ; he makes choice of Him above all things, and speaks largely in His commendation. Second, he desires to be united to Him, and where this desire is, there is an intercourse; he will open his mind to Him by prayer and go to Him in all his consultations for His counsel. Third, he places contentment in Him alone, because in his worst conditions he is in peace and quiet if he may have His countenance shine upon him. Fourth, he seeks to please Him because he labors to be in such a condition that God may delight in him. His love stirs up his soul to remove all things distasteful to Him. He asks as David did, "Is there yet any that is left of the house of Saul, that I may show him kindness for Jonathan's sake?" (2 Samuel 9:1).

We see by experience that there is a succession of love; he that loves for beauty will despise when he sees a better. So it is in the soul respecting heavenly and earthly things; when the soul sees more excellence and a satisfying fullness in heavenly things, then the love of earthly things, like Dagon, immediately falls down. So Paul says, "I account all things as dross and as dung in comparison of Christ."

When we love things baser than ourselves, it is like a clear stream that runs into a sink. As our love therefore is the best thing we have, and none deserves it more than God, so let Him have our love—yes the strength of our love, that we may love Him with all our souls and with all our mind and with all our strength.

The love of a wife to her husband may begin from the supply of her necessities, but afterwards she may love him also for the sweetness of his person. So the soul first loves Christ for salvation, but when she is brought to Him and finds what sweetness there is in Him, then she loves Him for Himself.

God comforts us in the exercise and practice of grace; we must not therefore snatch comforts before we be fit for them, when we perform precepts then God will bestow comforts. If we will make it good indeed that we love God, we must keep His commandments; we must not keep one but all. It must be universal obedience fetched from the heart-root, and that out of love.

When the love of Christ is manifested to us, and our love again to Christ is quickened by the Spirit, this causes an admiration in the soul when it considers what wonderful love is in Christ, and the Spirit witnesses that this love of Christ is set upon us. From hence it begins to admire: "How is it that You will manifest Yourself unto us and not unto the world? What is the reason You so love me, and not others?" When the soul has been with God on the mount and is turned from earthly things, then it sees nothing but love and mercy. Such grace constrains us to do all things out of love to God and goodwill to men.

# JOHN COTTON

## A Holy Fear of God and His Judgments

"'Hear this now, O foolish people, without understanding, who have eyes and see not, and who have ears and hear not: Do you not fear Me?' says the Lord" (Jeremiah 5:21–22).

We learn from this text what is the best frame of mind with which to entertain God's judgments. We are to adore the perfections of the glorious God who is displayed in them. We are to be afraid of them, deeply abhorring the divine displeasure and humbling ourselves under His mighty hand. We are to stand in such awe of Him that we renounce and abandon every evil way and rush to the Lord Jesus Christ as our only place of refuge.

"Kiss the Son, lest He be angry, and you perish in the way, when His wrath is kindled but a little. Blessed are all those who put their trust in Him" (Psalm 2:12). We learn from this text that it is not cowardly to be afraid of God's judgments, but very agreeable to true Christian courage.

God is no fit match for us to contend with. No one has ever hardened himself against Him and prospered (Job 9:4). He is our Creator; we are His creatures. We are as clay in the hands of the potter. He is the King of Kings and the Lord of Lords. God cannot err on His end, as the princes of this world may in the execution of their displeasure through impotency or want of knowledge, for He is infinite in knowledge, wisdom, and power, and there in no comparison between infinite and finite.

It is not cowardly, then, to fear God.

43

# THOMAS WATSON

## Body of Divinity

Glorifying God consists in four things: Appreciation, Adoration, Affection, and Subjection. This is the yearly rent we pay to the crown of heaven.

*Appreciation.* To glorify God is to set God highest in our thoughts, and to have a venerable esteem of Him. "You, Lord, are most high for evermore" (Psalm 92:8). "You are exalted far above all gods" (Psalm 97:9). There is in God all that may draw forth both wonder and delight; there is a constellation of all beauties. He is *prima causa*, the original and springhead of being, who sheds a glory upon the creature. We glorify God when we are God-admirers— when we admire His attributes, which are the glistering beams by which the divine nature shines forth; His promises, which are the charter of free grace, and the spiritual cabinet where the pearl of price is hid; the noble effects of His power and wisdom in making the world, which is called "the work of His fingers" (Psalm 8:3). To glorify God is to have God-admiring thoughts; to esteem Him most excellent and search for diamonds in this rock only.

Glorifying God consists in *adoration,* or worship. "Give unto the Lord the glory due unto His name; worship the Lord in the beauty of holiness" (Psalm 29:2). There is a twofold worship: 1) A civil reverence which we give to persons of honor. "Abraham stood up and bowed himself to the children of Heth" (Genesis 23:7). Piety is no enemy to courtesy. 2) A divine worship which we give to God

44

as His royal prerogative. "They bowed their heads, and worshipped the Lord with their faces towards the ground" (Nehemiah 8:6).

This divine worship God is very jealous of; it is the apple of His eye, the pearl of His crown, which He guards, as He did the tree of life, with cherubim and a flaming sword, that no man may come near it to violate it. Divine worship must be such as God Himself has appointed, else it is offering strange fire (Leviticus 10:1). The Lord would have Moses make the tabernacle "according to the pattern in the mount" (Exodus 25:40). He must not leave out anything in the pattern, nor add to it. If God was so exact and curious about the place of worship, how exact will He be about the matter of His worship! Surely here everything must be according to the pattern prescribed in His Word.

*Affection.* This is part of the glory we give to God, who counts Himself glorified when He is loved (Deuteronomy 6:5). "You shall love the Lord your God with all your heart, and with all your soul." There is a twofold love:

- *Amor concupiscentiae:* a love of concupiscence, which is self-love; as when we love another because he does us a good turn. A wicked man may be said to love God because He has given him a good harvest, or filled his cup with wine. This is rather to love God's blessing than to love God.

- *Amor amicitiae:* a love of delight, as a man takes delight in a friend. This is to love God indeed; the heart is set upon God, as a man's heart is set upon his treasure. This love is exuberant—not a few drops, but a stream. It is superlative; we give God the best of our love, the cream of it. "I would cause you to drink of spiced wine of the juice of my pomegranate" (Song of Solomon 8:2). . . . Thus to love God is to glorify Him. He who is the chief of our happiness has the chief of our affections.

*Subjection.* This is when we dedicate ourselves to God, and stand ready dressed for His service. Thus the angels in heaven glorify Him; they wait on His throne and are ready to take a commission from Him. Therefore, they are represented by the cherubim with wings displayed, to show how swift they are in their obedience. We glorify God when we are devoted to His service; our head studies for Him, our tongue pleads for Him, and our hands relieve His members. The wise men that came to Christ did not only bow the knee to Him, but presented Him with gold and myrrh (Matthew 2:11).

So we must not only bow the knee, give God worship, but bring presents of golden obedience. We glorify God when we stick at no service, when we fight under the banner of His gospel against an enemy, and say to Him as David to King Saul: "Your servant will go and fight with this Philistine" (1 Samuel 17:32).

A good Christian is like the sun, which not only sends forth heat, but goes its circuit round the world. Thus, he who glorifies God has not only his affections heated with love to God, but he goes his circuit, too; he moves vigorously in the sphere of obedience.

# THE POWER OF PRAYER

"We cannot all argue, but we can all pray; we cannot all
be leaders, but we can all be pleaders; we cannot all be
mighty in rhetoric, but we can all be prevalent in prayer."

—*An All-Round Ministry*

# JOHN BUNYAN

## A Discourse Touching Prayer

Prayer is a sincere, sensible, affectionate pouring out of the heart or soul to God—through Christ, in the strength and assistance of the Holy Spirit—for such things as God has promised, or according to the Word, for the good of the church, with submission, in faith, to the will of God. . . .

Why must *sincerity* be one of the essentials of prayer which is accepted of God? Because sincerity carries the soul in all simplicity to open its heart to God, and to tell Him the case plainly, without equivocation; to condemn itself plainly, without dissembling; to cry to God heartily, without complimenting. Sincerity is the same in a corner alone as it is before the face of the world. It knows not how to wear two faces, one for an appearance before men and another for a short snatch in a corner; but it must have God, and be with Him in the duty of prayer. It is not lip-labor that it regards, for it is the heart that God looks at, and that which sincerity looks at, and that which prayer comes from if it be that prayer which is accompanied with sincerity.

Second, it is a sincere and *sensible* pouring out of the heart or soul. It is not, as many take it to be, even a few babbling, prating, complimentary expressions, but a sensible feeling there is in the heart. Prayer has in it a sensibleness of diverse things; sometimes sense of sin, sometimes of mercy received, sometimes of the readiness of God to give mercy.

Third, prayer is a sincere, sensible, *affectionate* pouring out of the soul to God. Oh, the heat, strength, life, vigor, and affection that is in right prayer! "As the deer pants for the water brooks, so pants my soul for You, O God" (Psalm 42:1). . . . When the affections are indeed engaged in prayer, then the whole man is engaged, and that in such sort that the soul will spend itself to nothing, as it were, rather than go without that good desired—communion and solace with Christ.

Fourth, prayer is a sincere, sensible, affectionate, pouring out of the heart or soul to God through Christ, by the strength or *assistance of the Spirit.* For these things do so depend one upon another, that it is impossible that it should be prayer without a joint concurrence of them; for though it be never so famous, yet without these things, it is only such prayer as is rejected of God. For without a sincere, sensible, affectionate pouring out of the heart to God, it is but lip-labor; and if it be not through Christ, it falls far short of ever sounding well in the ears of God. So also, if it be not in the strength and assistance of the Spirit, it is but like the sons of Aaron, offering with strange fire (Leviticus 10:1–2).

Fifth, prayer is a sincere, sensible, affectionate pouring out of the heart, or soul, to God, through Christ, in the strength and assistance of the Spirit, *for such things as God has promised.* Prayer it is when it is within the compass of God's Word. But it is blasphemy, or at best vain babbling, when the petition goes against the book. David, therefore, still in his prayer, kept his eye on the Word of God. "My soul," he said, "cleaves to the dust; quicken me according to Your Word." And again, "My soul melts for heaviness, strengthen me according to Your Word" (Psalm 119:25–28). . . .

Sixth, *for the good of the church.* This clause reaches in whatsoever tends either to the honor of God, Christ's advancement, or His people's benefit. For God, and Christ, and His people are so linked together that if the good of the one be prayed for, to wit, the church, the glory of God, and the advancement of Christ must be included. . . .

Seventh, prayer must *submit to the will of God* and say, "Your will be done," as Christ taught us (Matthew 6:10). Therefore the people of the Lord in humility are to lay themselves and their prayers, and all that they have, at the foot of their God to be disposed of by Him as He in His heavenly wisdom sees best.

# CHRISTOPHER LOVE

## When Is Prayer Heard?

A man must be brought into a state of friendship or reconciliation with God before any prayer he makes can be accepted.

God does not accept the person for the prayer's sake, but the prayer for the person's sake. We read in Genesis 4:4: "God had respect unto Abel, and unto his offering." It was first to Abel and then his sacrifice. God accepted his service because his person was in a state of favor with Him. God is first pleased with the worker before He can accept the work. This is also laid down in Hebrews 11:5: "By faith Enoch was translated, that he should not see death, for before his translation he had this testimony, that he pleased God." Now without faith in Christ to justify your person, you cannot please God. The person justifies the works—make the tree good and the fruit must be good.

Until we are brought into that state of reconciliation, we have no share in the intercession, satisfaction, and righteousness of Jesus Christ. And till we have a share in them, our prayers cannot be accepted. Jacob could not receive the blessing from the father but in the garments of his elder brother; nor can we receive anything from the hands of God but in the robes of Christ. No prayer can be accepted by God but in and through the intercession of Jesus Christ.

If Christ is not an intercessor in heaven, no prayer will be heard on earth. In Revelation 8:3 it is written that there was "an angel that came and stood at the altar, having a golden censer, and there was given to him much incense, that he should offer it with the prayers of all saints upon the golden altar which was before the throne." The word in Greek has this purpose: that He should add in prayers to the prayers of the saints. It is as if the prayer of Christ and a believer were all one. In Isaiah 56:7 God promises, "I will bring My people to My holy mountain, and make them joyful in My house of prayer." Our prayers are but as so many ciphers that signify nothing until the intercession of Christ is added to them. Without that they cannot be accepted.

Till we are in a state of friendship and reconciliation, we do not have the assistance of God's Spirit to help us; and if we do not have the assistance of the Spirit, we shall never find acceptance with Him. All requests that are not dictated by the Spirit are but the breathings of the flesh, which God does not regard. Now, till we are reconciled to God, we cannot have the Spirit. Galatians 4:6: "And because you are sons, God has sent forth the Spirit of His Son into your hearts crying, 'Abba, Father.'"

# CHRISTOPHER LOVE

## When Is Prayer Heard?

If it is so that a man must be in a state of friendship before his prayers can be accepted, then understand that all that you ever do before that state is odious to God. Not only your sinful actions, but even your civil, your natural, yes, your religious actions. Not that they are so in themselves, or in regard of God, but in regard of the doer of them. Many prayers cannot turn one sin into a grace, but one sin willfully and resolutely continued in can turn all your prayers into sin. "The sacrifice of the wicked is an abomination to the Lord: how much more when he brings it with a wicked mind?" (Proverbs 21:27).

A diseased body turns food into corrupt humors which a healthy body turns into sound nourishment. I have read of a precious stone that had excellent virtue in it but lost all efficacy if it was put into a dead man's mouth. Prayer is an ordinance of great excellency, of great efficacy, but if it is in a dead man's mouth—if it comes out of the heart of one who is dead in trespasses and sins—it loses all its virtue. Water that is pure in the fountain is corrupted in the channel. . . .

Let this teach you not only to look to the fitness and disposedness of your heart in prayer, but also to make inquiry about what you are who prays. It is our duty, and it is very good to look to the qualification of the heart in prayer, to look to the qualification of the duty. But the main work is to look after the qualification of the person, and to see whether you are in a state of favor and reconciliation with God. For if the person is not in favor with God, you may be confident your petitions will not be heard nor accepted; God looks upon it as the corrupt breathings of your sinful and corrupt heart. You are to look therefore in the performance of a duty whether you can go to God in prayer as a Father.

There are many who look after the qualification of their duty, but few look after the qualification of the person to see whether they are justified or not, whether God is their Friend or not. But we should look mainly to this, for let the heart of a man be never so well disposed, yet if your person is not justified, your prayer cannot be accepted.

God does not care for the rhetoric of prayers (how eloquent they are), nor for the arithmetic of prayers (how many they are), nor for the logic of them (how rational and methodical they are), nor for the music of them (what a harmony and melody of words you have). God looks at the divinity of prayers, which is from the qualification of a person, from a justified person and in a sanctified manner. It is good to inquire: "Is my heart right? Is my mind composed? Are my affections raised and kindled in prayer?" Rather, chiefly inquire: "Is my person accepted by God?"

# MATTHEW HENRY

## A Method for Prayer

After ascribing glory to God in prayer, which is His due, we must next take shame to ourselves, which is our due, and humble ourselves before Him in the sense of our own sinfulness and vileness. Herein also we must give glory to Him as our Judge, by whom we deserve to be condemned—and yet hope, through Christ, to be acquitted and absolved.

In this part of our work, we must acknowledge the great reason we have to lie very low before God, to be ashamed of ourselves when we come into His presence, and to be afraid of His wrath, having made ourselves both odious to His holiness and obnoxious to His justice. We must take hold of the great encouragement God has given us to humble ourselves before Him with sorrow and shame, and to confess our sins.

We must therefore confess and bewail our original corruption in the first place: that we are the children of apostate and rebellious parents, and the nature of man is depraved and has wretchedly degenerated from its primitive purity and rectitude—such is our nature. We must lament our present corrupt dispositions to that which is evil, and our aversion to and impotency in that which is good.

We must look into our own hearts and confess with holy blushing the blindness of our understandings and their unaptness to admit the rays of the divine light. The stubbornness of our wills and their unaptness to submit to the rules of the divine law. The vanity of our thoughts and their neglect of those things which they ought to be conversant with and dwelling upon those things that are unworthy of them and tend to corrupt our minds. The carnality of our affections, their being placed upon wrong objects and carried beyond due bounds. The corruption of the whole man: irregular appetites towards those things that are pleasing to sense, and inordinate passions against those things that are displeasing, and an alienation of the mind from the principles, powers, and pleasures of the spiritual and divine life.

We must lament and confess our omissions of duty, our neglect of it and triflings in it; and that we have done so little since we came into the world of the great work we were sent into the world about—so very little to answer the end of our creation or of our redemption, of our birth and of our baptism; and that we have profited no more by the means of grace. We must likewise bewail our many actual transgressions, in thought, word, and deed.

We must confess and bewail the workings of pride in us. The breaking out of passion and rash anger. Our covetousness and love of the world. Our sensuality and flesh-pleasing. Our security and unmindfulness of the changes we are liable to in this world. Our fretfulness and impatience and murmuring under our afflictions. Our inordinate dejection and distrust of God and His providence. Our uncharitableness towards our brethren and unpeaceableness with our relations, neighbors, and friends—and perhaps injustice towards them. Our tongue sins. Our spiritual slothfulness and decay.

We must acknowledge the great evil that there is in sin, and in our sin; the malignity of its nature and its mischievousness to us. The sinfulness of sin. The foolishness of sin. The unprofitableness of sin. The deceitfulness of sin. The offense which by sin we have given to the holy God. The damage which by sin we have done to our own souls and their great interests.

57

# MATTHEW HENRY

## A Method for Prayer

O God, we are ashamed and blush to lift our faces to You, our God, for our iniquities have risen higher than our head, and our guilt has mounted up to the heavens. To us belongs open shame, because we have sinned against You.

Behold, we are of small account; what shall we answer You? We lay our hand on our mouth and put our mouth in the dust, for there may yet be hope, crying with the convicted leper under the law, "Unclean, unclean."

You put no trust in Your holy ones, and the heavens are not pure in Your sight; how much less one who is abominable and corrupt—man, who drinks injustice like water! When our eyes have seen the King, the Lord of hosts, we have reason to cry out, "Woe to us, for we are lost!"

Dominion and fear are with You; You make peace in Your high heaven. Is there any number to Your armies? Upon whom does Your light not arise? How then can man be in the right before God? How can he who is born of woman be pure? But You, You are to be feared! Who can stand before You when once Your anger is roused? You, our God, are a consuming fire; who considers the power of Your anger?

If we claimed to be in the right, our own mouth would condemn us; if we said, "We are blameless," You would prove us perverse. For if You contend with us, we could not answer You once in a thousand times. If we were not aware of anything against ourselves, yet we are not thereby acquitted, for He who judges us is the Lord, who is greater than our hearts and knows everything. But we ourselves know that we have sinned, Father, against heaven and before You, and are no longer worthy to be called Your children.

# COTTON MATHER

## The Diary of Cotton Mather

When I have been sitting in a room full of people, at a funeral, where they take not much liberty for talk, and where yet much time is most unreasonably lost, I have usually set my wits a work to contrive agreeable benedictions for each person in the company.

In passing along the street, I have set myself to bless thousands of persons, who never knew that I did it, with secret wishes after this manner sent unto Heaven for them. Upon the sight of:

- **A tall man:** "Lord, give that man high attainments in Christianity; let him fear God above many."
- **Children at play:** "Lord, let not these children always forget the Work which they came into the world upon."
- **A very little man:** "Lord, bestow great blessings upon that man, and above all, Your Christ, the greatest of blessings."
- **A man carrying a burden:** "Lord, help this man to carry a burdened soul unto his Lord-Redeemer."
- **A man on horseback:** "Lord, Your creatures do serve that man; help him to serve his Maker."
- **Young people:** "Lord, help these persons to remember their Creator in the days of their youth."
- **Young gentlewomen:** "Lord, make them wise virgins, as the polished stones of Your temple."

- **A shop-keeper, busy in the shop:** "Lord, let not the world cause that person to neglect the one thing that is needful."
- **A man who going by me took no notice of me:** "Lord, help that man to take a due notice of the Lord Jesus Christ, I pray thee."

# THOMAS MANTON

## A Treatise on the Life of Faith

There are none that pray aright, but those that pray in faith. Faith is all in all in prayer. "The prayer of faith shall save the sick" (James 5:15). And it is not prayer simply, but the faith in prayer that prevails with God for a gracious answer. "If you have faith, and doubt not . . . all things whatsoever you shall ask in prayer, believing, you shall receive" (Matthew 21:21–22). The grant and answer is suspended upon that condition, for God will not exercise His power till we rest upon it.

In short, faith and prayer are inseparable companions; like Hippocrates' twins, they live and die together. They are begotten together, and grow up together, and die together.

They are begotten together, for faith begins its life in crying unto God. The first grace that is acted is faith, and the first duty when grace is infused is prayer. "I will pour upon them the spirit of grace and supplication" (Zechariah 12:10). And after his conversion, the first news we hear of Paul is this: "Behold, he prays" (Acts 9:11). As the newborn babe falls a-crying; so, as soon as we are born again, the first work that is set upon is prayer.

More, prayer and faith grow up together, mutually strengthening and increasing and setting one another to work. "Trust in the Lord at all times, pour out your hearts before Him" (Psalm 112:6–8). Trust vents itself in prayer, and prayer increases trust—for in prayer the principles of confidence are solemnly drawn into the view of conscience.

Last, prayer and faith end together. When we come to die, faith is resolved into sight, and prayer into an uninterrupted praise.

# SAMUEL RUTHERFORD

## From the Sermon "Crying Unto Jesus"

"Behold, a woman of Canaan came out of the same coasts, and cried unto Him" (Matthew 15:22). In this prayer the Syro-Phoenician woman cried with intense feeling. Would it not have been more modest for her to speak gently to this soul-redeeming Savior, who hears before we pray, than to cry or shout? Was Christ so hard to be entreated? The disciples afterward complained of her crying after them, but there were reasons for her loud praying that are applicable to us.

First, need cannot blush. The pinching necessity of the saints is not bound by the law of modesty. Hunger cannot be ashamed. "I mourn in my complaint," says David, "and make a noise" (Psalm 54:2). "Like a crane or a swallow, so did I chatter," says Hezekiah. "I did mourn as a dove" (Isaiah 38:14).

Second, fervor is a heavenly ingredient in prayer, even though God hears prayer only as offered in Christ and not because of its warmth. An arrow drawn with full strength has a speedier issue. Therefore, the prayers of the saints are called their crying: "Out of the depths have I cried" (Psalm 130:1). Jesus, our pattern for prayer, offered up prayers and supplications with "strong crying and tears" (Hebrews 5:7).

Third, intense prayers prevail and are answered. "This poor man cried, and the Lord heard him, and saved him out of all his troubles" (Psalm 34:6). The cry adds wings to the prayer as a swift

64

courier speeds his message of life and death to the king during a time of war.

Fourth, there is a sort of violence offered to God in fervent prayer. "I will not let You go," said Jacob to his Lord (Genesis 32:26). When Moses was wrestling in prayer for the people, God answered, "Now therefore let Me alone" (Exodus 32:10). There is strength and muscles in such prayers, and by such prayers "the king is held in the galleries" (Song of Solomon 7:5).

# SAMUEL RUTHERFORD

## From the Sermon "Crying Unto Jesus"

There are many good reasons for urgent prayer, but we must consider some of the hindrances that keep poor sinners from this kind of praying. These will be stated in the form of objections:

*If prayers must be fervent, and even loud, what must become of me, who am often so confounded that I cannot utter one word?* In God's reckoning, groans are taken as prayer. "For He has looked down from the height of his sanctuary . . . to hear the groaning of the prisoner" (Psalm 102:19–20). And when the Spirit intercedes, it is with "groanings which cannot be uttered" (Romans 8:26). Faith sighs to heaven, and Christ receives sighs into His censer for prayer. Words are but the body, the outside of prayer, while sighs are nearer the heart.

*I have not so much as a voice.* Yes, but there are other voices besides those that are articulate. For example, there is a voice in tears: "The Lord has heard the voice of my weeping" (Psalm 6:8). A baby has no prayers for the breast, but a mother can interpret his weeping.

*Even weeping is often more than I can render.* Intensity of feeling frequently moves one to tears, but tears are not an indispensable sign of grief. Hezekiah could only chatter and moan (Isaiah 38:14). Sorrow does not always travel the same beaten road. Weeping is but the outward casing of sorrow, and there is often the most sorrow where there is the least weeping.

*All my ways of expressing prayer are imperfect.* In God's book, a look toward heaven or an uplifting of the eyes is set down as prayer: "In the morning will I direct my prayer unto You, and will look up" (Psalm 5:3). What is prayer but a pouring out of the soul to God? Faith will find another outlet if one is stopped. Feeling breaks out in looks when voice is lacking, just as smoke pours out of the windows when the door is shut. Dying Stephen looked up to heaven by the window of the soul to give notice that a poor friend was on his way, and that was prayer enough. If I were ready to sink into hell, I should wish no more than to send one longing look to heaven.

*My heart is so hard that I have no praying disposition.* Then pray that you may pray. If an overwhelmed heart refuses to come, go and tell Christ, beseeching Him to come and fetch the heart to Himself. It is Christ's eye directed to hard hearts that melts them. Although this is the lowest degree of prayer, it is of no importance to the essence of sincere praying as long as the soul expresses itself, whether in words, groans, sighs, looks, or tears. Prayer is an outpouring of the soul to God, and the very exercise brings along with it the needful affections.

*What should be done with incoherent utterance?* Broken petitions are set down in Scripture as prayer (Psalms 6:3; 109:4; 116:3). The causes of this incoherency in prayer are various. Sometimes it arises not from haste or unbelief, but from intensity of emotion. Love and longing have eagles' wings and fly where language would only creep like a snail.

It is not every part of a poor petitioner's supplication that belongs to the supplication. Out of fear, the poor man may speak broken words that cannot be understood by the prince. However, nonsense in prayer—when sorrow, blackness, and a dark, overwhelmed spirit dictate the words—is well received by God. Prayer is often in the womb of a sigh: "Lord, You have heard the desire of the humble"

67

(Psalm 10:17). When others cannot know what a groan means, God knows because His Spirit made the sigh. He first makes prayer as an Intercessor and then hears it as God.

*But is all my crying in prayer the result of the Spirit?* The flesh may come in and join in prayer, and some things may be said in haste, not in faith, as in that prayer "Has God forgotten to be gracious?" (Psalm 77:9). However, Christ washes sinners in His blood. He rejects those things that are wrong, but He washes their prayers and causes the Father to accept them. Thus, we should fervently lay our hearts before God.

# THOMAS GOUGE

## A Word to Sinners and a Word to Saints

Are you bound under any spiritual infirmities? Do what those sick and diseased persons did when Christ was upon the earth. They came to Him in faith, believing He was both able and willing to cure them; whereby they drew virtue from Him for their healing.

Are you troubled for the weakness of your faith, complaining that you have no assurance of your interest in Christ; no assurance of the pardon of your sins? Go to Christ by prayer for the increase of faith, believing that He is able and willing to strengthen your weak faith. And fear not; you will find such measure of strength added to you as Christ sees best, and as shall be sufficient for you.

Are you sensible of the working and stirring of corruption in yourself, fearing lest it should get dominion over you? Lay hold on that promise from Romans 6:14: "Sin shall not have dominion over you." And in confidence of His faithfulness who spoke those words, apply yourself to Christ by prayer, that He would make good that word to you; then stand still and see the salvation of God. Lust, as strong as it is, will not be able to stand before the prayer of faith. Only be careful that, when you have made your prayer, you set a watch.

Are you assaulted by the temptations of Satan, and do you fear that he may get the victory over you? Go to Christ by prayer for strength and support against the enemy, believing there is a power in Christ, and also a willingness in Him, to succor and strengthen you. Do this and you shall be sure to find, if not deliverance from temptations, yet grace sufficient to resist them and power to overcome them.

Lastly, are you troubled with a hard and obdurate heart? With a filthy and unclean heart? With a worldly and covetous heart? With a proud and barren heart? Go to Christ by prayer, believing there is a power and a willingness in Him to modify your hard and obdurate heart; to purify your filthy and unclean heart; to spiritualize your worldly and covetous heart; to humble your proud heart; and to make fruitful your barren heart. And doubt not that you shall find your hard and obdurate heart in some measure softened, your filthy and unclean heart in some measure purified, your worldly and covetous heart in some measure spiritualized, your proud heart in some measure humbled, and your barren heart in some measure made fruitful.

Certainly one special reason why many go drooping and groaning so long under the bondage of corruption, under the weight and burden of their spiritual maladies and diseases, is because they do not go to Christ by prayer for freedom from the same, or through the weakness of their faith, they do not believe Christ is able or willing to help and deliver them. For what Christ said to the poor man who came to Him in behalf of his possessed child, the same He says to you: "If you can believe, all things are possible to him that believes" (Mark 9:23).

# WILLIAM GURNALL

## The Christian in Complete Armor

To pray always is to pray in everything. Prayer is a universal duty with which, like a girdle, we are to compass in all our affairs. It is to be as bread and salt on our table—whatever else we have at our meal, those are not forgot to be set on. Whatever we do or would have, be it small or great, prayer is necessary.

But not as the heathen, who prayed for some things to their gods, and not for others. If poor, they prayed for riches; if sick, for health. But as for the good things of the mind, such as patience, contentment, and other virtues, they thought they could carve well enough in these for themselves without troubling their gods to help them. This poet, it seems, was of this mind:

> It is enough,
> To pray of Jove who gives and takes away
> That he may give me life and wealth:
> I will myself prepare the equal soul.

Oh, how proud is ignorance! Let God give the less, and man will do the greater.

But their folly is not so much to be wondered at compared with the irreligion of many among ourselves, who profess to know the true God and have the light of His Word to direct them. Some are so brutish in their knowledge that they hardly pray to God for anything. Maybe they look upon pardon of sin and salvation of

71

their souls as fruit on the top branches of a tree—out of the reach of their own arm. Therefore now and then they put up some slight prayers to God for them. But as for temporals, which seem to hang lower, they think they can pluck them by their own industry without setting up the ladder of prayer to come at them.

They that should see some—how busy they are in laying their plots, and how seldom in prayer—could not but think they expected their safety from their own policy, and not God's providence. Or, should they observe how hard they work in their shop, and how seldom and lazy they are at prayer for God's blessing on their labor in their closet, they must conclude these men promise themselves their estates more from their own labor than the divine bounty.

In a word, it is some great occasion that must bring them upon their knees before God in prayer. Maybe, when they have an extraordinary enterprise in hand wherein they look for strong opposition or great difficulty, in such a case God shall have them knocking at His door—when they are at their wits' end and know not how to turn. But in the more ordinary and common actions of their lives, they think they can please their master at their pleasures, and so pass by God's door without bespeaking His presence or assistance. Thus, one runs into his shop, and another into the field, and takes no notice that God is concerned in their employments.

This is not to "pray always." If you will, therefore, be a Christian, do not part stakes with God this way, committing the greater transactions of your life to Him, but trusting yourself with the less. Rather, "acknowledge God in all your ways, and lean not to your own understanding" in any. By this you shall give Him the glory of His universal providence, with which He encircles all His creatures and all their actions.

As nothing is too great to be above His power, so nothing is too little to be beneath His care.

# OCTAVIUS WINSLOW

## Words of Divine Comfort

"Cursed is the cheat who has an acceptable male in his flock and vows to give it, but then sacrifices a blemished animal to the Lord. 'For I am a great king,' says the Lord Almighty, 'and my name is to be feared among the nations'" (Malachi 1:14).

What a fearful anathema is this? But is it disproportioned to the sin it denounces? It is a fearful thing to attempt to deceive God; and yet how many religionists, unsuspectingly to themselves, are committing this sin! My soul, examine yourself, and see if there is anything in your dealings towards God unreal and deceptive, false and dishonoring; and if so, drag it to the Cross, and by its revealing light search it out, and by its crucifying power slay it.

But look at this sin. What is it?

It is the sin of making a solemn vow to God, and then attempting to palm upon Him a deception by offering to Him that which is an abomination in His sight. "You brought Me that which was torn, and the lame, and the sick; thus you brought an offering. Should I accept this of your hand?" (Malachi 1:13). Have you not often offered God a divided heart—a heart divided with the world, or the creature—while He is presented with but a scanty measurement of that love of which He originally and righteously claims the whole?

73

O Lord! Make my heart and its love true and constant to You! If there be a rival to this, gently, lovingly displace it, that I might give to You, the First and the Best of Beings, the first and the best of my love.

# MATTHEW HENRY

## A Method for Prayer

The Lord Jesus has taught us to pray not only with others, but for others. And the apostle has appointed us to make supplication for all the saints (Ephesians 6:18); many of his prayers in his epistles are for his friends. We must not think that when we are in this part of prayer, we may let fall our fervency and be more indifferent because we ourselves are not immediately concerned in it; rather, let a holy fire of love, both to God and man, here make our devotion yet more warm and lively.

We must pray for the whole world of mankind, the lost world, and thus we must honor everyone. And according to our capacity, we must do good to everyone (Galatians 6:10). We must pray for the propagation of the gospel in foreign parts and the enlargement of the church by the bringing in of many to it. For the conversion of the Jews. For all churches that are groaning under the yoke of Islamic tyranny. For the churches on the mission field. For the universal church, wherever dispersed, and for all the interests of it. For the conviction and conversion of atheists, deists, and infidels, and of all who are out of the way of truth, and of profane scoffers and those who disgrace Christianity by their vicious and immoral lives.

We must pray for the amending of everything that is amiss in the church, the reviving of primitive Christianity and the power of godliness, and, to that end, the pouring out of the Spirit. For the breaking of the power of all the enemies of the church and the defeating of all their designs against her. For the relief of suffering churches and the support, comfort, and deliverance of all who are persecuted for righteousness' sake. For the nations around us and all the countries of the world. For our own land and nation, which we ought in a special manner to seek the welfare of, that in its peace we may have peace.

We must be thankful to God for His mercies to our land. We must be humbled before God for our national sins and provocations. We must pray earnestly for national mercies. For the favors of God to us and the tokens of His presence among us, as that in which the happiness of our nation is bound up. For the continuance of the gospel among us and the means of grace, and a national profession of Christ's holy religion. For the continuance of our outward peace and tranquility, our liberty and plenty, for the prosperity of our trade, and a blessing upon the fruits of the earth.

We must pray for the success of all endeavors for the reformation of manners, the suppression of vice and profaneness, the support of religion and virtue, and the bringing of them into reputation. For the healing of our unhappy divisions and the making up of our breaches. For victory and success against our enemies abroad who seek our ruin. For all orders and degrees of men among us, and all we stand in any relation to. For our Head of State, that God will protect his person, preserve his health, and continue his life and government, long a public blessing. For the safe and righteous continuation of our civil government, that a blessing may attend it, that peace and truth may be established in our days and secured to posterity, and that the hopes of our adversaries and all their aiders and abettors may be extinguished. For the advisers, cabinet members, members of Congress or Parliament, the ambassadors and envoys abroad, and all who are employed in the conduct of public affairs.

# SAMUEL RUTHERFORD

## The Trial and Triumph of Faith

How shall we know when our prayers are answered? Hannah knew it by peace after prayer. Paul knew it by receiving new supply to bear the want of what he sought in prayer; he is answered that is more heavenly after prayer.

Liberty and boldness of faith is also a sign of an answered prayer. The Intercessor at the right hand of God cannot lose His own work; His Spirit groans in the saints. Does not my head accept what I set my heart on work to do? (Romans 8:23, 26–27, cf. Revelation 8:3).

We are heard and answered of God when we are not heard and answered of God. I pray for a temporal favor—victory to God's people in this battle—and they lose the day. Yet I am heard and answered, because I prayed for that victory, not under the notion of victory, but as linked with mercy to the church and the honor of Christ. So, the formal object of my prayers was a spiritual mercy to the church, and the honor of Jesus Christ. Now, the Lord, by the loss of the day, has shown mercy to His people in humbling them, and glorifies His Son in preserving a fallen people. So He heareth that which is spiritual in my prayers; He is not to hear the errors of them. Christ puts not dross in His censer of gold.

We are heard whenever we ask in faith; but let faith reach no further than God's will. When we make God's will our rule, He will do His own will; if He does not follow my will, it is to be noted that the creature's will divided from God's will, in things not necessary for salvation and God's glory, is no part of God's will and no asking of faith. . . .

Patience to wait on God until the vision speaks is also an answer. Some letters require no answer, but are mere expressions of the desires of the friend. The general prayers of the saints—that the Lord would gather in His elect, that Christ would come and marry the bride and consummate the nuptials—do refer to a real answer, when our husband, the King, shall come in person at His second appearance.

# WILLIAM PERKINS

## The Art of Prophesying

We have been considering the preaching of the Word. Now, finally, something should be said about leading in public prayer. This is the second aspect of prophesying. In it the minister is the voice of the people in calling upon God (1 Samuel 14:24; Luke 11:1).

In this connection we should note the following points:

1. The subject of public prayer should be, first, the deficiencies and sins of the people, and then the graces of God and the blessings they stand in need of (1 Timothy 2:1–2). Tertullian says, "We do all pray for all emperors, that they may obtain a long life, a quiet reign, a safe family, courageous armies, a faithful council, loyal subjects, a peaceable world, and whatsoever things are desired of a man and of Caesar." Again, "We pray for emperors for their ministers and powers, for the state of the time, for the quietness of their affairs, and for the delaying of their death." The Lord's Prayer covers these areas under six headings: God's glory, God's kingdom, our obedience, the preservation of life, the forgiveness of sins, and the strengthening of the spirit.

2. The form of prayer should be as follows: One voice, that of the minister alone, should lead in prayer, the congregation joining in silently but indicating their agreement at the end

by saying "Amen" (Nehemiah 8:6; Acts 4:24). This was the practice in the early church, as Justin says: "When the president has finished his prayers and thanksgivings, all the people present cry out with a favorable approbation, saying, 'Amen.'"

3. But the one voice which expresses the corporate prayers of the congregation needs to be understood (1 Corinthians 14:15). It should not lead in prayer in a jagged and abrupt fashion, but with a steady flow of petitions, so that empty repetitions are avoided (Matthew 6:7).

4. There are three elements in praying: Carefully thinking about the appropriate content for prayer; Setting the themes in an appropriate order; Expressing the prayer so that it is made in public in a way that is edifying for the congregation.

# COTTON MATHER

## The Duties of Parents to Their Children

Parents, is it your heart's desire that your children may be saved? Let it also be your prayer.

Prayer for the salvation of any sinners avails much. How much may it avail for the salvation of our sinful children? Much availed that prayer of David in 1 Chronicles 29:19: "Lord, give unto my son a perfect heart, to keep Your commandments." Parents, make such a prayer for your children. "Lord, give to my child a new heart, and a clean heart, and a soft heart, and a heart after Your own heart."

We have been told that children once were brought unto our Lord Jesus Christ, for Him to put His hands upon them; and He put His hands upon them and blessed them. Oh! Thrice and four times blessed children! Well, parent, bring your children unto the Lord Jesus Christ; it may be, He will put His blessing, and healing, and saving hands upon them. Then they are blessed, and shall be blessed for evermore!

Pray for the salvation of your children, and carry the names of every one of them, every day, before the Lord with prayers, the cries whereof shall pierce the very heavens. Holy Job did so! Job 1:5: "He offered according to the number of all his children; thus did Job continually."

Address heaven with daily prayers, that God would make your

children the temples of His Spirit, the vessels of His Glory, and the care of His holy angels.

Address the Lord Jesus Christ with prayers like them of old, that all the maladies upon the souls of your children may be cured, and that the evil one may have no possession of them. Yes, when you cast your eyes upon the little folks, often in a day dart up an ejaculatory prayer to heaven for them; "Lord, let this child be Your servant forever."

If your prayers are not presently answered, be not disheartened; remember the Word of the Lord in Luke 18:1, "That men ought always to pray, and not to faint." Redouble your importunity, until you speed for your child, as the poor woman of Canaan did. Join fasting to your prayer; it may be the evil in the soul of your child will not go out without such a remedy. David sets himself to fasting, as well as prayer, for the life of his child. Oh, do as much for the soul of your child!

Wrestle with the Lord. Receive no denial. Earnestly protest, "Lord, I will not let You go, except You bless this poor child of mine and make it Your own!" Do this until, if it may be, your heart is raised by a touch of heaven to a particular faith that God has blessed this child, and it shall be blessed and saved forever.

But is this all that is to be done? There is more. Parents, pray with your children, as well as for them. Family prayer must be maintained by all those parents that would not have their children miss of salvation, and that would not have the damnation of their children horribly fall upon themselves. Man, your family is a pagan family, if it be a prayerless family. And the children going down to the place of dragons from this your family will pour out their execrations upon you in the bottom of hell, until the very heavens be no more.

But, besides your family prayers, oh, parents, why should you not now and then take one capable child after another alone before the Lord? Carry the child with you into your secret chambers; make the child kneel down by you, while you present it unto the Lord, and implore His blessing upon it. Let the child hear the groans, and see the tears, and be a witness of the agonies wherewith you are travailing for the salvation of it. The children will never forget what you do; it will have a marvelous force upon them.

# MATTHEW HENRY

## A Method for Prayer

We pray, as we are taught, for all people, believing that this is good and pleasing in the sight of God our Savior who desires all people to be saved and to come to the knowledge of the truth and of Jesus Christ and who gave Himself as a ransom for all (1 Timothy 2:3–6).

Oh, look with compassion upon the world that lies in the power of the evil one, and let the ruler of this world be cast out, he who has blinded their minds.

Oh, let your way be known on earth, that barbarous nations may be civilized, and that those who live without God in the world may be brought to the service of the living God. And thus, let Your saving power be known among all nations. Let the peoples praise You, O God; yes, let all the peoples praise You. Let the nations be glad and sing for joy, for You judge the peoples with equity and guide the nations upon earth (Psalm 67:2–4).

Oh, let Your salvation and Your righteousness be revealed in the sight of the nations, and let all the ends of the earth see the salvation of our God (Psalm 98:2–3).

Oh, make the nations Your Son's heritage, and the ends of the earth His possession; for You have said, "It is too light a thing for Him to raise up the tribes of Jacob and to bring back the preserved of Israel"; but You will make Him as a light for the nations (Isaiah 49:6).

Let all the kingdoms of the world become the kingdom of the Lord and of His Christ (Revelation 11:15).

3

# EXHORTATIONS
# AND PROPHETIC WORDS

"We make alliances of peace where we ought to proclaim
war to the knife; we plead our constitutional temperament,
our previous habits, the necessity of our circumstances,
or some other evil excuse as an apology for being
content with a very partial sanctification, if indeed it be
a sanctification at all. We are slow also to rebuke sin in
others, and are ready to spare respectable sins, which
like Agag walk with mincing steps. The measure of our
destruction of sin is not to be our inclination, or the habit
of others, but the Lord's command. We have no warrant
for dealing leniently with any sin, be it what it may."

—*The Treasury of David*

# RICHARD BAXTER

## The Reformed Pastor

See that the work of saving grace be thoroughly wrought in your own souls. Take heed to yourselves, lest you be void of that saving grace of God which you offer to others, and be strangers to the effectual working of that gospel which you preach; and lest, while you proclaim to the world the necessity of a Savior, your own hearts should neglect Him, and you should miss of an interest in Him and His saving benefits.

Take heed to yourselves, lest you perish while you call upon others to take heed of perishing; and lest you famish yourselves while you prepare food for them. Though there is a promise of shining as the stars to those "who turn many to righteousness," that is but on supposition that they are first turned to it themselves. Their own sincerity in the faith is the condition of their glory, simply considered, though their great ministerial labors may be a condition of the promise of their greater glory. Many have warned others that they come not to that place of torment, while yet they hastened to it themselves. Many a preacher is now in hell who has a hundred times called upon his hearers to use the utmost care and diligence to escape it.

Can any reasonable man imagine that God should save men for offering salvation to others while they refuse it themselves, and for telling others those truths which they themselves neglect and abuse? Many a tailor goes in rags that makes costly clothes for others; and many a cook scarcely licks his fingers when he has dressed for others the most costly dishes. Believe it, brethren—God never saved any man for being a preacher, nor because he was an able preacher; but because he was a justified, sanctified man, and consequently faithful in his Master's work.

Take heed, therefore, to ourselves first, that you be that which you persuade your hearers to be, and believe that which you persuade them to believe, and heartily entertain that Savior whom you offer to them. He that bade you love your neighbors as yourselves did imply that you should love yourselves, and not hate and destroy yourselves and them.

# JOSEPH ALLEINE

## An Alarm to the Unconverted

Before a man has true faith, he is overcome by the world. He either bows down to mammon, idolizes his reputation, or is a lover of pleasure more than a lover of God. Here is the root of man's misery by the fall. He is turned aside to the creature and gives that esteem, confidence, and affection to the creature which is due to God alone.

O miserable man, what a deformed monster sin has made you! God made you a little lower than the angels; sin has made you little better than the devils! Sin has made you a monster that has his head and his heart where his feet should be—and his feet kicking against heaven—and everything out of place. The world which was formed to serve you now rules you! The deceitful harlot has bewitched you with her enchantments and made you bow down and serve her!

But converting grace sets all in order again. It puts God on the throne and the world at his footstool; Christ in the heart and the world under the feet. "I am crucified to the world, and the world to me" (Galatians 6:14). Before this change, all the cry was, "Who will show us any worldly good?" But now he prays, "Lord, lift You up the light of Your countenance upon me," and take the corn and wine whoever will" (Psalm 4:6–7). Before, his heart's delight and content were in the world. Then the song was: "Soul, take your ease—eat, drink, and be merry! You have much goods laid up for many years" (Luke 12:19). But now all this is withered, and there is no loveliness that we should desire it; and he tunes up with the sweet psalmist of Israel, "The Lord is the portion of my inheritance; the lines are fallen to me in a fair place, and I have a goodly heritage" (Psalm 16:5–6).

# THOMAS WATSON

## A Divine Cordial

Many love sin more than God. "They are haters of God, insolent, proud, and boastful. They are forever inventing new ways of sinning" (Romans 1:30).

What is there in sin that any should love it?

- *Sin is a debt.* "Forgive us our debts" (Matthew 6:12). Sin is a debt which binds over to the wrath of God! And will you love sin? Does any man love to be in debt?
- *Sin is a disease.* "The whole head is sick" (Isaiah 1:5). And will you love sin? Will any man hug a disease? Will he love his plague sores?
- *Sin is a pollution.* The apostle calls it "filthiness" (James 1:21). It is compared to leprosy and to poison of asps!
- *God's heart rises against sinners.* "My soul loathed them!" (Zechariah 11:8).
- *Sin is a hideous monster.* Lust makes a man brutish; malice makes him devilish! What is in sin to be loved? Shall we love deformity?
- *Sin is an enemy.* It is compared to a "serpent." Sin has five sharp stings: shame, guilt, horror, death, and damnation!

Will a man love that which seeks his death? Surely then it is better to love God than sin. God will save you, but sin will damn you! Is he not a fool who loves damnation?

But love to God will never let sin thrive in the heart. The love of God withers sin. The flower of love kills the weed of sin. How should we labor for that grace of love to God, which is the only corrosive to destroy sin!

# THOMAS HOOKER

## The Application of Redemption

There is great disconnect between the knowledge of two travelers: the first has, in his own person, taken a view of many coasts, passed through many countries, has there taken up his abode some time, and by experience has been an eyewitness of the extreme cold and scorching heats, has surveyed the glory and beauty of the one, the barrenness and meanness of the other—he has been in the wars and seen the ruin and desolation wrought there. The second traveler sits by his fireside and happily reads the story of these in a book, or views the proportion of these in a map.

The difference between the two is great, and the difference of their knowledge more than a little: the one saw the country really, the other only in the story. The one has seen the very place, the other only in the paint of the map drawn.

There is a similar difference in the right discerning of sin. The one has surveyed the compass of his whole course, searched the frame of his own heart, and examined the windings and turnings of his own ways. He has seen what sin is and what it has done—how it has made havoc of his peace and comfort, ruined and laid waste the very principles of reason and nature and morality, and made him a terror to himself. . . .

"To the pure all things are pure; but to the unbelieving there is nothing pure, but their very consciences are defiled." It is a desperate malignity in the temper of the stomach that should turn our meat and diet into diseases, the best cordials and preservatives into poisons, so that what in reason is appointed to nourish a man should kill him. Such is the venom and malignity of sin. Hence, it follows that sin is the greatest evil in the world, or indeed that can be. For, that which separates the soul from God, that which brings all evils of punishment and makes all evils truly evil and spoils all good things to us—that must be the greatest evil.

# JOHN COTTON

## A Holy Fear of God and His Judgments

Let our flesh now tremble for fear of God. Let us be afraid of His judgments. Let us at last hearken immediately to the exhortation to reform and amend our ways and doings. This we most certainly must do if we are to expect or even hope to be saved from destroying judgments.

My dear neighbors, are you trembling this day for fear of God? Are you now afraid of His judgments? Are you sensibly touched and deeply affected with the threatening tokens of the divine anger? I am sure you ought to be, and if you are not, you are stupid indeed!

Unto such I would now address myself, and with bowels of pity and concern I entreat and beseech you not to go on any longer in your unrepentant state. I advise such not to be deaf to God's voice unto them this week, but to be searching their hearts and trying their ways. I beseech you to no longer delay taking some suitable time to look within yourselves and reflect with all possible seriousness and solemnity of spirit upon all your past evil ways and doings. You are also to bring to your remembrance, and to especially mourn for, the carnality, the corruptions, and great wickedness of your evil hearts, realizing that carnal mind and heart within you in enmity against God. Oh, be persuaded to bring your hard, corrupt, and depraved hearts to God for softening, renewing, cleansing, and healing. Plead with Him that He will take away your hearts of stone and give you hearts of flesh! Oh, plead with God the gracious promises He has made to do so for those who will seek Him for it.

And as you bring unto the Lord your corrupt and wicked hearts, so come to Him also with the wickedness of your lives laying heavy upon your hearts—wickedness by which you have dishonored God, squelched the Spirit of God, and wounded your own souls. Oh, come with the utmost grief, distress, and anguish. Know and see the evil and bitterness of such ways and doings which your conscience must tell you have not been right. Abhor yourselves before God in the very remembrance of them. Judge and condemn yourselves before Him as utterly unworthy of any mercy or salvation from Him.

And having thus mourned for your provocations of God, earnestly implore divine pity and pardoning mercy through the merit of Christ for His sake alone. Resolve, by the help of divine grace, that you will cast away from you all your transgressions. Then you will have reason to hope to be saved from the judgments of God or hid under that shadow of His wings until the heat of His indignation is past.

Oh, what encouragement have we then to be humbling ourselves before God as we do this day. But what will all our confessions avail if we will not forsake (as well as confess) our sins? Let each one of us, then, from this day onward, set himself to reform and amend everything that is amiss. Let every one ask, "What have I done?" And, "Have I not done a great deal to bring down this new and tremendous judgment on the land?" If we do not, with the greatest possible concern of soul, do so, this will not be an acceptable day unto the Lord.

I trust God has a remnant of His reformed and faithful people here—a number of such that tremble at His Word and at His judgments. These are men of humble and contrite spirits, men of prayer and of holy conversation, men who are burdened over the sins of the times and of the place in which they live, men who are daily interceding with God for sparing mercy to a sinful land. And how many such are there in other towns and places, doing as we are doing here and have been in a very solemn manner all this week, who are this day pleading with God for mercy to a sinful people? But whether their intercessions shall prevail, God only knows.

Oh, that this might be a day of atonement to us and to our houses. Oh, that God would hear and answer our supplications to Him in this time of distress, while we are trembling before Him and greatly afraid of further terrible manifestations of His holy displeasure. Let us beg the Lord to show us what He would have us learn and do by this awful voice by which He has spoken to us. I hope, my neighbors, this is your great concern this day. I dare not any longer delay calling you thus together that we might once more unite in humbling ourselves before God and seek His face and favor.

# RICHARD BAXTER

## The Saint's Everlasting Rest

It was not only our interest in God, and actual enjoyment of Him, that was lost in Adam's fall, but all spiritual knowledge of Him and true disposition towards such a felicity. When the Son of God comes with recovering grace and discoveries of a spiritual and eternal happiness and glory, He finds no faith within man to believe it. Like the poor man who would not believe anyone had such a sum as a hundred pounds, it was so far above what he himself possessed. So men will hardly now believe there is such a happiness as once they had, much less as Christ has now procured.

When God would give the Israelites His Sabbaths of rest, in a land of rest, it was harder to make them believe it than to overcome their enemies and procure it for them. And when they had it, only as a small intimation and earnest of an incomparably more glorious rest through Christ, they yet believe no more than they possess, but say, with the epicure at the feast, *Surely there is no other heaven but this!*

. . . What is more welcome to men under personal afflictions, tiring duties, disappointments, or sufferings, than rest? It is not our comfort only, but our stability. Our liveliness in all duties, our enduring of tribulation, our honoring of God, the vigor of our love, thankfulness, and all our graces—yes, the very being of our religion and Christianity depend on the believing, serious thoughts of our rest.

And now, reader, whoever you are, young or old, rich or poor, I entreat you and charge you in the name of your Lord—who will shortly call you to a reckoning and judge you to your everlasting, unchangeable state—that you not give these things the reading only, and so dismiss them with a bare approbation; but that you set upon this work, and take God in Christ for your only rest, and fix thy heart upon Him above all. May the living God, who is the portion and rest of His saints, make our carnal minds so spiritual, and our earthly hearts so heavenly, that loving Him and delighting in Him may be the work of our lives. . . .

Nothing else can make him content. He has written vanity and vexation upon all his worldly enjoyments, and loss and dross upon all human excellencies. He has life and immortality now in pursuit. He pants for grace and glory, and has an incorruptible crown in view. His heart is set to seek the Lord. He first seeks the kingdom of God and His righteousness, and religion is no longer a casual matter with him, but his main care. Before, the world had the sway with him. He would do more for gain than godliness—more to please his friend or his flesh than the God that made him; and God must stand by until the world was first served. But now all must stand by; he hates father and mother, and life, and all, in comparison of Christ.

Well then, pause a little, and look within. Does not this concern you? You pretend to be for Christ—but does not the world sway you? Do you not take more real delight and contentment in the world than in Him? Do you not find yourself more at ease when the world is in your mind and you are surrounded with carnal delights, than when retired to prayer and meditation in your room, or attending upon God's Word and worship? There is no surer evidence of an unconverted state than to have the things of the world uppermost in our aim, love, and estimation.

# SAMUEL RUTHERFORD

## The Trial and Triumph of Faith

There are two parts in our human will: 1) The natural frame and constitution of it, and 2) The goodness of it. The will of angels and of sinless Adam was not essentially good, for then angels could never have turned devils. Therefore, the constitution of the will needs supervenient goodness and confirming grace, even when the will is at its best.

Grace, grace is now the only oil to our wheels. Christ has taken the castle, both in-works and out-works, when he has taken the will—the proudest enemy that Christ has out of hell. When Saul rendered his will, he rendered his weapon. This is mortification, when Christ runs away with your will. As Christ was like a man that had not a man's will, so Saul (Acts 9:6), "trembling and astonished, said, 'Lord, what will You have me to do?'" It is good when the Lord tramples upon Ephraim's fair neck (Hosea 10:11).

There is no goodness in our will now, except what it has from grace. And to turn the will from evil to good is no more nature's work than we can turn the wind from the east to the west. When the wheels of the clock are broken and rusted, it cannot go. When the bird's wing is broken, it cannot fly. When there is a stone in the sprent and in-work of the lock, the key cannot open the door. Christ must oil the wheels of our misordered wills, and heal them, and remove the stone, and infuse grace (which is wings to the bird). If not, the motions of our wills are all hell-ward.

# THOMAS BROOKS

## Apples of Gold

"My life passes more swiftly than a runner. It flees away" (Job 9:25).

Time is a precious talent which we are accountable for. Cato and other heathens held that account must be given not only of our labor, but also of our leisure. At the great day, it will appear that those who have spent their time in mourning over sin have done better than those who have spent their time in dancing; and those who have spent many days in pious humiliation better than those who have spent many days in idle recreations.

I have read of a devout man who, when he heard a clock strike, would say, "Here is one more hour past, which I have to answer for!" Ah! Just as time is very precious, so it is very short. Time is very swift; it is suddenly gone. The ancients emblemed time with wings, as it were, not running but flying! Time is like the sun, which never stands still, but is continually a-running his race. The sun did once stand still—but time never did. Time is still running and flying! It is a bubble, a shadow, a dream!

Sirs! If the whole earth whereupon we tread were turned into a lump of gold, it would not be able to purchase one minute of time! Oh, the regrettings of the damned for misspending precious time! Oh, what would they not give to be free, and to enjoy the means of grace one hour! Ah! With what attention, with what intention, with what trembling and melting of heart, with what hungering and thirsting would they hear the Word! Time, says Bernard, would be a precious commodity in hell, and the selling of it most gainful where for one day a man would give ten thousand worlds, if he had them.

# JONATHAN EDWARDS

## Discourse on the Preciousness of Time

Time ought to be esteemed by us very precious, because we are uncertain of its continuance. We know that it is very short, but we know not how short. We know not how little of it remains— whether a year, or several years, or only a month, a week, or a day. We are every day uncertain whether that day will not be the last, or whether we are to have the whole day.

There is nothing that experience verifies more than this. If a man had but little provision laid up for a journey or a voyage, and at the same time knew that if his provision should fail, he must perish by the way, he would be the more choice of it. How much more would many men prize their time if they knew that they had but a few months, or a few days, more to live! And certainly a wise man will prize his time the more, as he knows not but that it will be so as to himself.

This is the case with multitudes now in the world who at present enjoy health, and see no signs of approaching death: many such, no doubt, are to die the next month, many the next week—yes, many probably tomorrow, and some this night; yet these same persons know nothing of it, and perhaps think nothing of it, and neither they nor their neighbors can say that they are more likely soon to be taken out of the world than others. This teaches us how we ought to prize our time, and how careful we ought to be, that we lose none of it.

Ah! As you love your precious immortal souls, as you would escape hell and come to heaven; as you would be happy in life and blessed in death, and glorious after death; don't spend any more of your precious time in drinking and gabbing, in carding, dicing, and dancing! Don't trifle away your time, because time is a talent that God will reckon with you for.

You may reckon upon years, many years yet to come—when possibly you have not so many hours to live! It may be this night you will have your final summons, and then in what a sad case will you be! Will you not wish that you had never been born?

Sirs! Time let slip cannot be recalled!

# RICHARD BAXTER

## A Call to the Unconverted to Turn and Live

Is it not a strange thing that any man should be willing to die and be damned? Yes, but that is the case of the wicked—that is, of the greatest part of the world. But you will say this cannot be, for nature desires the preservation and felicity of itself, and the wicked are more selfish than others, not less. Therefore how can any man be willing to be damned?

To which I answer: It is a certain truth that no man can be willing to experience any evil if he perceives it to be evil, but only as it has some appearance of good—much less can any man be willing to be eternally tormented. Misery, as such, is desired by none.

And yet, for all that, it is most true what God teaches us: that the cause, the reason why the wicked die and are damned, is because they *will* die and be damned. And this is true in several respects.

They will go the way that leads to hell, though they are told by God and man whither it goes and where it ends; and though God has so often professed in His Word that if they hold on in that way, they shall be condemned. They shall not be saved unless they turn. "There is no peace, says the Lord, unto the wicked. The way of peace they know not; there is no judgment in their goings; they have made them crooked paths; whosoever goes therein shall not know peace" (Isaiah 59:8). They have the word and the oath of the living God for it: that if they will not turn, they shall not enter into His rest. And yet wicked they are, and wicked they will be. . . .

105

Is this not the truth of your case, sinners? You would not burn in hell, but you will kindle the fire by your sins and cast yourselves into it. You would not be tormented with devils forever, but you will do that which will certainly procure it, in spite of all that can be said against it. It is just as if you would say: "I will drink this poison, but I will not die. I will cast myself headlong from the top of a steeple, but I will not kill myself. I will thrust this knife into my heart, but I will not take away my life. I will put this fire into the thatch of my house, but I will not burn it." So it is with wicked men; they *will* be wicked, and they *will* live after the flesh and the world, and yet they would not be damned.

But do you not know that the means do lead to the end? And that God has by His righteous law concluded that you must repent or perish? He that will take poison may as well say plainly, "I will kill myself." For it will prove no better in the end, though perhaps he loved it for the sweetness of the sugar that was mixed with it and would not be persuaded that it was poison; but it is not his conceits and confidence that will save his life.

So, if you will be drunkards or fornicators or worldlings or live after the flesh, you may as well say plainly, "We will be damned." For so you will be, unless you turn. Would you not rebuke the folly of a thief or murderer that would say, "I will steal and kill, but I shall not be hanged," when he knows that if he does the one, the judge in justice will see that the other be done? If he says, "I will steal and murder," he may as well say plainly, "I will be hanged."

In the same way, if you will go on in a carnal life, you may as well say plainly, "We will go to hell."

# COTTON MATHER

## The Duties of Parents to Their Children

The case inquires, "What may be done by pious parents to promote the piety and salvation of their children?" You will take it for granted that the answer to it will tell you also, "What should be done." For you will readily grant that in such an important case as this, all that may be done should be done!

Parents, if you do not first become pious yourselves, you will do nothing to purpose to make your children so. Except you yourselves walk in the way of the Lord, you will be very careless about bringing your children to such a walk. It is not a Cain, or a Cham, or any enemy of God that will do anything to make his children become the children of God. Oh, parents, in the name of God, look after your own miserable souls. How should those wretched people do anything for the souls of their children who never did anything for their own?

Parents, consider the condition of your children, and the loud cry of their condition unto you to endeavor their salvation! What an army of powerful thoughts do at once now show themselves to besiege your hearts and subdue them unto a just care for the salvation of your children. Know you not that your children have precious and immortal souls within them? They are not all flesh. You that are the parents of their flesh must know that your children have spirits also, whereof you are told in Hebrews 12:9 that God is the Father of them, and in Ecclesiastes 12:7 that God is the Giver of them.

The souls of your children must survive their bodies and are transcendently better and higher and nobler things than their bodies. Are you solicitous that their bodies may be fed? You should be more solicitous that their souls may not be starved, or go without the Bread of Life. Are you solicitous that their bodies may be clothed? You should be more solicitous that their souls may not be naked, or go without the garments of righteousness.

Are you loath to have their bodies laboring under infirmities or deformities? You should be much more loath to have their souls pining away in their iniquities. Man, are your children but the children of swine? If you are regardless of their souls, truly you do call them so!

# THOMAS BROOKS

## Apples of Gold

"I thought in my heart, 'Come now, I will test you with pleasure to find out what is good.' But that also proved to be meaningless. 'Laughter,' I said, 'is foolish. And what does pleasure accomplish?'" (Ecclesiastes 2:1–2).

Solomon's question bids a challenge to all the masters of mirth to produce any one satisfactory fruit which it affords, if they could.

The hearts of young men usually are much given up to pleasure. Sensual pleasures are only seeming and apparent pleasures—but the pains which attend them are true and real. He who delights in sensual pleasures shall find his greatest pleasures become his bitterest pains. Pleasures pass away as soon as they have wearied out the body, and they leave it as a bunch of grapes whose juice has been pressed out. Xerxes, being weary of all pleasures, promised rewards to the inventors of new pleasures, which being invented, he nevertheless remained unsatisfied.

As a bee flies from flower to flower and is not satisfied, and as a sick man moves from one bed to another for ease, and finds none—so men given up to sensual pleasures go from one pleasure to another but can find no contentment, no satisfaction. "Everything is so weary and tiresome! No matter how much we see, we are never satisfied. No matter how much we hear, we are not content!" (Ecclesiastes 1:8).

There is a curse of unsatisfiableness that lies upon the creature.

Honors cannot satisfy the ambitious man, nor riches the covetous man, nor pleasures the voluptuous man. Man cannot take off the weariness of one pleasure by engaging in another pleasure.

Pleasures seem solid in their pursuit, but are mere clouds in the enjoyment.

# WILLIAM BATES

## The Danger of Prosperity

The experience of all ages has verified that none are exposed to more dangerous trials than the prosperous in this world. The great tempter has found the temptations of prosperity so insinuative and prevailing with men that he attempted our blessed Savior; expecting, by the pleasant prospect of the kingdoms of this world, and their glory, to have fastened an impression upon His spirit and tainted His inviolable purity. But he found nothing in our Savior—not the least irregular inclination to his allurements—and could work nothing upon Him.

It is otherwise with men born of the flesh, in whom there is a carnal heart (the center of apostasy and corruption) that is easily enticed and overcome by charming complacencies. Prosperity is a disguised poison—pleasant to the unwary sense, but deadly in the operation. And it is all the more pernicious in its effects because it is viewed as less dangerous in the opinions of men. The temptations of prosperity are so frequent and favored by us that they give vigor to the inward enemy, the sensual affections, and boldness to the malicious tempter. They foment the carnal appetites that defile and debase the soul and are the more rebellious and exorbitant the more they are gratified.

Prosperity is the strongest obstacle against the conversion and reformation of sinners. While they are plying their various pleasures, they have neither will nor leisure to advert to the voice

111

of conscience, so reproachful and stinging to them. And many times prosperity stupefies conscience so that men are fearless of divine judgments when involved in sensual security. They will not reverence and obey God's authority until they feel His power; they abuse His blessings to pride and vanity, idleness and luxury, and are hardened in their impenitence, dyed with the deepest tincture ingratitude. They drive on through a course of sin, till death puts a period to their lusts. How destructive, how penal is prosperity to such graceless souls? When God rains snares upon the wicked, when the affluence of this world is abused to satisfy their vicious desires, it is a sad forerunner of the shower of fire and brimstone and the horrible tempest that shall overwhelm them at last.

Others in prosperity are not openly profane and boldly vicious, yet are corrupted and insensibly destroyed by it. They over-value and over-delight in the good things of this world, and please themselves in an opinionative felicity in their present state. They enjoy the world with more appearance of reason and less sensuality than the riotous and luxurious; but their conversation with so many charming objects alienates them from God. They do not sanctify Him in their hearts, placing their highest esteem upon His most amiable excellencies and their dearest delight in communion with Him. They look upon religion as a sour severity, and they count nothing delightful but what is suitable to the fleshly affections. . . .

And how many by the deceitfulness of riches are apt to imagine that they possess with dominion what they receive in trust? They might be rich in good works, and if their hearts were according to their ability as fruitful as paradise, yet they are as barren as the sands of Africa. They are in a mighty debt for so many received blessings, for which their account will be heavy and undoing with the highest Lord.

These and many other considerations make it evident how dangerous prosperity is to the most that enjoy it here. It is therefore a point of high and holy wisdom how to manage prosperity so as to avoid the impendent evils that usually follow it, and to improve it for our eternal advantage.

# THOMAS GOODWIN

## From the Sermon "The Vanity of Thoughts"

The vanity of the mind appears in curiosity: a longing and itching to be fed with and to know, and then delighting to think of things that do not at all concern us. . . . Thus men, not contenting themselves with the wonders of God discovered in the depth of His Word and works, will launch into another sea and world of their own making, and there they sail with pleasure, as many of the school-men [Scholastics] did in some of their speculations, spending their precious wits in framing curious webs out of their own bowels.

Take another instance: those who have leisure and ability to read much. They should ballast their hearts with the Word and take in those more precious words and wisdom and sound knowledge to profit themselves and others; to build upon their own souls; and be enabled to serve their country. But what do their curious fancies carry them to be versed in? Nothing but play-books, jeering pasquils, romances, and feigned stays which are the curious needlework of idle brains. So they load their heads with "apes and peacocks' feathers" instead of pearls and precious stones. As Solomon says: "The heart of him that has understanding seeks knowledge, but the mouth of fools feeds on foolishness" (Proverbs 15:14). Like the chameleon, such men live on air and wind.

And there are others who, out of mere curiosity to know and please their thoughts, listen after all the news that flies up and down the world. They scum all the froth that floats in foolish men's mouths and please themselves only with talking, thinking, and hearing of it. I do not condemn all herein: some of their ends are good, and they can make use of it to do as Nehemiah did, who inquired how things went at Jerusalem in order to rejoice with God's people, mourn with them, pray for them, and to know how to fashion their prayers accordingly.

But I condemn that curious itch that is in those who listen after such news merely to please their fancies, which are much delighted with new things, though they concern them not. Such the Athenians were (Acts 17:21). How do some men long all week until they have events and issues, and make it a great part of the happiness of their lives to study the state more than their own hearts and affairs of their callings. Such men take actions of state as their text to study the meaning of, and to preach on wherever they come! I speak of those that yet lay not to heart the miseries of the church of Christ, nor help them with their prayers, if at any time they happen.

A similar curiosity is seen in many who desire to know the secrets of other men, which yet would do them no good to know, and who study men's actions and ends not to reform them, or do good to them, but to know them and think and muse upon them when alone, with pleasure.

This is curiosity and a vanity of the thinking power. It is indeed a great sin when much of men's most pleasing thoughts are spent on things that concern them not. For the things we ought to know, and which do concern us, are enough to take up all our thoughts alone, neither shall we have any to spare. Thoughts are precious things, the immediate fruits and buds of an immortal nature, and God has given us power to coin them—to lay them out in things that concern our own good, and of our neighbors, and His own glory—and thus not to spend them is the greatest waste in the world. Examine what corn you put in to grind, for God ought to have toll of all.

# THOMAS BROOKS

## A Word in Season to Suffering Saints

Covetousness is explicit idolatry. Covetousness is the darling sin of our nation. This leprosy has infected all sorts and ranks of men. Covetousness, being idolatry and the root of all evil, is highly provoking to God.

Whatever a man loves most and best, that is his god. The covetous man looks upon the riches of the world as his heaven—his happiness, his great all. His heart is most upon the world, his thoughts are most upon the world, his affections are most upon the world, and his discourse is most about the world.

He who has his mind taken up with the world and chiefly delighted with the world's music, he has also his tongue tuned to the same key, and takes his joy and comfort in speaking of nothing else but the world and worldly things. If the world is in the heart, it will break out at the lips. A worldly minded man speaks of nothing but worldly things. "They are of the world, therefore they speak of the world" (1 John 4:5). The love of this world oils the tongue for worldly discourses and makes men forget God, neglect Christ, despise holiness, and forfeit heaven.

Ah! The time, the thoughts, the strength, the efforts, which are spent upon the world and the things of the world—all while sinners' souls lie a-bleeding and eternity is hastening upon them!

I have read of a greedy banker who was always best when he was most in talking of money and the world. Being near his death, he was much pressed to make his will. Finally he dictates: "First, I bequeath my own soul to the devil for being so greedy for the muck of this world. Secondly, I bequeath my wife's soul to the devil for persuading me to this worldly course of life. Thirdly, I bequeath my pastor's soul to the devil because he did not show me the danger I lived in, nor reprove me for it."

"People who want to get rich fall into temptation and a trap and into many foolish and harmful desires that plunge men into ruin and destruction" (1 Timothy 6:9).

# CHRISTOPHER LOVE

## Weak Measures of Grace in Christians

A weak Christian does not have clear insight into the close and spiritual failings which cleave to his performances. He sees his gifts and takes notice of his affections, but he does not see the vanity of his mind, the unsoundness of his ends, his carnal dependence upon his duty, self-love, and vainglory. But in the course of time, a grown Christian takes notice of these things in himself. An experienced Christian will take as much notice of his failing in duty as of his ability in it; and though he discerns an enlargement of gifts and graces in himself at times, yet he still discerns much spiritual pride, popular applause, ostentation of gifts, and too much forwardness in setting out his parts (which a weak Christian seldom perceives).

To have a scrupulous conscience about matters of indifference argues for a weak Christian; for so the apostle calls them "weak in the faith" who bind the conscience when the Scripture leaves it free. One believer thought he might eat anything, and another doubted the lawfulness of eating sundry things. Now those who doubted, the apostle called weak; and the weak conscience is apt to be defiled. Not to know our liberty, and to abuse our liberty, is an argument that we have but little grace. Young converts call more things sins than ever God did; they perplex and entangle themselves merely in indifferent things. It is true, there ought to be a conscientious tenderness in all Christians—tenderness of conscience is our duty. But a tormenting, entangling scrupulosity is our infirmity. And yet, as a weak Christian is better than no Christian, a weak faith is better than a seared conscience.

To be so intently set on the exercises of religion as to neglect our particular callings is a sign we are but weak in grace. It was a good saying of that famous man of God, Dr. Richard Sibbes: "I like that Christian well that will hear much and live much, that will pray much and work much." In young converts the affections are strong and stirring, and they think they can never hear enough. Many times they neglect the duties of their callings, which argues their weakness and infirmity. An experienced, grown Christian is regular in his general and particular callings, so that the one shall not jostle and hinder the others.

To hold men's persons in admiration argues weakness in grace. Such were the Corinthians. The apostle called them children, babes; though they had the life of Christians, yet they had but little of the strength of Christians. They were carnal; they favored the flesh more than the Spirit. Ignorance is often a cause of admiration. Weak Christians who have but little knowledge are apt to be so taken with men's persons that one cries, "I am of Paul," and another, "I am of Apollos," and so they fall into sin, condemned of combining the faith of Christ with respect of persons so as to cry up one minister and cry down others. To idolize some and despise others argues that you are in weak faith. A solid Christian loves all good ministers and can condemn none.

To be easily seduced and led away into error also argues weakness in grace. The apostle Paul calls those children who are "tossed to and fro and carried about with every wind of doctrine" (Ephesians 4:14). Weakness of head argues that grace is not very strong in your heart. . . .

Last, a weak Christian is one who cannot bear reproof. Sharp weather discovers whether you are of a weak or sound body. So a sharp reproof will discover whether you are of a weak spiritual

119

temper and constitution. When Nathan came to David, he could bear the reproof though the prophet told him to his face that he was the man who had sinned. Asa, though a good man, could not endure the faithful reproof of a prophet, but was wroth with the seer and put him in the prison house.

# THOMAS MANTON

## A Treatise on the Life of Faith

Here is reproof to them that will not pray, when God allows us—yes, commands us—to pray in faith, and with a confidence that we shall speed the better. If there were but a loose possibility, we should pray. "Repent therefore of this wickedness, and pray God, if perhaps the thought of your heart may be forgiven" (Acts 8:22). If it is a very great difficulty, yet pray. So is the example in Joel 2:14: "Who knows, but the Lord will return, and repent, and leave a blessing behind Him?" Faith can stand upon one weak leg; if there be but a "maybe," we should go to the throne of grace.

I reprove those who do not look for any success in prayer—who pray only out of course and throw away their prayers, as children shoot away their arrows and never look after them anymore; those who do not gather up the fruit of their prayers. "In the morning will I direct my prayer unto You, and will look up" (Psalm 5:3). The same in Habakkuk 2:1: "I will stand upon my watch, and set me upon the tower and will watch to see what he will say unto me." He was spying and observing what came in by his dealing with God in prayer; he was looking to see the blessing coming.

Besides, when we do not look after the success of our prayers, we lose many gracious experiences that would confirm our faith. "The word of the Lord is a tried word" (Psalm 18:30). I have found that it is not time lost to go and plead the promises with

121

God. And it will awaken our love. It will quicken us to holy living and a life of praise.

Last, I reprove those who have many doubts and dark thoughts about what they pray for, and about the mercy and power of God; this is an evil incident to God's own children. There is a twofold unbelief: a reigning unbelief, and a doubting unbelief. The reigning unbelief is in those that were never acquainted with God. "You have said, 'It is in vain to serve God, and what profit is it that we have kept His ordinances?'" (Malachi 3:14). But then there is a doubting unbelief, which is a weakness left upon the saints that, though it makes their prayers very uncomfortable, yet it does not make void their prayers. "O you of little faith! Wherefore did you doubt?" (Matthew 14:31). Peter ventured out of the ship at Christ's call, but his feet were ready to sink ever and anon. David was surprised with this unbelief, but the Lord heard him (Psalm 31:22).

If faith be weak, we must not cease to pray, but pray the more that faith may be confirmed, and that we may be assured of God's favor, and may grow up into a confidence in this duty.

# SAMUEL RUTHERFORD

## From a Letter to the Lady Cardoness

Worthy and well-beloved in the Lord: Grace, mercy, and peace be to you. I long to read a letter from you, so that I may know how your soul prospers. My desire and longing is to hear that you walk in the truth, and that you are content to follow the despised but most lovely Son of God.

I cannot but recommend Him to you, as your Husband, your Well-beloved, your Portion, your Comfort, and your Joy. I say this of the Lovely One, because considering what He has done for me, I can say nothing else. He has watered with His sweet comforts an oppressed prisoner. He was always kind to my soul, but never so kind as now, in my greatest extremities. I dine and sup with Christ. He visits my soul with the visitations of love, even in the middle of the night.

I am completely convinced that what I am now suffering for is nothing less than Christ's own truth, and Christ's own way to heaven. I exhort you in the name of Christ to continue in the truth which I delivered to you. Make Christ sure to your soul, for your day draws near to the end. Many slide back now who seemed to be Christ's friends, and prove themselves dishonest to Him. Be faithful to the death, and you shall have the crown of life. This span-length of your days (of which the Spirit of God speaks, Psalm 39:5) will, within a short time, come to a finger breadth, and at length to nothing. Oh, how sweet and comfortable will the feast of a good conscience be to you, when your eyes will be clouded, your face become pale, and your breath turn cold. Then your poor soul will come sighing to the windows of the house of clay of your dying body, and will long to be let out, and to have the jailer to open the door that the prisoner may be set free! You draw close to the shore: look to your accounts and ask your Guide to take you to the other side.

Don't let the world be your portion; who are you to be satisfied with dead clay? You are not an illegitimate child, but a rightful heir of the King. Therefore set your heart on your inheritance. Go up beforehand and see your lodging. Look through all your Father's rooms in heaven, because in your Father's house are many dwelling places. Men take a sight of lands before they buy them. I know that Christ has made the bargain already, but think kindly of the house you are going to, and see it often. Set your heart on things that are above, where Christ is at the right hand of God.

Stir up your husband to mind his own country at home. Counsel him to deal mercifully with the poor people of God under him. They are Christ's, and not his; therefore desire him to show them merciful dealing and kindness, and to be good to their souls. I desire you to write to me. It may be that my parish forget me; but my witness is in heaven that I dare not, I do not forget them. They are my sighs in the night and my tears in the day. I think myself like a husband plucked from the wife of his youth. O Lord, be my judge: what joy would it be to my soul to hear that my ministry has left the Son of God among them, and that they are walking in Christ!

# THOMAS WATSON

## Body of Divinity

This is to be laid down for a proposition: that there shall be a day of judgment. "For we must all appear before the judgment-seat of Christ" (2 Corinthians 5:10). This is the grand assize; the greatest appearance that ever was. Adam shall then see all his posterity at once. We must all appear; the greatness of men's persons does not exempt them from Christ's tribunal; kings and captains are brought in trembling before the Lamb's throne. We must all appear, and appear in our own persons, not by proxy.

How does it appear that there shall be a day of judgment? There are two ways:

1. *By the testimony of Scripture.* "For God shall bring every work into judgment, with every secret thing" (Ecclesiastes 12:14). "For he comes, for he comes to judge the earth" (Psalm 96:13). The reduplication denotes the certainty. "I beheld until the thrones were cast down, and the Ancient of days did sit, whose garment was white as snow. . . . The judgment was set, and the books were opened" (Daniel 7:9–10).

2. *It appears from the petty sessions kept in a man's own conscience.* When a man does virtuously, conscience excuses him; when he does evil, conscience arraigns and condemns

him. Now, what is this private session kept in the court of conscience but a certain forerunner of that general day of judgment when all the world shall be summoned to God's tribunal?

But you ask, "Why must there be a day of judgment?" So that there may be a day of retribution in which God may render to everyone according to his work. Things seem to be done very unequally in the world: the wicked prosper as if they were rewarded for doing evil, and the godly suffer as if they were punished for being good. Therefore, for vindicating the justice of God, there must be a day wherein there shall be a righteous distribution of punishments and rewards to men, according to their actions.

Who shall be judge? The Lord Jesus Christ. "The Father has committed all judgment to the Son" (John 5:22). It is an article of our creed that "Christ shall come to judge the living and the dead." It is a great honor put upon Christ; He who was Himself judged shall be judge. He who once hung upon the cross—He shall sit upon the throne of judgment! He is fit to be judge, as He partakes of both the manhood and Godhead:

1. *Of the manhood.* Being clothed with the human nature, He may be visibly seen of all. It is requisite the judge should be seen. "Behold, He comes with clouds, and every eye shall see Him" (Revelation 1:7).

2. *As He partakes of the Godhead.* He is of infinite knowledge to understand all causes brought before Him, and of infinite power to execute offenders. He is described with seven eyes (Zechariah 3:9) to denote His wisdom, and an iron rod (Psalm 2:9) to denote His power. He is so wise that He cannot be deceived, and so strong that He cannot be resisted.

When will the time of judgment be? The time of the general judgment is a secret kept from the angels. "Of that day and hour knows no man, no, not the angels of heaven" (Matthew 24:36). But it cannot be far off. One great sign of the approach of the day of judgment is, "That iniquity shall abound." Sure then that day is near at hand, for iniquity never more abounded than in this age, in which lust grows hot and love grows cold.

When the elect are all converted, then Christ will come to judgment. As he who rows a ferry-boat stays until all the passengers are taken in, and then rows away, so Christ stays until all the elect are gathered in, and then He will hasten away to judgment.

# JESUS CHRIST:
## SAVIOR AND FRIEND

"In life He is my life, and in death He shall be the death of
death; in poverty Christ is my riches; in sickness He makes
my bed; in darkness He is my star, and in brightness He is my
sun; He is the manna of the camp in the wilderness, and He
shall be the new corn of the host when they come to Canaan."

—*Morning and Evening*

# JOHN FLAVEL

## Fountain of Life Opened Up

There is no doctrine more excellent in itself, or more necessary to be preached and studied, than the doctrine of Jesus Christ, and Him crucified. All other knowledge, no matter how much it is magnified in the world, is and ought to be esteemed but dross in comparison with the excellency of the knowledge of Jesus Christ. "In Him are hid all the treasures of wisdom and knowledge" (Colossians 2:3).

Eudoxus was so affected with the glory of the sun that he thought he was born only to behold it. How much more should a Christian judge himself born only to behold and delight in the glory of the Lord Jesus? Let the doctrine of Christ be considered absolutely, and then these lovely properties with which it is naturally clothed will render it superior to all other sciences and studies.

The knowledge of Jesus Christ is the very marrow and kernel of all the Scriptures—the scope and center of all divine revelations. Both Testaments meet in Christ. The ceremonial law is full of Christ, and all the gospel is full of Christ. The blessed lines of both Testaments meet in Him, and how they both harmonize and sweetly concentrate in Jesus Christ is the chief scope of that excellent epistle to the Hebrews. This argues the unspeakable excellence of this doctrine, the knowledge whereof must needs therefore be a key to unlock the greatest part of the sacred Scriptures.

For it is in the understanding of Scripture, much as it is in the knowledge men have in logic and philosophy, that if a scholar comes to understand the bottom-principle upon which, as upon its hinge, the controversy turns, the true knowledge of that principle shall carry him through the whole controversy and furnish him with a solution to every argument. Even so, the right knowledge of Jesus Christ, like a clue, leads you through the whole labyrinth of the Scriptures.

# OCTAVIUS WINSLOW

## None Like Christ

There is no friend like Christ! The truth upon which we have been endeavoring to concentrate your thoughts is one of great practical influence. It chimes with every event, circumstance, and situation of your life. Let your faith deal with it as a divine verity, as a practical reality, that in whatever position God places you, He intends, by His dealings in providence and by His teaching in grace, to bring you into the deeper experience of this the most precious of all experimental and practical truths: "No one can meet my case like Christ."

Whatever, through this year, your position may be—and I will hypothetically place it—let faith reason thus:

- I am in great adversity. Why should I resort to the help of man? He may fail me, but there is none like Christ.

- I am in profound grief and my heart is melted within me. Why should I repair to the soothing of human sympathy? It may disappoint me, but there is none like Christ.

- I am in a great strait. Insurmountable difficulties and inextricable perplexities weave their network around my path, and I am at my wit's end. Why should I betake myself to human counsel? It may mislead me, but there is none like Christ.

- My future looks dark and lowering. Disease undermines my health, my energies failing, and the duties, responsibilities, and labors for which I have taxed my utmost powers all lie untouched and neglected. Yet why should I despond? There is none like Christ.

- My temporal circumstances are narrowing. Resources fail me; poverty, with its humiliating attendants, stares me in the face. Yet why should I yield to unbelief? There is none like Christ.

- I am approaching the solemn hour of death. Heart and flesh are failing me, and the veil of eternity is slowly rising to my view. Yet why should I fear, and tremble, and shrink back? I have committed my soul to my Savior, and there is none like Christ.

# THOMAS BROOKS

## The Golden Key to Open Hidden Treasures

Christ was truly made a curse for us, and He did bear both in His body and soul that curse which by reason of the transgression of the law was due to us. Therefore I may well conclude this head with that saying of Jerome: "The Lord's injury is our glory."

The more we ascribe to Christ's suffering, the less remains of ours. The more painfully that He suffered, the more fully we are redeemed. The greater His sorrow was, the greater our solace. His dissolution is our consolation, His cross our comfort, His annoyance our endless joy. His distress in soul is our release, His calamity our comfort, His misery our mercy, His adversity our felicity, His hell our heaven.

Christ is not only accursed, but "a curse." And this expression is used both for more significancy and usefulness to note out the truth and realness of the thing, and also to show the order and way He took for bringing us back unto that blessedness which we had lost. The law was our righteousness in our innocent condition, and so it was our blessedness. But the first Adam, falling away from God by his first transgression, plunged himself into all unrighteousness and so inwrapped himself in the curse (James 1:13–15). Now Christ, the second Adam, that He may restore the lost man into an estate of blessedness, became that for them which the law is unto them—namely, a curse. Beginning where the law ends, and so going backward to satisfy the demands of the law to

135

the uttermost, He becomes first a curse for them, and then their righteousness, and so their blessedness (Romans 10:4).

Christ's becoming a curse for us stands in this, that whereas we are all accursed by the sentence of the law because of sin, He now comes in our place and stands under the stroke of that curse which of right belongs to us. So that it no longer lies on the backs of poor sinners, but on Him for them and in their stead.

Therefore He is called a "surety" (Hebrews 7:22). The surety stands in the room of a debtor, malefactor, or him who is any way liable to the law. Such is Adam and all his posterity. We are by the doom of the law evil-doers and transgressors, and upon that score we stand indebted to the justice of God and lie under the stroke of His wrath. Now the Lord Jesus, seeing us in this condition, steps in and stands between us and the blow; yes, He takes this wrath and curse off from us and unto Himself. Christ Jesus does not expect that we should pay the debt ourselves—but He takes it wholly to Himself. As a surety for a murderer or traitor, or some other notorious malefactor that has escaped prison and has run away, He undergoes whatever the malefactor is chargeable with for satisfying the law. Even so, the Lord Jesus Christ stands surety for us renegade malefactors, making Himself liable to all that curse which belongs to us, that He might both answer the law fully and bring us back again to God.

As the first Adam stood in the place of all mankind fallen, so Christ the second Adam stands in the room of all mankind which is to be restored. He sustains the person of all those who spiritually descend from Him and unto whom He bears the relation of a head (Ephesians 1:22–23).

# WILLIAM PERKINS

## The Order of Salvation and Damnation

Now follows the union of the two natures in Christ, which especially concerns His mediation—for by this union it comes to pass that His humanity did suffer death upon the cross in such sort as He could neither be overcome, nor perpetually overwhelmed by it. Three things belong to this uniting of Natures.

First is *conception,* by which His human nature was by the wonderful power and operation of God both immediately (that is, without man's help) and miraculously framed of the substance of the virgin Mary. Luke 1:35: "And the angel answered and said unto her, 'The Holy Ghost shall come upon you, and the power of the Highest shall overshadow you: therefore also that holy thing which shall be born of you shall be called the Son of God.'"

The Holy Ghost cannot be said to be the Father of Christ because He did minister no matter to the making of the humanity, but only fashioned and framed it of the substance of the virgin Mary.

Second is *sanctification,* whereby the same human nature was purified—that is, altogether severed by the power of the Holy Ghost from the least stain of sin, to the end that it might be holy, and He made fit to die for others. As the apostle writes in 1 Peter 3:18: "For Christ also has once suffered for sins, the just for the unjust, that He might bring us to God, being put to death in the flesh but quickened by the Spirit." And 1 Peter 2:22: "Who did no sin, neither was guile found in His mouth."

137

Third is *assumption*, whereby the Word (that is, the second person of the Trinity) took upon Him flesh and the seed of Abraham. Namely, that His human nature to the end, that it being destitute of a proper and personal substance, might in the person of the Word obtain it, subsisting, and as it were, being supported of the Word forever. John 1:14: "And the Word was made flesh and dwelt among us, and we beheld His glory, the glory as of the only begotten of the Father, full of grace and truth."

In the assumption, we have three things to consider:

1. *The difference of the two natures of Christ.* For the divine nature, as it is limited to the person of the Son, is perfect and actually subsisting in itself; the human nature, which consists in whole of body and soul, neither subsists in itself, nor by itself.

2. *The manner of union.* The person of the Son did, by assuming the human nature, create it, and by creating assumed it, communicating His subsistence unto it; the like example of union is nowhere to be found.

3. *The product of the Union.* Whole Christ, God and man, was not made a new person of the two natures, as of parts compounding a new thing; but remained still the same person. Now where the ancient Fathers termed Christ a compound person, we must understand them not properly, but by proportion. For as the parts are united in the whole, so these two natures do concur together in one person, which is the Son of God.

By this we may see that Christ is [the] one [and] only Son of God, not two: yet in two respects He is the Son of God. As He is the eternal Word, He is by nature the Son of the Father. As He is a man, the same Son also, yet not by nature or by adoption, but only by personal union (Luke 1:35).

# OCTAVIUS WINSLOW

## The Titles of Christ

If the creation of the world demanded the power of the Almighty God, much more its redemption. What was essentially required in the case? The harmony of the Divine attributes, the honor of the Divine government, the vindication of the Divine law, the satisfaction of Divine justice—in a word, the endurance of the wrath of God and the penalty of a death the most ignominious and painful.

But more even than this. There was involved in the accomplishment of the salvation of the Church the bearing of her sins, the bringing in of a new and an everlasting righteousness, the endurance of the curse, and the full payment of the great debt due to God. All this demanded the utmost resources of the Deity. There must be Divine wisdom, Divine power, and Divine love.

But Jesus was equal to the undertaking, and accomplished it. To Almighty God, the salvation of countless myriads, even at such a cost, and by such a sacrifice, was not an impossible thing. To any other and finite being, it would, it must have been, an impossibility. If the Almighty God had not undertaken it, the entire universe of fallen beings must have perished forever. But here was a work worthy of Jesus, worthy of His divine love and infinite power.

It is a glorious work, even for a created being, to save. The highest benefactor and the truest philanthropist is he who instrumentally saves a soul from death. To plant a single gem in the Savior's crown; to heighten, by one songster, the hallelujah of the

Lamb; to occupy a solitary mansion in the Father's house with a ransomed tenant—oh, it were worth the toil and suffering of a life!

What, then, must have been the joy that was set before Him of saving myriads from endless death—of studding the many crowns worn at His appearing with countless jewels, of peopling heaven with the redeemed of earth, and of securing an eternal revenue of glory to His Father. He willingly endured the cross, despising the shame!

Who but the Almighty God could have sustained the burden of all the sins of the elect? Who could have exhausted the curse, have borne the condemnation, and have suffered the penalty— and yet have risen again from the grave? Oh yes, salvation was a mighty work; but Jesus was Almighty to achieve it. God placed our salvation on One that was mighty, strong to deliver, mighty to save. One single sin would have sunk the Church to the bottomless abyss; but Jesus bore all the sins of the whole elect of God. And although the tremendous load crushed His humanity to the death, His Godhead bore Him up, carried Him successfully through, and landed Him safe in heaven amid the acclaim of angels and the hallelujahs of saints.

The suffering and slain victim is now the triumphant and enthroned victor over hell, death, and the grave!

# JEREMIAH BURROUGHS

## The Incomparable Excellencies and Holiness of God

What need we all have of Jesus Christ! If God is glorious in holiness, we should all say, "Who can stand before so holy a God!" Were it not for the holiness of the blessed mediator who stands between the Father and us, and presents His infinite satisfaction to the Father for our sins, and clothes us with His righteousness— woe, woe unto us!

If you could possibly imagine that all of the excellencies of heaven and earth were put into one creature except holiness, if that creature had only the least drop of uncleanness and unholiness in it, God would eternally hate that creature. Were there not a mediator between that creature and God, God would eternally let out His wrath upon it. For God is so glorious in holiness that He infinitely hates filthiness. We wonder when we hear of the great misery threatened to wicked men, but we would not wonder if we knew God's holiness.

God so infinitely hates sin that He instantly sent all the angels that fell down in chains of eternal darkness and refused to enter into the least parley with them or to be reconciled with them. Now what is the reason that, though we have so much uncleanness in us, God is pleased to be reconciled to us and admits us into His presence and gives us hope to see His face with joy to all eternity? It is this: because we have a mediator and they have none. Were it not for that, we could weep streams of blood from our eyes and God would hate and abhor us. His wrath would eternally seize us.

Therefore, though you may rejoice in inherent holiness, let your hearts be particularly upon the perfect holiness of Jesus Christ and offer that up to God. Though you have much uncleanness in yourself and in your duties (for what is it for us to offer duty to the holy God), let this comfort you: you do not have to deal with God in yourself, but through Christ, and in Him you have liberty to come. You may look upon God's face with boldness.

This is the great mystery of godliness revealed in the gospel: that, notwithstanding the infiniteness of God's holiness, there is a way for us polluted creatures to look upon this God with joy. This mystery is only taught in the gospel. Though men now think they can come and cry to you, and you come to see your uncleanness, your heart will sink down in eternal despair. You will not be able to endure beholding God then. And if you are not acquainted with God in this way of reconciliation, you will be undone forever. Therefore, study the mystery of the gospel. Make use of Christ that the glory of God's holiness may not be to your terror but to your comfort.

# RICHARD SIBBES

## The Bruised Reed

Objection: If Christ will have His victory, why is it thus with the church of God, and with many a gracious Christian? The victory seems to be with the enemy.

To understand this, we should remember, firstly, that God's children usually, in their troubles, overcome by suffering. Here lambs overcome lions, and doves overcome eagles, by suffering, that herein they may be conformable to Christ, who conquered most when He suffered most. Together with Christ's kingdom of patience there was a kingdom of power.

Secondly, this victory is by degrees, and therefore they are too hasty-spirited that would conquer as soon as they strike the first stroke, and be at the end of their race at the first setting forth. The Israelites were sure of their victory in their journey to Canaan, yet they must fight it out. God would not have us quickly forget what cruel enemies Christ has overcome for us. "Slay them not, lest my people forget," says the Psalmist (59:11), so that, by the experience of that annoyance we have by them, we might be kept in fear to come under their power.

Thirdly, God often works by contraries: when He means to give victory, He will allow us to be foiled at first; when He means to comfort, He will terrify first; when He means to justify, He will condemn us first; when He means to make us glorious, He will abase us first. A Christian conquers, even when he is conquered.

When he is conquered by some sins, he gets victory over others more dangerous, such as spiritual pride and security.

Fourthly, Christ's work, both in the church and in the hearts of Christians, often goes backward so that it may go forward better. As seed rots in the ground in the winter time, but after comes up better, and the harder the winter the more flourishing the spring. So we learn to stand by falls, and to get strength by weakness discovered. We take deeper root by shaking. And, as torches flame brighter by moving, thus it pleases Christ, out of His freedom, in this manner to maintain His government in us. Let us herein labor to exercise our faith, so that it may answer Christ's way of dealing with us. . . . Let us assure ourselves that God's grace, even in this imperfect state, is stronger than man's free will in the state of original perfection. It is founded now in Christ, who, as He is the author, so will He be the finisher, of our faith (Hebrews 12:2). We are under a more gracious covenant.

What some say of rooted faith, *fides radicata,* that it continues, while weak faith may come to nothing, seems to be contradicted by this Scripture. For, as the strongest faith may be shaken, so the weakest, where truth is, is so far rooted that it will prevail. Weakness with watchfulness will stand when strength with too much confidence fails. Weakness, with acknowledgement of it, is the fittest seat and subject for God to perfect His strength in; for consciousness of our infirmities drives us out of ourselves to Him in whom our strength lies.

From this it follows that weakness may be consistent with the assurance of salvation. The disciples, notwithstanding all their weaknesses, are bidden to rejoice that their names are written in heaven (Luke 10:20). Failings, with conflict, in sanctification should not weaken the peace of our justification and assurance of salvation. It matters not so much what ill is in us, as what good; not what corruptions, but how we regard them; not what our particular failings are so much as what the thread and tenor of our lives are, for Christ's dislike of that which is amiss in us turns not to the hatred of our persons but to the victorious subduing of all our infirmities.

Some have, after conflict, wondered at the goodness of God that so little and such trembling faith should have upheld them in so great combats, when Satan had almost caught them. And, indeed, it is to be wondered at how much a little grace will prevail with God for acceptance, and over our enemies for victory, if the heart is upright. Such is the goodness of our sweet Savior that He delights to show His strength in our weakness.

# STEPHEN CHARNOCK

## The Necessity of Regeneration

Christ came to destroy the works of the devil: "For this purpose the Son of God was manifested, that He might destroy the works of the devil" (1 John 3:8). These works are two: sin, and the misery consequent upon it. Upon the destruction of sin necessarily follows the dissolution of the other, which was knit with it. If the sinful nature were not taken away, the devil's works would not wholly be destroyed; or if the sinful nature were taken away, and a righteous nature not planted in the stead of it, he would still have his ends against God in depriving God of the glory He ought to have from the creature. And the creature could not give God the glory He was designed by His creation to return, unless some nature were implanted in him whereby he might be enabled to do it.

Would it then bring honor to this great Redeemer to come short of His end against Satan and let all the trophies of Satan remain—the errors of the understanding, perversity of the will, disorder of the affections, and confusion of the whole soul? Or if our Savior had only removed these things, how would the works of the devil be destroyed if we remain open to his assaults and liable the next moment to be brought into the same condition—which we surely would be, were it not for a righteous and divine nature bestowed upon us.

What is more, Christ came to bring us to God: "For Christ also has once suffered for sins, the just for the unjust, that He might bring us to God" (1 Peter 3:18). Was this to bring us to God with all our pollutions—the cause for which God cast us off? No, it was to bring us in such a garb that we might be fit to converse with Him. Can we be so without a new nature and a spiritual likeness to God? If a man were to bring another to a prince for a favorable introduction, would that man bring him into the prince's presence in a slovenly and sordid habit—such a garb which he knew was hateful to the prince? No, and neither will our Savior, nor can He, bring sinners in such a plight to God. Because it is more contrary to the nature of God's holiness to have communion with such than it is contrary to the nature of light to have communion with darkness (1 John 1:5–7).

# THOMAS BROOKS

## The Unsearchable Riches of Christ

Oh, those riches of grace and goodness that are in Christ—how do they satisfy the souls of sinners! A pardon does not more satisfy a condemned man, nor bread the hungry man, nor drink the thirsty man, nor clothes the naked man, nor health the sick man than the riches of Christ do satisfy the gracious man.

John 4:13–14: "Whoever drinks of this water shall thirst again: but whoever drinks of the water that I shall give him shall never thirst; but the water that I shall give him shall be in him a well of living water springing up to everlasting life." Grace is a perpetual flowing fountain. Grace is compared to water. Water serves to cool men when they are in a burning heat, and so grace cools the soul when it has been scorched and burned up under the sense of divine wrath and displeasure. Water is cleansing, so is grace; water is fructifying, so is grace; and water is satisfying, it satisfies the thirsty, and so does grace. "Show us the Father, and it suffices us," according to John 14:8.

Ecclesiastes 5:10: "He who loves silver shall not be satisfied with silver; nor he who loves abundance with increase. This is also vanity." If a man is hungry, silver cannot feed him; if naked, it cannot clothe him; if cold, it cannot warm him; if sick, it cannot cure him—much less then is it able to satisfy him. Oh! but the riches of Christ are soul-satisfying riches. A soul rich in spirituals, rich in eternals, says, "I have enough, though I have not this and that temporal good."

# THOMAS MANTON

## Man and Sin

"For when we were yet without strength, in due time Christ died for the ungodly" (Romans 5:6). In this chapter there are two parts: in the first, the apostle lays down the comfortable fruits and privileges of a justified estate; in the second, he argues the firmness of these comforts, because they are so rich that they are scarce credible, and hardly received. The apostle represents the firmness and soundness of these comforts by a double comparison: by comparing Christ with Christ; and Christ with Adam.

In comparing Christ with Christ, three considerations do occur:

1. *The efficacy of His love toward us before justification, with the efficacy of His love toward us after justification.* The argument stands thus: If Christ had a love for us when we were sinners, and His love prevailed with Him to die for us, how much more may we expect His love when made friends?

2. *The efficacy of the death of Christ, and the efficacy of the life of Christ.* It is absurd to think that Christ rising from the dead, and living in heaven, should not be as powerful to save, and bring us to God, as Christ dying was to reconcile us to Him.

3. *The privative mercy, or being saved from hell, with the positive mercy, or obtaining a title to heaven.* "And not only so,

but we also joy in God through our Lord Jesus Christ, by whom we have now received the atonement" (5:11).

For the comparison between Christ and Adam, the sum of it is that Christ is more able to save than Adam is to destroy, and therefore justified persons need to fear nothing. As Adam was a public person and root of mankind, so is Christ a public person. For Adam was "the figure of Him that was to come" (5:14). Adam was a public person, but a finite person, having no intrinsic value in himself and only represented all of us by divine institution. But Christ, beside the institution of God, was an infinite person, and therefore there is a "much more" upon Christ. His sacred virtue exceeds that cursed influence of Adam in many particulars, amply set down in the latter end of the chapter by the apostle.

# JOHN BUNYAN

## Grace Abounding to the Chief of Sinners

Once as I was walking to and fro in a good man's shop, bemoaning of myself in my sad and doleful state, afflicting myself with self-abhorrence for this wicked and ungodly thought; lamenting, also, this hard hap of mine that I should commit so great a sin; greatly fearing I would not be pardoned; praying, also, in my heart, that if this sin of mine did differ from that against the Holy Ghost, the Lord would show it me.

And being now ready to sink with fear, suddenly there was, as if there had rushed in at the window, the noise of wind upon me, but very pleasant, and as if I heard a voice speaking, "Didst thou ever refuse to be justified by the blood of Christ?" And my whole life and profession past was, in a moment, opened to me, wherein I was made to see that designedly I had not. So my heart answered groaningly, "No." Then fell, with power, that word of God upon me: "See that you refuse not Him that speaks" (Hebrews 12:25).

This made a strange seizure upon my spirit; it brought light with it, and commanded a silence in my heart of all those tumultuous thoughts that before did use, like masterless hell-hounds, to roar and bellow and make a hideous noise within me. It showed me, also, that Jesus Christ had yet a word of grace and mercy for me—that He had not, as I had feared, quite forsaken and cast off my soul. Yes, this was a kind of chide for my proneness to desperation; a kind of a threatening me if I did not, notwithstanding my sins and the heinousness of them, venture my salvation upon the Son of God.

But as to my determining about this strange dispensation, what it was I knew not; from whence it came I knew not. I have not yet, in twenty years' time, been able to make a judgment of it. I thought then what here I shall be loath to speak. Verily, that sudden rushing wind was as if an angel had come upon me; but both it and the salvation I will leave until the day of judgment. Only this I say: it commanded a great calm in my soul and persuaded me there might be hope; it showed me, as I thought, what the sin unpardonable was, and that my soul had yet the blessed privilege to flee to Jesus for mercy. . . .

Still my life hung in doubt before me, not knowing which way I should tip; only this I found my soul desire, even to cast itself at the foot of grace by prayer and supplication. But, oh! it was hard for me now to bare the face to pray to this Christ for mercy, against whom I had thus most vilely sinned. It was hard work, I say, to offer to look Him in the face against whom I had so vilely sinned; and, indeed, I have found it as difficult to come to God by prayer after backsliding from Him as to do any other thing. Oh, the shame that did now attend me! Especially when I thought I am now going to pray to Him for mercy that I had so lightly esteemed but a while before!

I was ashamed, yes, even confounded because this villainy had been committed by me; but I saw there was but one way with me: I must go to Him and humble myself unto Him and beg that He, of His wonderful mercy, would show pity to me and have mercy upon my wretched sinful soul.

# SAMUEL RUTHERFORD

## From a Letter to Lady Kenmure

Madam: grace, mercy, and peace be to you. . . .

Madam, in regard to yourself, I am encouraged when people complain about their failures, so long as they are trying to do something about them. This is because I see many people who think that holiness is satisfied, if they merely complain, and then do nothing. It is as if saying "I am sick" could cure an invalid. These people seem to think that complaining about failure was a magic charm to eradicate guilt! I am glad that you are wrestling and struggling on in this dead age, when many have lost tongue, arms, and legs for Christ.

I urge you, Madam, a nearer communion with Christ, and a growing communion. There are curtains to be opened in Christ that we have never seen before, and new layers of love in Him. I despair that I will ever make it to the far end of that love, there are so many layers in it. Therefore dig deep, and sweat, and labour. Take pains for Him, and set aside as much time as you can in each day for Him. Christ will be won with labour.

I, His exiled prisoner, sought Him, and He has taken pity on me, and made a moan for me, as He does for His own. I do not know what to do with Christ. His love surrounds me and overwhelms me. I am burdened by it; but oh, how sweet and lovely is that burden! I dare not keep it inside me. I am so in love with His love, that if His love were not in heaven, I would not be willing to go there. Oh, what pondering, what telling there is in Christ's love!

I fear nothing now so much as losing Christ's cross, and the showers of love that accompany it. I wonder how it could be that such a slave could be exalted to a place of honor, at His own elbow. Oh that I should ever kiss such a fair, fair, fair face as Christ's! But I dare not refuse to be loved. There is nothing within me that is the cause for Him to look upon me and love me. God never gained anything from me. His love cost me nothing. Oh, the many pounds of His love under which I am sweetly pressed!

Now, Madam, let me tell you that most people only have a stage Christianity. They consider it to be a mask easily put on or taken off. I myself thought it would be an easy thing to be a Christian, and that seeking God would only be like a jaunt next door. But oh the windings, the turnings, the ups and downs that He has led me through! And even so, it still seems as if it will be a long way to the shore.

He speaks in my inmost being during the night. When I awake, I find His love arrows, that He shot at me, sticking in my heart. Who will help me to praise? Who will come to lift up with me, and set on high, His great love? And yet I find that a flood of challenges will come in at midsummer and question me. But it is only to keep a sinner in order.

As for friends, I would not think the world to properly be the world if friends did not leave me. Using God's wisdom, I hope to use the world as an intelligent employer uses an untrustworthy employee. He does not trust him with money or anything important that he might steal. I pray to God that I will not trust this world with my joys, comforts, or confidence. If I did, it would put Christ out of His proper place in my heart. Indeed, Madam, from my few experiences I counsel you to give Christ the authority over all the business of your life. Fasten all your burdens on the peg fastened in

David's house (Isaiah 22:23). Woe to me if ever the world should teach me anything about consolation. Away, away, with any such false teachers. Christ then would laugh at me and say: "Now you're warned. Be careful who you trust."

# THOMAS GOODWIN

## The Riches of God's Love to His Elect

As God loves us in Christ, His love is described in a manner *the same with which He loves Himself*. There is a union between Jesus Christ and us, and there is also a union between God and us. John 17:23 says, "I in them, and You in me." In the same way that our Lord and Savior Christ loved His people so that, if His people were hurt, He takes it as if it were done to Himself ("Saul, Saul, why do you persecute Me?"), so you shall find that God Himself speaks as if His people and He were all one.

It is not only as John writes: "God knows them that are His." These are great words; they are deep words, and deep expressions. But you shall find that God in the Old Testament speaks in the person of His people, as well as Christ does in the New Testament. The union between Christ and His people is such, and His love such, that what was done to them, He reckons cloned to Himself; it is the same between God and us also. "Yours they were," says Christ, "and You gave them to Me." They are more God's therefore than Christ's—or first God's, and then given unto Christ. Therefore, in Isaiah 63:9 God is said to be afflicted as His people are afflicted. Yes, the salvation of His people God accounts His salvation (Isaiah 49:6).

And though God loves Himself with a natural love, yet His love to us is now in a manner naturalized, because he is become a father to us. He was happy in Himself, and He might be so without us forever; yet now He speaks as if that the want of us would make Him imperfect. "Who shall separate us from the love of God?" The word implies a separation, like the rending of the soul from the body; and as the soul would be imperfect without the body, so the love that God bears us would make Him, too, if there could be a separation.

Therefore in Zephaniah 3:17 He is said to "rest in His love." If He did not enjoy us, He would never be at rest. To these kind of expressions, my brethren, does the Scripture rise.

# JEREMIAH BURROUGHS

## Christ Is All in All

All good is in God, true, but how shall we come to partake of that good? There is such a distance between you and God that, were not Christ in the middle, you would never come together. But Christ has come between and joined you together so that all is yours because you are Christ's and Christ is God's.

Think of God as the Fountain of all good, and Christ, as it were, the Cistern, and from Him are pipes converged to every believer. Faith sucks at the mouth of every pipe and draws from God, but it comes from God through Christ. The Father fills the Son with all good and so it comes from the Father, through the Son, by faith unto the soul of every believer. . . .

There is no coming to the Father except by Christ, and Christ takes a believer by the hand and leads him to the Father, and so he comes to have boldness. He is the way of conveying good to us by His intercession, for He is now and shall forever be at the right hand of the Father in glory making intercession for His people. That is, He is continually presenting before the Father the work of His mediation, His merits, what He has done and suffered and is, as it were, pleading with His Father for the conveyance of all needful mercy and good unto the souls and bodies of His people, whom He has redeemed.

It is as if Christ should every moment eternally speak thus to the Father: "Father, behold, here is my blood, my merits, my death, all my sufferings, the work of my humiliation. It is for these. Yes, for this poor soul and for that poor soul particularly." Know that Christ thinks not only of the lump of believers in general, but particularly of every believer, and is continually presenting His infinite merits before the Father to plead with Him to supply of all grace and mercy to us. Thus He becomes an infinite way of conveying good to the souls of His people, and to be all and in all to them both here and eternally.

# CHRISTOPHER LOVE

## A True Map of Man's Miserable State by Nature

Every man who is out of Christ comes from a base origin. He does not have his origin from the Spirit, but from the flesh. He does not proceed from God who is the Father of lights, but from the devil who is the prince of darkness.

He is base because he commits base actions. All the actions and services of a Christ-less man, at best, are but as filthy rags and dead works. A man, in his unconverted state, is the slave and drudge of the devil—a worker of wickedness, still fulfilling the desires of the flesh and of the mind, being given over to vile affections.

He is a base man who is without Christ because he aims at base ends in whatever he does, and that happens in two ways. 1) In this world he aims at base ends in his hearing, reading, praying, and profession of religion. He minds himself and his own ends in all that he does. 2) All his actions tend to base ends in another world. As the actions of a man in Christ tend to salvation, so the actions of a Christ-less man tend to damnation.

Second, a man without Christ is not only a base man, but a bondman. This Christ tells you in John 8:36, "If the Son shall make you free, then are you free indeed," intimating that if you do not have an interest in Christ to free you from the slavery of sin and Satan, you are slaves indeed. This bondage and slavery, likewise, consists in three particulars: they are slaves to sin, to the devil, and to the law.

1. **Every Christ-less man is a slave to sin.** In John 8:34 Jesus says, "Verily I say unto you, whosoever commits sin is the servant of sin," and in 2 Peter 2:19, "While they promise them liberty, they themselves are servants of corruption, for of whom a man is overcome, of the same he is brought into bondage." Every man, by nature, is a slave to his lusts, a slave to sin, and to the creatures. God made man over all the creatures, but man has made himself servant to all the creatures by sin.

2. **He is not only in bondage and slavery to sin, but to the devil, too.** The last two verses of 2 Timothy 2 say: "in meekness instructing those that oppose themselves, if God will give them repentance, to the acknowledging of the truth, so that they may recover themselves out of the snare of the devil, who are taken captive by him at his will."

3. **He is in bondage to the law;** that is, he does nothing in obedience to the law. And this is the great misery of a man without Christ. He is bound to keep the whole law of God. There is a very strange expression in Revelation 18:10–16. Saint John tells there that all those who did worship the beast shall cry, "'Woe and alas,' for Babylon is fallen, and shall cry for the slaves and souls of men." All wicked men are slaves to the antichrist, to sin, and to the law—and this is the great misery of an unregenerate man.

# CHRISTOPHER LOVE

## A True Map of Man's Miserable State by Nature

You are a beggarly man without Jesus Christ, for all the treasures of grace and mercy are hid and locked up in Christ as in a common magazine or storehouse. Colossians 2:3 states: "In Him are hid all the treasures of wisdom and knowledge." If you are out of Christ, you have nothing. As it says in Revelation 3:17, "You say you are rich and increased in goods, and have need of nothing; but you know not that you are poor, and wretched, and miserable, and blind, and naked."

You will grant that he is a poor and beggarly man that lacks these four things: meat for his belly, clothes for his back, money for his purse, and a house to put his head in. Why, in all these respects, every man who is out of Christ is a beggarly man.

1. **A beggarly man is one who has no meat to put in his belly,** and all you who have no interest in Jesus Christ are beggarly in this regard, because you do not feed upon that bread of life, nor drink of the water of life, the Lord Christ, whose flesh is meat indeed, and whose blood is drink indeed, without which your souls will starve for hunger.

2. **You will say he is a poor man who has no clothes to put upon his back,** and thus every man out of Christ is not only poor, but naked. That man who is not clothed with

the long robes of Christ's righteousness is a naked man, and is exposed to the wrath and vengeance of Almighty God. Those men have a cloak to cover their sinful nakedness and shame who are clothed with the robes of Christ's righteousness. It is said of Jacob that he obtained the blessing from his father by being clad in the garments of his eldest brother, and so we are only blessed by God our Father as we are clothed with the robes of our elder brother Jesus Christ.

3. **That man is a beggarly man who has no money in his purse.** So, though your purses are full of gold, if your hearts are not full of grace, you are very beggarly men. Grace is the only true riches (Luke 16:11). All the durable riches are bound up in Christ.

4. **Last, he is a beggarly man who does not have a house to put his head in,** who is destitute of a house to lodge in and a bed to lie on. So, you who have no interest in Christ, when your days are expired and death comes, you do not know what to do or where to go. You cannot say with the godly man that, when death takes you from here, you shall be received into everlasting habitations. You cannot say that Christ has gone before to prepare a place for you in heaven.

So, then, in these four particulars you see that a Christ-less man is a very beggarly man, having neither food for his body, nor clothes for his back, nor money for his purse, nor a house to put his head in—unless it is a dungeon of darkness with devils and damned spirits.

# THOMAS MANTON

## From the Sermon "Be Not Soon Shaken in Mind"

The time of Christ's coming to judgment must be patiently expected, not rashly defined or determined. For this is the error that the apostle opposes with such earnestness. . . .

It was an arrogant presumption when some early Christians fixed the time of Christ's arrival; much more, it was a sin to fix the time. "For of that day and hour knows no man; no, not the angels of heaven, but my Father only" (Matthew 24:36). The peremptory time of the Day of Judgment God keeps to Himself, and it is arrogance for any to define it and set a time, when God has resolved to keep it secret.

The fixing of that time did a great deal of hurt. For the present it drew away their minds from their calling, because they expected a sudden coming of the Lord. Ill impressions either destroy or weaken necessary duties. The least error gratifies Satan and the interest of his kingdom, for he is the father of lies. It might shake their faith in other things when their credulity was disproved by the event; the gospel might be brought into contempt when their error only was confuted; many men who have been peremptory in fixing times, afterwards have thrown off their religion.

More, it did but engender strife among Christians; it begat wranglings and disputes in the church. "He is proud, knowing nothing, but doting about questions and strifes of words, whereof comes envy, strife, railing, and evil surmising" (1 Timothy 6:4).

Therefore, let us not fix times for Christ's return. Many of the ancients were too bold this way, and we are apt to it. Lactantius peremptorily said the world would endure but two hundred years after his time. So many will fix the time of the calling of the Jews, and the destruction of Antichrist, without evident grounds and reasons. What God has revealed is enough to bear us out in our duty and suffering. In other things let us patiently wait; we see reason to do so when we consider how many men have proved false prophets.

And yet, let us not put off the time, and set it at too great a distance. Distant things, though never so great, will hardly move us; that which men put off they do in effect put away. They put far off the evil day, and they would not let it come near their minds to have any operation upon them. Look, as the stars, those vast globes of light, by reason of the distance between us and them, do seem but as so many spangles; so we have but a weak sight of what is set at a great distance, and their operation on us will be but small. The closer things are, the more they will work upon us.

One that looks upon what God has revealed of this as sure and near, he is more affected with it than others are. Therefore set yourselves at the entrance of that world, where you must everlastingly be, and watch, and be ready. They that put it off are apt to loiter in their work. If Christ's coming be not near at hand, certainly the time of our departure is at hand, and it will not be long ere it comes about.

# OCTAVIUS WINSLOW

## None Like Christ

Does the world challenge you thus: "What is your Beloved more than another beloved?" Your answer is at hand: My Beloved bore my sins, opened in His heart a fountain in which I am washed whiter than snow. My Beloved sustains my burdens, counsels my perplexities, heals my wounds, dries my tears, supplies my needs, bears with my infirmities, upholds my steps, and cheers my pathway to the tomb. My Beloved will be with me in the valley of the shadow of death, and with His presence I shall fear no evil. My Beloved has gone to prepare a place for me in the many-mansioned house of my Father, and will come again and receive me to Himself—that where He is, I may be also. My Beloved will walk with me in the gold-paved streets of the New Jerusalem, will lead me to fountains of living waters, and will wipe every tear from my eyes.

This is my Beloved, and this is my Friend!

Therefore stand firm. Yet have we need of constant vigilance, lest we should not always and in everything give Christ the pre-eminence. The rival interests and the antagonistic forces of the world and the flesh are in perpetual play. These demand that, with the prophet, we should "stand continually upon the watchtower in the daytime, and be set in our wards whole nights" (Isaiah 21:8).

Should you discover any encroachment of your worldly calling upon the claims Christ has to your time and service—any rival affections to the claims He has to your whole heart, any secret demur to the claims He has to your unreserved obedience; should you, in a word, detect the undue ascendency or influence of any one being or object whose presence and power tends to shade the beauty, lessen the attractions, weaken the supremacy, or share the throne of Christ in your soul—that being and that object must be relinquished at once and forever!

# MISSIONS AND EVANGELISM

"'Oh!' says one, 'I am not my brother's keeper.' No, I will tell you your name: it is Cain. You are your brother's murderer; for every professing Christian who is not his brother's keeper is his brother's killer. And be you sure that it is so, for you may kill by neglect quite as surely as you may kill by the bow or by the dagger."

—*We Endeavour*

# WILLIAM PERKINS

## Cases of Conscience

In the work effecting the salvation of man, ordinarily there are two special actions of God: the giving of the first grace, and after that, the giving of the second. The former of these two works has ten actions:

1. God gives man the outward means of salvation, especially the ministry of the Word. And with it, He sent some outward and inward cross to break and subdue the stubbornness of our nature, that it may be made pliable to the will of God. This we may see in the example of the jailer in Acts 16. And of the Jews that were converted at Peter's sermon in Acts 2.

2. This done, God brings the mind of man to consideration of law, and therein generally to see what is good and what is evil; what is sin and what is not sin.

3. Upon a serious consideration of the law, He makes a man particularly to see and know his own peculiar and proper sins, whereby he offends God.

4. Upon the site of sin He strikes the heart with legal fear. (Now these four actions are indeed no fruits of grace, for a reprobate may go thus far; they are works of preparation

going before grace. The other actions which follow are effects of grace.)

5. The fifth action of grace therefore is to stir up the mind to serious consideration of the promise of salvation propounded and published in the gospel.

6. After this is the kindling of the heart with some sense of the sparks of faith—that is, a will and desire to believe, and in grace to strive against doubting and despair. Now in the same instant, when God begins to kindle the heart with any sparks of faith, then also He justifies the sinner, and with this begins the work of sanctification.

7. Then, so soon as faith is put into the heart, there is presently a combat: for a fight of doubting, despair, and distrust. And in this combat, faith shows itself by fervent, constant, and earnest invocation for pardon. After invocation follows the strength and prevailing of this desire.

8. Furthermore, God in mercy quite unsettles the conscience, as touching the salvation of the soul, and the promise of life, whereupon it rests and stays in itself.

9. Next, after this settled assurance and persuasion of mercy, falls a storing up of the heart to evangelical sorrow, according to God—that is, a grief for sin because it is sin, and because God is offended. And then the Lord works repentance, whereby the sanctified heart turns itself on Him. And though this repentance be one of the last in order, yet it is itself first: as when a candle is brought into our room,

we first see the light before we see the candle, and yet the candle must needs be before the light can be.

10. Lastly, God gives a man grace to endeavor to obey His commandments by new obedience. And by these degrees does the Lord give the first grace.

The second work of God tending to salvation is the giving of the second grace, which is nothing itself, but the continuance of the first grace given. . . . And this, if we regard man in himself, is very necessary. For as fire, without supply of matter where it is fed and contained, would soon go out, so unless God of His goodness should follow His children, and by new and daily supplies continue His first grace in them, they would undoubtedly lose the same, and finally fall away.

# RICHARD BAXTER

## The Reformed Pastor

Must I turn to my Bible to show a preacher where it is written that a man's soul is worth more than a world, much more therefore than a hundred pounds a year? And how much more are many souls worth? Or that both we and all that we have are God's and should be employed to the utmost for His service? Or that it is inhuman cruelty to let souls go to hell for fear my wife and children should fare somewhat the harder, or live at lower rates, when, according to God's ordinary way of working by means, I might do much to prevent their misery if I would but a little displease my flesh—that which all who are Christ's have crucified with its lusts?

Every man must render to God the things that are God's, and that, let it be remembered, is all he is and all he possesses. How are all things sanctified to us but in the separation and dedication of them to God? Are they not all His talents, and must be employed in His service? Must not every Christian first ask, *In what way may I most honor God with my substance?* Do we not preach these things to our people? Are they true as to them, and not as to us?

Yea more, is not the church-maintenance devoted, in a special manner, to the service of God for the church? And should we not then use it for the utmost furtherance of that end? If any minister who has two hundred pounds a year can prove that a hundred pounds of it may do God more service if it be laid out on himself, or wife and children, than if it maintain one or two suitable assistants to help forward the salvation of the flock, I shall not presume to reprove his expenses. But where this cannot be proved, let not the practice be justified.

And I must further say that this poverty is not so intolerable and dangerous a thing as it is pretended to be. If you have but food and raiment, must you not therewith be content? And what would you have more than that which may fit you for the work of God? It is not being clothed in purple and fine linen, and faring sumptuously every day, that is necessary for this end. "A man's life consists not in the abundance of the things that he possesses" (Luke 12:15).

If your clothing be warm, and your food be wholesome, you may be as well supported by it to do God service as if you had the fullest satisfaction to your flesh. A patched coat may be warm, and bread and water are wholesome food. He that wants not these, has but a poor excuse to make for hazarding men's souls so that he may live on dainties.

# JONATHAN EDWARDS

## From the Sermon "Sinners in the Hands of an Angry God"

Are there not many here who have lived long in the world and are not to this day born again? Are there not many here who are aliens from the commonwealth of Israel, and have done nothing ever since they have lived but treasure up wrath against the day of wrath? Oh, sirs, your case, in an especial manner, is extremely dangerous. Your guilt and hardness of heart is extremely great. Do you not see how generally persons of your years are passed over and left, in the present remarkable and wonderful dispensation of God's mercy? You have need to consider yourselves and awake thoroughly out of sleep. You cannot bear the fierceness and wrath of the infinite God.

And you, young men and young women, will you neglect this precious season which you now enjoy, when so many others of your age are renouncing all youthful vanities, and flocking to Christ? You especially have now an extraordinary opportunity; but if you neglect it, it will soon be with you as with those persons who spent all the precious days of youth in sin, and are now come to such a dreadful pass in blindness and hardness. And you, children, who are unconverted, do not you know that you are going down to hell, to bear the dreadful wrath of that God who is now angry with you every day and every night? Will you be content to be the children of the devil, when so many other children in the land are converted, and are become the holy and happy children of the King of kings?

And let every one that is yet out of Christ, and hanging over the pit of hell—whether they be old men and women, or middle aged, or young people, or little children—now hearken to the loud calls of God's Word and providence. This acceptable year of the Lord, a day of such great favor to some, will doubtless be a day of as remarkable vengeance to others. Men's hearts harden, and their guilt increases apace at such a day as this, if they neglect their souls; and never was there so great danger of such persons being given up to hardness of heart and blindness of mind. God seems now to be hastily gathering in His elect in all parts of the land; and probably the greater part of adult persons that ever shall be saved will be brought in now in a little time, and that it will be as it was on the great out-pouring of the Spirit upon the Jews in the apostles' days. The elect will obtain, and the rest will be blinded.

If this should be the case with you, you will eternally curse this day, and will curse the day that ever you were born, to see such a season of the pouring out of God's Spirit, and you will wish that you had died and gone to hell before you had seen it. Now undoubtedly it is, as it was in the days of John the Baptist, that the axe is in an extraordinary manner laid at the root of the trees, that every tree which brings not forth good fruit may be hewn down and cast into the fire.

Therefore, let every one that is out of Christ now awake and fly from the wrath to come. The wrath of Almighty God is now undoubtedly hanging over a great part of this congregation. Let everyone fly out of Sodom: "Haste and escape for your lives; look not behind you, escape to the mountain, lest you be consumed."

# THOMAS BROOKS

## Apples of Gold

If they deserve a hanging who feast their slaves and starve their wives, who make provision for their enemies but none for their friend; how will you escape hanging in hell, who make provision for everything, yes, for all your lusts—but make no provision for your immortal souls? What shall we think of those who sell their precious souls for toys and trifles which cannot profit?

Ah! Do not pawn your souls, do not sell your souls, do not exchange away your souls, do not trifle and fool away your precious souls! They are jewels, worth more than a thousand worlds! If they are safe, all is safe; but if they are lost, all is lost: God lost, and Christ lost, and heaven lost—and that forever!

Now if you are resolved to spend your strength in the service of sin and the world, then know that no tongue can express, no heart can conceive that trouble of mind, that terror of soul, that horror of conscience, that fear and amazement, that weeping and wailing, that crying and roaring, that sighing and groaning, that cursing and howling, that stamping and tearing, that wringing of hands and gnashing of teeth which shall certainly attend you when God shall bring you into judgment. Yes, judgment for all your looseness and lightness, for all your wickedness and wantonness, for all your profaneness and baseness, for all your neglect of God, your grieving the Comforter, your trampling underfoot the blood of a Savior, for your prizing earth above heaven, and the pleasures of this world above the pleasures which are at God's right hand.

Oh! How you will wish in that day when your sins shall be charged on you—when justice shall be armed against you, when conscience shall be gnawing within you, when the world shall be a flaming fire about you, when the gates of heaven shall be shut against you and the flame of hell ready to take hold of you, when angels and saints shall sit in judgment upon you and forever turn their faces from you, when evil spirits shall be terrifying you and Jesus Christ forever disowning you.

How you will wish in that day that you had never been born, or that you might now be unborn, or that your mothers' wombs had been your tombs! Oh, how you will then wish to be turned into a bird, a beast, a stock, a stone, a toad, a tree! How you will say, "Oh that our immortal souls were mortal! Oh that we were nothing! Oh that we were anything but what we are!"

# THOMAS WATSON

## The Beatitudes

"When the sentence for a crime is not quickly carried out, the hearts of the people are filled with schemes to do wrong" (Ecclesiastes 8:11).

God forbears punishing—therefore men forbear repenting. He does not smite upon their back by correction—therefore they do not smite upon their thigh by humiliation (Jeremiah 31:19). The sinner thinks thus: "God has spared me all this while; surely He will not punish me." "He says to himself: 'God has forgotten; He covers His face and never sees!'" (Psalm 10:11).

In infinite patience God sometimes adjourns His judgments a while longer. He is not willing to punish (2 Peter 3:9). God is like the bee, which naturally gives honey—but stings only when it is provoked. But alas, how is His patience abused! God's patience hardens most. Because God stops the vial of His wrath, sinners stop the conduit of tears!

To be hardened under God's patience makes our condition far worse. Incensed justice will revenge abused patience! God was patient towards Sodom, but when they did not repent, He made the fire and brimstone flame about their ears. Sodom, which was once the wonder of God's patience, is now a standing monument of God's severity. Long forbearance is no forgiveness. God may keep off the stroke awhile, but His justice is not dead—it only sleeps. God has leaden feet but iron hands. The longer God is taking His blow, the sorer it will be when it comes. The longer a stone is falling, the heavier it will be at last. The longer God is whetting His sword, the sharper it cuts!

How dreadful will their condition be, who sin because God is patient with them. For every crumb of His patience, God puts a drop of wrath into His vial. The longer God forbears with a sinner, the more interest he is sure to pay in hell.

# JONATHAN EDWARDS

## Discourse on Procrastination

What dismal calamities and miseries mankind are subject to for lack of behaving every day as if it did not depend on any future day!

The way of the world is for one day to foolishly depend on another—yes, on many others. And what is the consequence? Why, the consequence with respect to the greater part of the world is that they live all their days without any true peace or rest of soul. They are all their lifetime subject to bondage through fear of death. And when death sensibly approaches, they are put into a terrible fright.

They have a dismal view of their past; the ill improvement of their time, and the sins they have been guilty of, stand staring them in the face and are more frightful to them than so many devils. And when they look forward into that eternity whither they are going, how dismal is the prospect! Oh, how their hearts shrink at the thought of it! They go before the judgment-seat of God as those that are dragged there, while they would gladly, if they could, hide themselves in the caves and dens of the earth.

And something is worse yet than all the disquietude and terror of conscience in this world: the consequence of a contrary behavior, with respect to the bulk of mankind, is their eternal perdition. They flatter themselves that they shall see another day, and then another, and trust to that until finally most of them are swallowed up in hell to lament their folly to all eternity in the lake that burns with fire and brimstone. Consider how it was with all the foolish virgins who trusted to the delay of the bridegroom's coming. When he came, they were surprised and found unprepared, having no oil in their lamps; and while they went to buy, those who were ready went in with him to the marriage and the door was shut against them. They came afterwards crying in vain: "Lord, Lord, open to us."

# THOMAS WATSON

## The Beatitudes

"If anyone would come after Me, he must deny himself and take up his cross daily and follow Me" (Luke 9:23).

Self-denial is the highest sign of a sincere Christian. Hypocrites may have great knowledge and make large profession—but it is only the true-hearted saint who can deny himself for Christ.

Self-denial is the foundation of godliness, and if this foundation is not well-laid, the whole building will fall. If there is any lust in our souls which we cannot deny, it will turn at length either to scandal or apostasy. Self-denial is the thread which must run along through the whole work of piety.

A man must deny self-esteem. Every man by nature has a high opinion of himself. He is drunk with spiritual pride. A proud man disdains the cross. He thinks himself too good to suffer. Oh, deny self-esteem! Let the plumes of pride fall off!

A man must deny carnal self. This I take to be the chief sense of the text. He must deny carnal ease. The flesh cries out for ease. It is loath to put its neck under Christ's yoke or stretch itself upon the cross. The flesh cries out: "Oh! The cross of Christ is heavy! There are nails in that cross which will lacerate, and fetch blood!" We must deny our self-ease, and be as a deaf adder, stopping our ears to the charmings of the flesh! Those who lean on the soft pillow of sloth will hardly take up the cross.

This self-denying frame of heart is very hard. This is "to pluck out the right eye." It is easier to overcome men and devils, than to overcome self. "Stronger is he who conquers himself, than he who conquers the strongest walled city."

Self is the idol, and how hard it is to sacrifice this idol and to turn self-seeking into self-denial! But though it is difficult, it is essential. A Christian must first lay down self before he can take up the cross.

Alas! How far are they then from self-denial, who cannot deny themselves in the least things; who in their diet or apparel, instead of martyring the flesh, pamper the flesh! Instead of taking up the cross, take up their cups! Is this self-denial, to let loose the reins to the flesh? Oh, Christians, as ever you would be able to carry Christ's cross, begin to deny yourselves.

"Everyone who has given up houses or brothers or sisters or father or mother or children or property, for My sake, will receive a hundred times as much in return and will have eternal life!" (Matthew 19:29). Here is a very choice bargain!

# COTTON MATHER

## What Must I Do to Be Saved?

Oh! Set your hearts to these things. They are not vain things; your lives, the very lives of your souls are concerned in them. If your hearts may now fall in with these things, and formed and shaped according to the evangelical mold of them, lo, this day salvation is come unto your souls. Glorious Lord, incline the hearts of our people to do what must be done so that Your salvation may be bestowed upon them.

First this must be done: you must come to be bitterly sensible that you lack a glorious Christ for your Savior. We read in John 7:37, "If any man thirst, let him come unto me." Truly, no man will come to Christ until a thirst or a pungent and painful sense of the lack of Christ be raised in him.

You must feel the burden of your sin, lying on you; and you must cry out, "Oh, 'tis a heavy burden—too heavy for me!" You must see God angry with you, sin binding you, hell gaping for you; and you must utterly despair of helping yourself out of the confusion that is come upon you.

You must be filled with sorrow for what you have done; with horror at what you are exposed unto. The cry of your uneasy souls must be that in Romans 7:24: "O wretched man that I am, who shall deliver me!"

You must be no strangers to such soliloquies as these: *I have sinned; I have sinned, and woe is unto me that I have sinned; I have lost the knowledge of God and lost the image of God and lost the favor of God. My sin renders me obnoxious to the vengeance of God. Lust enchants me and enslaves me; Satan tyrannizes over me. I am in hourly hazard of an eternal banishment from God into outer darkness, into the place of dragons. Oh! Wretched man that I am: I can do nothing to deliver myself. I perish, I perish, except a glorious Christ be my deliverer.*

The degree of this distress on the minds of them that shall be saved is various. There is a variety in that [preparatory] work, which does distress the elect of God in their coming to a Savior. Converts do sometimes needlessly distress themselves, and even deceive themselves, by insisting too much on the measure of this preparation. But so much of this work, as will render us restless without a Christ; so much of this work, as will render a whole Christ precious to us before there must be so much in our experience, if we would be saved.

# RICHARD BAXTER

## The Reformed Pastor

How many around you are blindly hastening to perdition while your voice is appointed to be the means of arousing and reclaiming them! The physician has no excuse who is doubly bound to relieve the sick, when even every neighbor is bound to help them.

Brothers, what if you heard sinners cry after you in the streets: "O sir, have pity on me, and afford me your advice! I am afraid of the everlasting wrath of God. I know I must shortly leave this world, and I am afraid lest I shall be miserable in the next." Could you deny your help to such poor sinners? What if they came to your study door and cried for help, and would not go away till you had told them how to escape the wrath of God? Could you find in your hearts to drive them away without advice? I am confident you could not.

Why, alas! Such persons are less miserable than they who will not cry for help. It is the hardened sinner, who cares not for your help, that most needs it; and he that has not so much life as to feel that he is dead, nor so much light as to see his danger, nor so much sense left as to pity himself—this is the man that is most to be pitied.

Look upon your neighbors around you and think how many of them need your help in no less a case than the apparent danger of damnation. Suppose that you heard every impenitent person whom you see and know about you crying to you for help: "As ever you pitied poor wretches, pity us, lest we should be tormented in the flames of hell. If you have the hearts of men, pity us." Now, do for them what you would do if they followed you with such expostulations. Oh, how can you walk and talk and be merry with such people, when you know their case?

Oh, then, for the Lord's sake, and for the sake of poor souls, have pity on them and bestir yourselves, and spare no pains that may conduce to their salvation.

# JOSEPH ALLEINE

## A Sure Guide to Heaven

Dearly beloved, I gladly acknowledge myself a debtor to you, and am concerned, as I would be found a good steward of the household of God, to give to everyone his portion. But the physician is most concerned for those patients whose case is most doubtful and hazardous; and the father's pity is especially turned towards his dying child. So unconverted souls call for earnest compassion and prompt diligence to pluck them as brands from the burning (Jude 23). Therefore it is to them I shall first apply myself in these pages.

But from where shall I fetch my argument? With what shall I win them? Oh, that I could tell! I would write to them in tears, I would weep out every argument, I would empty my veins for ink, I would petition them on my knees. Oh, how thankful should I be if they would be prevailed with to repent and turn.

How long have I labored for you! How often would I have gathered you! This is what I have prayed for and studied for these many years: that I might bring you to God. Oh, that I might now do it! Will you yet be entreated?

But, O Lord, how insufficient I am for this work. Alas, with what shall I pierce the scales of Leviathan, or make the heart feel that is hard as the nether millstone? Shall I go and speak to the grave and expect the dead will obey me and come forth? Shall I make an oration to the rocks, or declaim to the mountains, and think to move them with arguments? Shall I make the blind to see?

But, O Lord, You can pierce the heart of the sinner. I can only draw the bow at a venture, but You direct the arrow between the joints of the harness.

Slay the sin and save the soul of the sinner that casts his eyes on these pages.

# THOMAS GOUGE

## The Young Man's Guide Through the Wilderness
## of This World

An Epistle to the Youth of England and Wales:

I fear you are not in such a condition of your souls that I may apply these words to you without exception: "I have written unto you, young men, because you are strong, and the Word of God abides in you, and you have overcome the wicked one" (1 John 2:14). Yet the searcher of hearts knows that I have written to you out of an earnest desire that it might be so.

Myself, and others that stand upon the brink of eternity by reason of age, can see better than yourselves (because we have had experience of it) that your youthful time is a dangerous time. However you may now rejoice, if you do not take heed you may contract such guilt to your souls as to make you mourn hereafter; yes, even forever (Proverbs 5:11–3).

You are apt to put off convictions and the calls of grace in hopes of a longer life; you seem to be unwilling yet to repent because you are too confident that you shall not yet die, as if holiness were not a thing in season for such as you.

But does God put off doing good to you until you are old? Is He not now preserving you, and providing for you while you are young? Why then will you put off doing service to Him until you are old? What horrible unthankfulness is this to God. What ground have you to think that you shall live so long? Or that you shall, without fail, die God's servants if you live now as slaves to sin and Satan?

# THOMAS WATSON

## A Divine Cordial

It is better to love God than the world.

If you set your love on worldly things, they will not satisfy. You may as well satisfy your body with air as your soul with earth! If the globe of the world were yours, it would not fill your soul. Will you set your love on that which will never give you contentment? Is it not better to love God? He will give you that which shall satisfy your soul to all eternity!

If you love worldly things, they cannot remove trouble of mind. If there is a thorn in the conscience, all the world cannot pluck it out. King Saul, being perplexed in mind, all his crown jewels could not comfort him (1 Samuel 28:15). But if you love God, He can give you peace when nothing else can. He can apply Christ's blood to refresh your soul. He can whisper His love by the Spirit, and with one smile scatter all your fears and disquiets.

If you love the world, you love that which may keep you out of heaven. "How hard it is for those who have wealth to enter the kingdom of God!" (Mark 10:23). Prosperity, to many, is like a large sail to a small boat, which quickly overturns it. By loving the world you love that which will endanger you. But if you love God, there is no fear of losing heaven. He will be a Rock to hide you, but not to hurt you. By loving Him, we come to enjoy Him forever.

You may love worldly things, but they cannot love you in return. You love gold and silver, but your gold cannot love you in return. You give away your love to the creature and receive no love back. But if you love God, He will love you in return. "If any man loves Me, My Father will love him, and We will come unto him, and make Our abode with him" (John 14:23). God will not be behindhand in love to us. For our drop of love to Him, we shall receive an ocean of His love!

While you love the world, you love that which is infinitely below the worth of your souls. When you lay out your love upon the world, you hang a pearl upon a swine—you love that which is inferior to yourself. As Christ speaks in another sense of the birds of the air, "Are you not much better than they?" (Matthew 6:26), so I say of worldly things: are you not much better than they? You love a fair house or a beautiful garment—are you not much better than they? But if you love God, you place your love on the most noble and sublime object; you love that which is better than yourselves. God is better than the soul, better than angels, better than heaven!

You may love the world and receive hatred for your love. Would it not vex one to lay out money upon a piece of ground which, instead of bringing forth grain or fruit, should yield nothing but nettles? Thus it is with all earthly things—we love them, and they prove nettles to sting us! We meet with nothing but disappointment. But if we love God, He will not return hatred for love. "I love those who love Me" (Proverbs 8:17). God may chastise His children, but He cannot hate them. Every believer is part of Christ, and God can as well hate Christ as hate a believer.

You may over-love the creature. You may love wine too much, and silver too much; but you cannot love God too much. It is our sin that we cannot love God enough. How weak is our love to God! If we could love God far more than we do, yet it can never be proportionate to His worth; so there is no danger of excess in our love to God.

You may love worldly things, and they die and leave you. Riches take wings! Relations drop away! There is nothing here abiding. The creature has a little honey in its mouth, but it has wings! It will soon fly away. But if you love God, He is "a portion forever" (Psalm 73:26). As He is called a Sun for comfort, so a Rock for eternity. Thus we see that it is better to love God than the world.

# OCTAVIUS WINSLOW

## The Atonement

The sin of rejecting the Savior is, to the writer's mind, the sin of sins. The sin of thinking lightly of Christ—of turning the back upon God's unspeakable gift, of refusing to receive, love, and obey His only and well-beloved Son—is the sin which seems, like Aaron's rod, to swallow up every other. It is the master sin; the sin on which the great indictment will be made out against the ungodly world in the day when God shall make inquisition for blood. It is a sin, too, of which the devils have never been guilty. To them the Savior has never been sent. Before their eyes the cross has never been lifted. Along their gloomy coasts no tidings of redeeming mercy have ever echoed.

To reject the Savior, then—to turn your back upon the cross, to heed not the glad tidings of redemption, and to die in that state—is to pass to the judgment, guilty of a sin from the charge of which even Satan himself will be acquitted! "This is the condemnation, that light is come into the world, and men love darkness rather than light, because their deeds are evil" (John 3:19). . . .

In rejecting Christ you turn your back upon God Himself. Has He not declared it? "He that hates me hates my Father also" (John 15:23). "For the Father judges no man, but has committed all judgment unto the Son: that all men should honor the Son, even as they honor the Father. He that honors not the Son, honors not the Father who has sent Him" (John 5:22–23).

Behold in what light the word of truth places the sin of hating, honoring not, and rejecting the Lord Jesus, the Son of God, and the Redeemer of men. We beseech you: ponder well the sin of turning your back upon God's "unspeakable gift."

# RICHARD BAXTER

## A Call to the Unconverted to Turn and Live

God takes pleasure in men's conversion and salvation, but not in their death or damnation. He would rather they turn and live than go on and die. I shall first teach you how to understand this, and then clear up the truth of it to you.

First, you must observe these following things:

1. A simple willingness, or complacency, is the first act of the will, following the simple apprehension of the undertaking before it proceeds to compare things together. But the choosing act of the will is a following act, and it supposes the comparing practical act of the understanding. And these two acts may often be carried to contrary objects without any fault at all in the person.

2. An unfeigned willingness may have diverse degrees. Some things I am so far willing of that I will do all that lies in my power to accomplish them; and some things I am truly willing another should do, yet I will not do all that I am able to procure them, having many reasons to dissuade me.

3. The will of a ruler, as such, is manifested in making and executing laws. But the will of a man in his simple and

natural capacity, or as absolute lord of his own, is manifested in desiring or resolving events.

4. A ruler's will, as lawgiver, is first and principally that his laws be obeyed, and not at all that the penalty be executed on any—but only on supposition that they will not obey his laws. But a ruler's will, as judge, supposes the law already either kept or broken; and therefore he resolves on rewards or punishments accordingly.

Having given up these necessary distinctions, I shall next apply them to the case in hand through the following propositions:

1. It is in the glass of the word and creatures that in this life we must know God; and so, according to the nature of man, we ascribe to Him understanding and will, removing all the imperfections that we can because we are capable of no higher positive conceptions of Him.

2. On the same grounds, we do (with the Scripture) distinguish between the acts of God's will as diversified from the respects or the objects, though as to God's essence they are all one.

3. And all the more bold because, when we speak of Christ, we have more ground for it from human nature.

4. And thus we say that the simple complacency, will, or love of God is to all that is naturally or morally good according to the nature and degree of its goodness. And so He has pleasure in the conversion and salvation of all, which yet will never come to pass.

5. And God, a ruler and lawgiver of the world, has so far a practical will for their salvation as to make them a free gift of Christ and life, and an act of oblivion for all their sin, if they will not unthankfully reject it—and to command His messengers to offer this gift to all the world, and persuade them to accept it.

Yet God resolves, as lawgiver, that those who will not turn shall die. And as judge, when their day of grace is past, He will execute that decree.

# JONATHAN EDWARDS

## From the Sermon "The Peace Which Christ Gives His True Followers"

You that have hitherto spent your time in the pursuit of satisfaction in the profit or glory of the world, or in the pleasures and vanities of youth, have this day an offer of that excellent and everlasting peace and blessedness Christ has purchased with the price of His own blood.

As long as you continue to reject those offers and invitations of Christ, and continue in a Christ-less condition, you never will enjoy any true peace or comfort; you will be like the prodigal who in vain endeavored to be satisfied with the husks that the swine did eat. The wrath of God will abide upon you, and misery will attend you wherever you go; you never will be able to escape.

Christ gives peace to the most sinful and miserable that come to Him. He heals the broken in heart and binds up their wounds. But it is impossible that they should have peace while they continue in their sins. There is no peace between God and them; for, as they have the guilt of sin remaining in their souls, and are under its dominion, so God's indignation continually burns against them. Therefore they travail in pain all their days. While you continue in such a state, you live in dreadful uncertainty of what will become of you—and you live in continual danger. When you are in the enjoyment of things most pleasing to you, where your heart is best suited and most cheerful, yet you are in a state of condemnation.

You hang over the infernal pit, with the sword of divine vengeance hanging over your head, having no security one moment from utter and remediless destruction.

What reasonable peace can anyone enjoy in such a state as this? Even though you clothe him in gorgeous apparel or set him on a throne, or at a prince's table, and feed him with the rarest dainties the earth affords—how miserable is the ease and cheerfulness that such have! What a poor kind of comfort and joy is it that such take in their wealth and pleasures for a moment, while they are the prisoners of divine justice and wretched captives of the devil! They have none to befriend them, being without Christ; they are aliens from the commonwealth of Israel, strangers from the covenant of promise—having no hope and without God in the world!

I invite you now to a better portion. There are better things provided for the sinful, miserable children of men. There is a surer comfort and more durable peace: comfort that you may enjoy in a state of safety and on a sure foundation. There is a peace and rest that you may enjoy with reason, and with your eyes open. You may have all your sins forgiven, your greatest and most aggravated transgressions blotted out as a cloud and buried as in the depths of the sea, that they may never be found more. And being not only forgiven, but accepted to favor, you become the objects of God's complacency and delight; being taken into God's family and made His children, you may have good evidence that your names were written on the heart of Christ before the world was made, and that you have an interest in that covenant of grace that is well ordered in all things and sure. Within this covenant is promised no less than life and immortality, an inheritance incorruptible and undefiled, a crown of glory that fades not away.

Being in such circumstances, nothing shall be able to prevent your being happy to all eternity; having for the foundation of your hope that love of God which is from eternity to eternity, and His promise and oath, and His omnipotent power—things infinitely firmer than mountains of brass. The mountains shall depart and the hills be removed; yes, the heavens shall vanish away like smoke and the earth shall wax old like a garment. Yet these things will never be abolished.

# JOSEPH ALLEINE

## A Sure Guide to Heaven

And now, beloved, let me know your mind. What do you intend to do? Will you go on and die, or will you turn and lay hold on eternal life? How long will you linger in Sodom? How long will you halt between two opinions? Have you not yet resolved whether Christ or Barabbas, whether bliss or torment, whether this vain and wretched world or the paradise of God be the better choice? Is it a disputable case whether the Abana and Pharpar of Damascus be better than all the streams of Eden, or whether the vile pool of sin is to be preferred before the water of life, clear as crystal, proceeding out of the throne of God and of the Lamb?

Can the world in good earnest do for you what Christ can? Will it stand by you to eternity? Will pleasures, lands, titles, and treasures descend with you? If not, had you not need look after something that will? What do you mean to stand wavering? Shall I leave you at last, like Agrippa, only almost persuaded? You are forever lost if left here; as good be not at all, as not altogether a Christian. How long will you rest in idle wishes and fruitless purposes? When will you come to a fixed, firm, and full resolve? Do you not see how Satan cheats you by tempting you to delay? How long has he drawn you on in the way of perdition!

Well, do not put me off with a dilatory answer; tell me not later. I must have your immediate consent. If you are not now resolved, while the Lord is treating with you and inviting you, much less likely are you to be later, when these impressions are worn off and you are hardened through the deceitfulness of sin. Will you give me your hand? Will you set open the door and give the Lord Jesus the full and ready possession? Will you put your name unto His covenant? What do you resolve upon? If you still delay, my labor is lost, and all is likely to come to nothing. Come, cast in your lot; make your choice.

"Now is the accepted time; now is the day of salvation; today, if you will hear His voice." Why should not this be the day from which you are able to date your happiness? Why should you venture a day longer in this dangerous and dreadful condition? What if God should this night require your soul? Oh, that you might know in this day the things that belong to your peace, before they be hid from your eyes! This is your day, and it is but a day. Others have had their day and have received their doom; and now are you brought upon the stage of this world, here to act your part for your eternity. Remember, you are now upon your good behavior for everlasting; if you do not make a wise choice now, you are undone forever. What your present choice is, such must be your eternal condition.

And is it true indeed? Are life and death at your choice? Why, then, what hinders but that you should be happy? Nothing does or can hinder but your own willful neglect or refusal. It was the saying of the eunuch to Philip: "See, here is water, what hinders me to be baptized?" So I may say to you: See, here is Christ; here is mercy, pardon, life. What hinders but that you should be pardoned and saved?

# THOMAS WATSON

## The Doctrine of Repentance

There is no better sign of true repentance than a holy antipathy against sin. Sound repentance begins in love to God—and ends in the hatred of sin.

How may true hatred of sin be known? When a man's heart is set against sin. Not only does the *tongue* protest against sin, but the *heart* abhors it. However lovely sin is painted, we find it odious—just as we abhor the picture of one whom we mortally hate, even though it may be well drawn.

Suppose a dish be finely cooked and the sauce good—yet if a man has an antipathy against the meat, he will not eat it. So let the devil cook and dress sin with pleasure and profit, yet a true penitent has a secret abhorrence of it, is disgusted by it, and will not meddle with it.

True hatred of sin is universal. There is a dislike of sin not only in the judgment, but in the will and affections. Many a one is convinced that sin is a vile thing, and in his judgment has an aversion to it—yet he tastes sweetness in it, and has a secret delight in it. Here is a disliking of sin in the judgment and an embracing of it in the affections! Whereas in true repentance, the hatred of sin is in all the faculties, not only in the mind, but chiefly in the will: "I do the very thing I hate" (Romans 7:15). Paul was not free from sin—yet his will was against it.

He who truly hates one sin hates all sins. He who hates a serpent hates all serpents. "I hate every false way" (Psalm 119:104). Hypocrites will hate some sins which mar their credit. But a true convert hates all sins—gainful sins, complexion sins, the very stirrings of corruption. A holy heart detests sin for its intrinsic pollution. Sin leaves a stain upon the soul. A regenerate person abhors sin not only for the curse, but for the contagion. He hates this serpent not only for its sting, but for its poison. He hates sin not only for hell, but as hell.

Those who have no antipathy against sin are strangers to repentance. Sin is in them, as poison in a serpent, which, being natural to it, affords delight. How far are they from repentance who, instead of hating sin, love sin! To the godly sin is as a thorn in the eye; to the wicked sin is as a crown on the head. "They actually rejoice in doing evil" (Jeremiah 11:15). Loving of sin is worse than committing it. What is it that makes a swine love to tumble in the mire? Its love of filth. Oh, how many there are who love the forbidden fruit! They love their sin—and hate holiness.

There should be a deadly antipathy between the heart and sin. What is there in sin that may make a penitent hate it? Sin is the accursed thing, the most deformed monster! Look upon the origin of sin, from whence it comes. It fetches its pedigree from hell: "He who commits sin is of the devil" (1 John 3:8). Sin is the devil's special work. How hateful is it to be doing that which is the special work of the devil—indeed, that which makes men into devils!

# THOMAS GOUGE

## The Christian Householder

Let this exhortation stir up all Christian parents and masters of families to be careful that their whole house does faithfully serve the Lord, as well as themselves. Let them take up Joshua's resolution, "As for me and my house, we will serve the Lord." As you would not be guilty of the body and blood of your children, and your servants' souls—and as you would not have them cry out against you in everlasting fire—see that you bring them up in the fear and admonition of the Lord.

Oh! Let religion be in your families, not as a matter of small importance, only to be mined by the bye, or at leisure hours when the world will give you leave; but let it be the tending business of the house. Oh, let your houses be nurseries for the church of God. Yes, let it be said of your houses that this man and that man was born there. And, if you would that your children should bless you, that your servants should bless you, then set up religion and piety in your families. And, as ever you would be blessed, or be a blessing to them, let your hearts and your houses be the temples of the living God in which His worship may be duly performed.

Yes, every parent, master, and governor should, in the body politic of his own house, be that which the heart is in the natural body of man. As it communicates life and vital spirits to the rest of the members, so must the master of the household endeavor to impart the spiritual life of grace to all that are members of his body politic, and his house, by a constant conscionable performance of holy and religious duties there—and this would make it a little church.

For maintaining the worship of God makes every house to become a sanctuary, a house of God. Hence, diverse pious governors in the New Testament are said to have churches in their houses (Aquila and Priscilla, for example, and Nimphas). As in respect of the saints in their houses, so it was in respect of the worship of God among them. Oh, what an honor will this be to us, when, upon this account, our habitations shall be called churches rather than private houses—temples of God rather than the dwellings of men!

# JOSEPH ALLEINE

## An Alarm to the Unconverted

Conversion turns the balance of the judgment, so that God and His glory outweigh all carnal and worldly interests. It opens the eye of the mind and makes the scales of its native ignorance fall off. It turns men from darkness to light. The man who before saw no danger in his condition now concludes himself lost and forever undone (Acts 2:37)—except renewed by the power of grace. He who formerly thought there was little hurt in sin now comes to see it to be the chief of evils. He sees the unreasonableness, the unrighteousness, the deformity and the filthiness of sin so that he is affrighted with it, loathes it, dreads it, flees from it, and even abhors himself for it (Job 42:6; Ezekiel 36:31; Romans 7:15).

He who could see little sin in himself, and could find no matter for confession, now sees the rottenness of his heart—the desperate and deep pollution of his whole nature. He cries: "Unclean! Unclean! Lord, purge me with hyssop, wash me thoroughly, create in me a clean heart." He sees himself altogether filthy, corrupt both root and branch (Psalm 14:3; Matthew 7:17–18). He discovers the filthy corners that he was never aware of and sees the blasphemy, and theft, and murder, and adultery that is in his heart, of which before he was ignorant. Hitherto he saw no form or loveliness in Christ, no beauty that he should desire Him. But now he finds the Hidden Treasure and will sell all to buy this field. Christ is the Pearl he seeks.

Now, according to this new light, the man is of another mind, another judgment, than he was before. Now God is all with him. He has none in heaven or in earth like Him. He truly prefers Him before all the world. His favor is his life, the light of His countenance is more than corn and wine and oil—the good that he formerly enquired after and set his heart upon (Psalm 4:6–7).

A hypocrite may come to yield a general assent that God is the chief good; indeed, the wiser heathens, some few of them, have at least stumbled upon this. But no hypocrite comes so far as to look upon God as the most desirable and suitable good to him, and thereupon to acquiesce in Him. This is the convert's voice: "The Lord is my portion, says my soul. Whom have I in heaven but You? And there is none upon earth that I desire beside You. God is the strength of my heart and my portion forever" (Lamentations 3:24; Psalm 73:25–26).

Conversion turns the bias of the will both as to means and end. The intentions of the will are altered. Now the man has new ends and designs. He now intends God above all, and desires and designs nothing in all the world so much as that Christ may be magnified in him. He counts himself more happy in this than in all that the earth could yield: that he may be serviceable to Christ, and bring Him glory. This is the mark he aims at: that the name of Jesus may be great in the world.

Reader, do you read this without asking yourself whether it be this way with you? Pause a while and examine yourself.

6

# GOD'S WORD
# AND CHRISTIAN DOCTRINE

"If my compass always points to the North, I know
how to use it; but if it veers to other points of the
compass, and I am to judge out of my own mind
whether it is right or not, I am as well without the thing
as with it. If my Bible is right always, it will lead me
right; and as I believe it is so, I shall follow it."

—*Barbed Arrows*

# STEPHEN CHARNOCK

## Discourse on the Word, the Instrument of Regeneration

The gospel is an instrument to unlock the prison doors and take them off the hinges, to strike off the fetters and draw out the soul to a glorious liberty. It is by the voice of the archangel that men shall rise in their bodies; it is by the voice of the Son of God in the Word that men rise in their souls. Nothing else ever wrought such miraculous changes: to make lions become lambs; to make beloved idols be cast away with indignation; to make its entrance like fire and consume old lusts in a short time. These have been undeniable realities which have created affection and astonishment in some enemies as well as friends.

The Word has a more excellent instrumentality in it than other providences of God, because it is a higher manifestation. Every creature conducts us to the knowledge of God by giving us notice of His power, wisdom, and goodness (Romans 1:20). The declaration of His works in the world is instrumental to make men seek Him. Every day's providence declares His patience, every shower of rain His merciful provision for mankind, every day's preservation of the world under a load of sin manifests His mercy. The heavens have a tongue, and the rod has a voice; the design of all is to lead men to repentance (Romans 2:4).

If these, therefore, be some kind of instruments upon the hearts of considering men, the gospel is a discovery superior to all these in manifesting not only a God of nature, but a God of grace. It was designed for a choicer and nobler work. The heavens and providence are instruments to instruct us; the Word an instrument to renew us.

But the Word is not a natural instrument that works by any natural efficacy, as food does nourish, the sun shines, the air and water cools, or as a sharp knife cuts if applied to fit matter. If the Word were natural, it would not be of grace. Though the shining of the sun or the healing by a plaster are acts of the goodness and mercy of God, yet the Scripture calls them not by that higher title: acts of grace.

If the operation were natural, the gospel would never be without its effect wherever it was preached; just as the sun, wherever it shines in any land, both enlightens and warms. Our Savior then would have had more success, since the gospel could not have greater natural efficacy than from His lips; yet the number of His converts were probably not much above five hundred, for so many He appeared to after His resurrection (1 Corinthians 15:6), when many thousands in that land heard His voice and saw His miracles. . . .

Lastly, were the Word natural, the wisest men—men of the sharpest understandings—could not resist it. No man can hinder the sun's shining upon him when he is under the beams of it; it would warm him whether he like it or not. Yet have not such men been the most desperate opposers of the Word in all ages of the world, as well as in the times of the apostles?

The Word is not then a natural instrument, but a moral instrument.

# WILLIAM PERKINS

## The Art of Prophesying

The excellency of the nature of Scripture can be described in terms of its perfection, or purity, or its eternity.

Its *perfection* consists either in its sufficiency or its purity. Its sufficiency is so complete that nothing may be either added to it or taken from it which belongs to its proper purpose: "For I testify to everyone who hears the words of the prophecy of this book: if anyone adds to these things, God will add to him the plagues that are written in this book; and if anyone takes away from the words of the book of this prophecy, God shall take away his part from the Book of Life, from the holy city, and from the things which are written in this book" (Revelation 22:18–19).

The *purity* of Scripture lies in the fact that it stands complete in itself, without either deceit or error: "The words of the Lord are pure words, like silver tried in a furnace of earth, purified seven times" (Psalm 12:6).

The *eternity* of the Word is its quality of remaining inviolable. It cannot pass away until everything it commands has been fully accomplished (Matthew 5:18).

The exceptional character of the influence of Scripture lies in two things:

1. Its power to penetrate into the spirit of man: "For the word of God is living and powerful, and sharper than any two-edged

sword, piercing even to the division of soul and spirit, and of joints and marrow, and is a discerner of the thoughts and intents of the heart" (Hebrews 4:12).

2. Its ability to bind the conscience—that is, to constrain it before God either to excuse or accuse us of sin: "There is one lawgiver, who is able to save and to destroy" (James 4:12); "The Lord is our judge, the Lord is our lawgiver, the Lord is our King; He will save us" (Isaiah 33:22).

The Word of God is in the Holy Scriptures. The Scripture is the Word of God written in a language appropriate for the church by men who were immediately called to be the clerks or secretaries of the Holy Spirit: "For prophecy never came by the will of man, but holy men of God spoke as they were moved by the Holy Spirit" (2 Peter 1:21).

We speak of it as canonical Scripture because it is, as it were, a canon—that is, a rule or line used by a master workman, by the aid of which the truth is first discovered, and then examined. Consequently the supreme, final determination and judgment of all controversies in the church ought to be made by it.

# THOMAS MANTON

## From the Sermon "God's Word in Our Hearts"

One duty and necessary practice of God's children is to hide the Word in their hearts. "This book of the Law shall not depart out of your mouth, but you shall meditate upon it day and night" (Joshua 1:8). "Receive, I pray you, the law from His mouth, and lay up His words in your heart" (Job 22:22).

Lay up His words as we would do choice things, that they may not be lost. And lay them up as a treasure to be used upon all occasions. Lay them up in the heart; let them not swim in the brain or memory only, but let the affections be moved therewith. "Let the Word of Christ dwell in you richly" (Colossians 3:16). Be so diligent in the study of the Scripture that it may become familiar with us by frequent hearing, reading, meditating, and conferring about it. As a stranger, let it not stand at the door, but receive it into an inner room. To be strangers to the Word of God, and little conversant in it, is a great evil.

What is it to hide the Word in our hearts?

1. **To understand it and to get a competent knowledge of it.** We take things into the soul by the understanding: "When wisdom enters into your heart, and knowledge is pleasant unto your soul" (Proverbs 2:10).

2. **When it is assented unto by faith.** The Word is settled in the heart by faith, otherwise it soon vanishes.

3. **When it is kindly entertained.** Christ complained, "You seek to kill Me, because My Word has no place in you" (John 8:37). Men are so possessed with lust and prejudice that there is no room for Christ's Word. Though it break in upon the heart with evidence and power, yet it is not entertained there, but cast out again as an unwelcome guest.

4. **When it is deeply rooted.** Many men have flashes for a time: their affections may be much aloft, and they may have great elevations of joy, but no sound grace. The Word must be settled into a standing affection if we would have comfort and profit from it.

There are two reasons why one great duty and practice of the saints is to hide the Word in their hearts. First, that we may have it ready for our use. We lay up principles that we may lay them out upon all occasions. When the Word is hidden in the heart, it will be ready to break out in the tongue and practice, and it will be forthcoming to direct us in every duty and exigency. When persons run to the market for every pennyworth, it does not make good housekeepers. To be seeking of comforts when we should use them, or to run to a book, is not so blessed as to hide it in the heart. "A good scribe which is instructed unto the kingdom of heaven . . . brings forth out of his treasure things new and old" (Matthew 13:52). He not only has this year's growth, but the last year's gathering (for so is the allusion); he has not only from hand to mouth, but a good stock by him. So should it be with the Christian, which is a very great advantage. . . .

The second reason is because God does so in the work of conversion. "I will put My laws into their mind, and write them in their hearts" (Hebrews 8:10). The mind is compared to tables of stone, and the heart to the ark; and so this is required of us to "write them upon the table of your heart" (Proverbs 7:3).

# THOMAS MANTON

## From the Sermon "God's Word in Our Hearts"

I want to persuade you to study the Scripture, that you may get understanding and hide the Word in your hearts for gracious purposes. This is the Book of books: let it not lie idle. The world can as well be without the sun as the Bible—Psalm 19 speaks first of the sun, then of the Law of God, which is to the Christian as the sun is to the outward world. Consider the great use of the Word for informing the understanding and reforming the will. The Word of God is able "to make the man of God perfect, and thoroughly furnished" (2 Timothy 3:17).

Meditate often on it: "Mary kept all these sayings" (Luke 2:19). How did she keep them? She "pondered them in her heart." Musing makes the fire to burn, and deep and constant thoughts are operative. The hen which straggles from her nest when she sits a-brooding produces nothing; it is a constant incubation which hatches the young. So when we have only a few straggling thoughts and do not brood upon the Truth—when we have flashes only, like a little glance of a sunbeam upon a wall—it does nothing. But serious thoughts, through the Lord's blessing, will do the work. Urge the heart again and again. Ask: is this a Truth? What will become of me if I disregard it? Is this the Word of God, and does it find no more entertainment in my heart?

Receive God's Word in love. The apostle makes this to be the ground of apostasy: "because they received not the love of the truth" (2 Thessalonians 2:10). Oh, let it soak into the affections. If it lies only in the tongue or in the mind, only to make it a matter of talk and speculation, it will be soon gone. The seed which lies upon the surface, the fowls of the air will pick it up. Therefore hide it deeply; let it soak further and further.

I also want to direct you what to do in reading God's Word. It is a notable preservative against sin, and an antidote against the infection of the world: "The Law of God is in his heart, none of his steps shall slide" (Psalm 37:31). As long as truth is kept lively and active, and in view of conscience, we shall not slide—or not so often. We have many temptations to divert us from obedience, but we are in safety when the Law of God is in our hearts. Every time you read the Scripture you should lay up something. The best way to destroy ill weeds is by planting the ground with right seed.

Then for promises: what have you hidden in your heart for comfort against desertions and afflictions? In a time of trial you will find one promise gives more comfort and support than all the arguments that can be produced by reason. "This is my comfort in my affliction: Your Word hath quickened me" (Psalm 119:50). He had a word to support him; therefore let us treasure up the promises.

So it is in hearing God's Word. Do not hear lightly, but hide the Word in your heart, so that it is not embezzled by your own negligence, forgetfulness, or running into carnal distractions; that it be not purloined by Satan, and that he may not snatch away the good Seed out of your soul. When the Word is preached, there is more company present than is visible; there are angels and demons in the assembly. Whenever the sons of God meet together, Satan is there, too. The devil is present to divert the mind by wandering thoughts, by raising prejudices that we may cast out the Word—or by excuses, delays, evasions, putting it off to others when we begin to have some sense of our sin and danger. The devil is loath to let us go too far, lest Christ get a subject into His kingdom. Therefore let us labor to get something into the heart by every sermon: some fresh consideration is given out to set you to work in the spiritual life. It is sad to consider how many have heard much, and yet laid up little or nothing at all; it may be they have laid it up in their notebooks, but not laid up the Word in their hearts.

# JONATHAN EDWARDS

## Discourse on Christian Knowledge

There is no other way by which any means of grace whatsoever can be of any benefit except by knowledge. All teaching is in vain without learning. Therefore the preaching of the gospel would be wholly to no purpose if it conveyed no knowledge to the mind.

There is an order of men which Christ has appointed on purpose to be teachers in His church. But they teach in vain if no knowledge in these things is gained by their teaching. It is impossible that their teaching and preaching should be a means of grace, or of any good in the hearts of their hearers, other than by knowledge imparted to the understanding. Otherwise it would be of as much benefit to the listeners as if the minister should preach in some unknown tongue. . . .

No speech can be a means of grace except by conveying knowledge. Otherwise the speech is as much lost as if there had been no man there, and if he that spoke had spoken only into the air. Therefore hearing is absolutely necessary to faith, because hearing is necessary to understanding: "How shall they believe in Him of whom they have not heard?" (Romans 10:14).

In like manner, there can be no love without knowledge. It is not according to the nature of the human soul to love an object which is entirely unknown. The heart cannot be set upon an object of which there is no idea in the understanding. The reasons that induce the soul to love must first be understood before they can have a reasonable influence on the heart.

God has given us the Bible, which is a book of instructions. But this book can be of no manner of profit to us unless it conveys some knowledge to the mind; it can profit us no more than if it were written in the Chinese or Tartarian language, of which we know not one word. So the sacraments of the gospel can have a proper effect no other way than by conveying some knowledge. They represent certain things by visible signs. And what is the end of signs, but to convey some knowledge of the things signified?

Such is the nature of man: that no object can come at the heart but through the door of the understanding. And there can be no spiritual knowledge of that of which there is not first a rational knowledge. It is impossible that anyone should see the truth or excellence of any doctrine of the gospel, if he does not know what that doctrine is. A man cannot see the wonderful excellence and love of Christ in doing such and such things for sinners unless his understanding is first informed about how those things were done. He cannot have a taste of the sweetness and excellence of divine truth unless he first has a notion that there is such a thing.

# STEPHEN CHARNOCK

## Discourse on the Word, the Instrument
## of Regeneration

How admirable, then, is the power of the gospel! It is a quickening Word, not dead; a powerful Word, not weak; a sharp-edged Word, not dull; a piercing Word, not cutting only skin deep. What welcome work does it make when a door of utterance and a door of entrance are both opened together! It has a mighty power to out-wrestle the principalities of hell and demolish the strongholds of sin in the heart. It is a Word of which it may be said, as the psalmist said of the sun, "His circuit is to the ends of the earth, and there is nothing hidden from the heat thereof" (Psalm 19:6). What a powerful breath is that which can make a dead man stand upon his feet and walk!

If you should find your faces, by looking in a glass, transformed into an angelical beauty, would you not imagine some strange and secret virtue in that glass? How powerful is this gospel Word, which changes a beast into a man, a devil into an angel, a clod of earth into a star of heaven!

It is above the power of all moral philosophy. The wisdom of the heathens never equaled the gospel in such miracles; the political government of the best states never made such alterations in the hearts of men. How excellent is that gospel which has done that for the renewing of millions of souls, which all the wit and wisdom of the choicest philosophers could never effect upon one heart! All other lectures can do no more than allay the passions, not change them; bring them into an order fit for human society, not beget them for a divine fellowship; not draw them forth out of a principle of love to God and fix them upon so high an end as the glory of God that is invisible. This is the glorious begetting by the gospel that enables men not only to moral actions, but inspires with divine principles and ends, and makes men highly delight in the ways they formerly abhorred. . . .

The gospel is above the power of the law. The natural law sees not Christ; the Mosaic law dimly shows Him far off; the gospel brings Him near, to be embraced by us and us to be divinely changed by Him. The natural law makes the model and frame of a man, the Mosaic adds some colors and preparations, and the gospel conveys spirit into them. The natural law begets us for the world, the Mosaic law kills us for God, and the gospel raises up to life. The natural law makes us serve God by reason, the Mosaic by fear, and the gospel by love.

It is by the gospel, and not by the law, that those three graces which are the main evidences of life are settled in the soul. It begets faith, whereby we are taken off from the stock of Adam and inserted in Christ; hope, whereby we flourish; and love, whereby we produce fruit. By faith we have life; by hope, strength; by love, liveliness and activity. All these are the fruits of the gospel administration.

# THOMAS GOUGE

## The Principles of the Christian Religion

The chief end of this treatise is to contribute some help to parents and masters of families in the discharge of that great and necessary duty of instructing their children and servants in the principles of the Christian religion. I know of no fitter persons to whom to dedicate this work than to such who are chiefly concerned in the duty and most obliged to see it done. And I write this so that I may have an opportunity to stir you up to a constant and conscionable performance of it, which you will find very advantageous to the spiritual good of your families here, and to their eternal happiness hereafter.

For by catechizing, a good and sure foundation is laid. Now it is necessary that in all buildings a good foundation be laid, lest, for want of it, the building should come to ruin—as our Savior expressed in Matthew 7:26–27.

The use of a catechism is the easiest and most compendious way of conveying knowledge into the heads and hearts of your children and servants. Why is it that many old people are so grossly ignorant of fundamental truths, even those that are necessary to salvation, if it is not due to a lack of being catechized in their youth? In addition, the most intelligent hearers are usually found to be those who, in a timely matter, were instructed in the principles of religion.

Those that profess the faith are thereby enabled to render a reason of the hope that is in them. For a catechism that is well composed contains the sum and substance of all that Christians believe. Thereby the persons under your charge will be so well grounded in the truths that they will not easily be made a prey, either to atheists or papists or other seducers. For such will be the more likely to hold fast the truths which they have been taught out of the Word of God. Whereas we find by experience that those who were never well catechized are too soon drawn aside from the truth in order to embrace erroneous and heretical doctrines.

Oh, how the consideration of these singular benefits of family instruction should stir up parents and masters speedily to set upon the work, and to make a continuance of it. Without such work, how can you expect God's blessing upon your family? How can you expect that your children and servants, who know not the God of their fathers, should serve Him with honest and upright hearts? How can you expect that the gross ignorance, which is naturally in your children and servants, should be dispelled, and that they should be enlightened with the knowledge of the true God and of His Son, Jesus Christ? And how can you expect that your children should be kept from running into all manner of sin and wickedness if you do not train them up in the knowledge and fear of God, in the nurture and admonition of the Lord?

Certainly every parent and master has as great a charge of the souls of those under his roof as the minister has of the souls in his flock. And a dreadful thing it must be, to be guilty of the blood of souls.

# WILLIAM PERKINS

## The Order of Salvation and Damnation

There are three persons: the Father, the Son, and the Holy Ghost. Matthew 3:16–17: "And Jesus, when He was baptized, went up straightway out of the water: and, lo, the heavens were opened unto Him, and He saw the Spirit of God descending like a dove and lighting upon Him: And lo a voice from heaven, saying, 'This is my beloved Son, in whom I am well pleased.'"

The Father is a person without beginning from all eternity, begetting the Son (Hebrews 1:3; Psalm 2:7). In the generation of the Son, these properties may be noted: 1) He that begets and He that is begotten are together, and to one before another in time. 2) He that begets communicates with Him that is begotten, not some one part, but His whole essence. 3) The Father begot the Son not out of Himself, but within Himself.

The incommunicable property of the Father is to be unbegotten—to be a Father and to beget. He is the beginning of actions, because He begins every action of Himself, effecting it by the Son and the Holy Ghost (1 Corinthians 8:6).

The Son is the second person, begotten of the Father from all eternity (Hebrews 1:5; Colossians 1:15; Romans 8:32). Although the Son is begotten of His Father, yet nevertheless He is of and by Himself very God: for He must be considered either according to His essence, or according to His filiation or sonship. In regard of His essence, he is of and by Himself very God; for the deity which is common to all the three persons is not begotten. But as He is a person, and the Son of the Father, He is not of Himself, but from another, for He is the eternal Son of His Father. And thus He is truly said to be very God of very God.

For this cause He is said to be sent from the Father (John 8:42; Philippians 2:6). For this cause also He is the Word of the Father, not a vanishing, but an eternal Word. Because as a word is, as it were, begotten of the mind, so is the Son begotten of the Father, and also because He brings glad tidings from the bosom of His Father.

The Holy Ghost is the third person, proceeding from the Father and the Son (John 15:26; Romans 8:9). And albeit the Father and the Son are two distinct persons, yet are they both but one beginning of the Holy Ghost. What may be the essential difference between proceeding and begetting, neither the Scriptures determine nor the Church knows.

The incommunicable property of the Holy Ghost is to proceed. His proper manner of working is to finish an action, effecting it as from the Father and the Son.

# THOMAS MANTON

## Man and Sin

Certainly to remedy so great an evil requires an almighty power and the all-sufficiency of grace; therefore it is good to see how conversion is described in Scripture.

Sometimes it is described as enlightening the mind: "And the eyes of your understandings being enlightened" (Ephesians 1:18). Man, the wisest creature on this side of heaven, is stark blind in the things of God. Though he has the light of nature and can put on the spectacles of art (and dress his notions of divine things by the glass of the Word), yet before the cure is wrought, something must be done upon the faculty: the eyes of our understandings must be enlightened, as well as the object revealed. Yes!

But this infusion of light is not all; the Scriptures speak also of opening the heart: "He opened the heart of Lydia" (Acts 16:14). God does not only knock at the heart, but opens it. He knocks many times by the outward means, but finds no entrance. Yes, as one that would open a door—he tries key after key, till he has tried all the keys in the bunch. So does God use means after means; but until He puts His fingers upon the handles of the lock, the door is not opened to Him.

Well, then, the mind must be enlightened, and the heart opened. If these words are not emphatical enough, you will find conversion also expressed by regeneration: "Except a man be born again, he cannot see the kingdom of God" (John 3:3). Mark that: we must not only be reformed, but regenerated. Now because generation is an ordinary work of nature, and often falls out in the course of second causes, therefore it is expressed by the metaphor of resurrection (Ephesians 2:5). But that which has been may be again; therefore it is called a creation.

Further, conversion is expressed by victory (1 John 4:4), or by the beating and binding of the "strong man," by one that is "stronger than he" (Luke 11:21–22); also by "bringing into captivity every proud thought" (2 Corinthians 10:5).

All these expressions does the Scripture use to set out the mystery of grace. One expression may not be heeded enough, and therefore are many types and figures of it used—so that what is lacking in one notion may be supplied by another. And let us gather them up a little. There must be not only light in the mind, but the heart must be moved; and that not a little stirred, but changed, fashioned anew, born again. And because generation supposes a previous disposition in the matter, not only is it called "regeneration," but the term "resurrection" is used, in which the matter is wholly unprepared. But yet because still here is matter to work upon, therefore it is called creation, which was a making all things out of nothing. God works faith where there is no faith, and repentance where was no repentance; he "calls the things that are not as though they were." But now because sin makes us worse than nothing, and as in creation, as there was nothing to help, so there was nothing to resist and hinder—therefore it is expressed by victory. It implies opposition to God's work, and the resistance that there is in the heart of man until it be overpowered by grace.

# WILLIAM GURNALL

## The Christian in Complete Armor

What kind of faith is it that will enable the Christian to "quench all the fiery darts of the evil one," i.e., the devil? Historical faith cannot do this, and therefore is not it. This is so far from quenching Satan's fiery darts that the devil himself, the one that shoots them, has this faith. "The devils believe, and shudder" (James 2:19).

Temporary faith cannot do it. This is far from quenching Satan's fiery darts; indeed, this faith is itself quenched by them. It makes a goodly blaze of profession and "endures for a while" (Matthew 13:21), but soon disappears.

Miraculous faith, this falls just as short as the former. Judas' miraculous faith, which he had with other of the apostles (for all that we can read), enabled him to cast devils out of others, but left himself possessed of the devil of covetousness, hypocrisy, and treason—yes, a whole legion of lusts that hurried him down the hill of despair into the bottomless pit of perdition.

Only one kind of faith remains, which is what the apostle is referring to; that is justifying faith. This indeed is the grace that makes him, whoever has it, the devil's match. Satan has not so much advantage of the Christian by the transcendence of his natural abilities, as he has of Satan in this cause and this his weapon. The apostle is confident to give the day to the Christian before the fight is fully over: "You have overcome the wicked one" (1 John

2:13); that is, you are as sure to do it as if you were now mounted on your triumphant chariot in heaven. The knight shall overcome the giant; the saint, Satan. And the same apostle tells us what will win the day: "This is the victory that overcomes the world, even our faith" (1 John 5:4).

# JOSEPH ALLEINE

## The Gospel in a Map

Hear, O you ends of the earth; the mighty God, the Lord, has spoken. Gather My saints unto Me, those who have made a covenant with Me by sacrifice (Psalm 50:1, 5). Behold, I establish My covenant between Me and you (Genesis 17:7). By My holiness have I sworn that I will be your covenant Friend. I lift up My hand to heaven. I swear I live forever, and because I live you shall live also (John 14:19).

I will be yours (Jeremiah 32:38–40): your refuge and your rest (Jeremiah 50:6; Psalm 90:1; Psalm 46:1), your patron and your portion (Psalm 73:26; Isaiah 25:4–5), your heritage and your hope, your God and your guide (Psalm 48:14). While I have, you shall never lack; and what I am to Myself, I will be to you (Psalm 34:9–10). You shall be My people, a chosen generation, a kingdom of priests, a holy nation, a peculiar treasure unto Me above all people (Exodus 19:5–6; 1 Peter 2:9). . . .

My livery shall you wear, and the stamp of My own face shall you carry (Ezekiel 36:25–26; Ephesians 4:24); I will make you My witness and the epistles of Christ unto the world (2 Corinthians 3:3). You shall be chosen vessels to bear My name before the sons of men. And that you may see that I am in earnest with you, see, I make with you an everlasting covenant, ordered in all things and sure (2 Samuel 23:5). And I do here solemnly deliver it to you as My act and deed, sealed with sacred blood (1 Corinthians 11:25) and ratified with the oath of a God (Hebrews 6:17) who cannot lie, and who knows no place for repentance (Titus 1:2).

Come, you blessed ones, receive the instrument of your salvation: take the writings, behold the seals; here are the conveyances of the kingdom. Fear not, the donation is full and free. See, it is written in blood, founded on the all-sufficient merits of your Surety (Hebrews 9), in whom I am well pleased (Matthew 3:17) and whose death makes this testament unchangeable forever, so that your names can never be put out, nor your inheritance alienated, nor your legacies diminished. Nothing may be altered, nothing added, nothing subtracted—no, not forever (Galatians 3:15–17). . . .

Here I seal to you your pardons. Though your sins are as many as the sands and as mighty as the mountains, I will drown them in the deeps of My bottomless mercies (Micah 7:19). I will be merciful to your unrighteousness. I will multiply your pardon (Hebrews 8:12; Isaiah 55:7); where your sins have abounded, My grace shall superabound. Though they be as scarlet, they shall be white as snow; though red like crimson, they shall be as wool (Isaiah 1:18). Behold, I declare Myself satisfied and pronounce you absolved (Job 33:24). The price is paid, your debts are cleared, your bonds are canceled (Isaiah 43:25; Colossians 2:13–14).

Whatever the law, conscience, or the accuser has to charge upon you, I here exonerate and discharge you. I am He who blots out your transgressions for My name's sake. Who shall lay anything to your charge when I acquit you? Who shall impeach you when I proclaim you guiltless (Romans 8:33–34)? Sons, daughters, be of good cheer; your sins are forgiven you (1 John 2:12). . . .

Here I sign your release from the house of bondage (Romans 6:17–18; 1 Corinthians 7:22). Come forth, you captives; come forth and hope, for I have found a ransom (Job 33:24). . . . Arise, O redeemed of the Lord; put off the clothing of your captivities; arise and come away.

The dark and noisome prison of sin shall no longer detain you (John 8:34–36). I will loosen your fetters and knock off your bolts. Sin shall not have dominion over you (Romans 6:14). I will heal your backslidings, I will subdue your iniquities (Micah 7:19; Jeremiah 3:12), I will sanctify you wholly (1 Thessalonians 5:23–24), and I will put My fear in your hearts so that you shall not depart from Me (Jeremiah 32:40). . . .

From the strong and reeking jail of the grave I deliver you. O death, I will be your plague. O grave, I will be your destruction (Hosea 13:14). My beloved shall not ever see corruption (Psalm 16:10). I will change your rottenness into glory and make your dust arise and praise Me (Daniel 12:2–3; Isaiah 26:19). What is sown in weakness, I will raise in power; what is sown in corruption, I will raise in incorruption; what is sown a natural body, I will raise a spiritual body (1 Corinthians 15:42–44). This very flesh of yours, this corruptible flesh, shall put on incorruption; and this mortal flesh shall put on immortality (1 Corinthians 15:53). Death shall be swallowed up in victory and mortality [shall be swallowed up] of life (1 Corinthians 15:54; 2 Corinthians 5:4).

The Complete Works of Richard Sibbes

We may observe the ingeniousness of the church in laying open her own state. It is the disposition of God's people to be ingenious in opening their state to God, as in David, Nehemiah, Ezra, and so on. The reason is thus:

1. By a free and full confession we give God the honor of His wisdom in knowing of our own condition, secret and open. We give Him the honor of mercy that will not take advantage against us; the honor of power and authority over us, if He should show His strength against us in judgment. We yield unto Him the glory of all His chief prerogatives, whereupon Joshua moved Achan to a free confession: "My son, give glory to God" (Joshua 7:19).

2. We shame Satan, who first takes away shame of sinning, and then takes away shame for sin. He tempts us not to be ashamed to do what we are ashamed to confess, so we, by silence, keep Satan's council against our own souls. If we accuse ourselves, we put him out of office who is the "accuser of the brethren" (Revelation 12:10).

3. We prevent, likewise, malicious imputations from the world. Augustine answered roundly and well when he was

upbraided with the sins of his former age: "What you find fault with," he said, "I have condemned myself before."

This ingenious dealing eases the soul, giving vent to the grief of it. While the arrow's head sticks in the wound, it will not heal. Sin unconfessed is like a broken piece of rusty iron in the body. It must be gotten out, or else it will, by ranking and festering, cause more danger. It is like poison in the stomach—if it be not presently cast up it will infect the whole body. Is it not better to take shame to ourselves now, than to be shamed hereafter before angels, devils, and men?

# JOHN FLAVEL

## Pneumatologia: A Treatise on the Soul of Man

What manner of being is this soul of mine? Whence came it? Why was it infused into this body, and where must it abide when death has dislodged it out of this frail tabernacle? There is a natural aversion in man to such exercises of thought as these, although in the whole universe of beings in this lower world, a more noble creature is not to be found.

The soul is the most wonderful and astonishing piece of divine workmanship. It is no hyperbole to call it the breath of God, the beauty of men, the wonder of angels, and the envy of devils. One soul is of more value than all the bodies in the world.

The nature of it is so spiritual and sublime that it cannot be perfectly known by the most acute and penetrating understanding, assisted in the search by all the aid philosophy can contribute.

It is not my design in this discourse to treat of the several faculties and powers of the soul, or to give you the rise, natures, or numbers of its affections and passions: but I shall confine my discourse to its general nature and original.

The soul is variously denominated from its several powers and offices, as the sea from the several shores it washes. . . . It is a vital, spiritual, and immortal substance, endowed with an understanding, will, and various affections; it is created with an inclination to the body and infused thereinto by the Lord. . . .

The soul is a spiritual and immortal substance, endued with an understanding. This is the noble and leading faculty of the soul; we are not distinguished from brutes by our senses, but by our understanding. As grace sets one man above another, so understanding sets the meanest man above the best of brutes. Strange and wonderful things are performed by the natural instinct and sagacity of beasts, yet what is said of one is true of them all: "God has not imparted understanding to them" (Job 39:17).

The soul is a jewel which adorns none but rational creatures: men and angels.

# ROBERT BOLTON

## Heart Surgery

"Now when they heard this, they were pricked in their heart, and said unto Peter and to the rest of the apostles, Men and brethren, what shall we do?" (Acts 2:37).

In these words, there is shown a thorough wounding of the hearts of these men when they had heard of the greatness of their sin. Therefore observe that contrition in a new-born soul is ordinarily in proportion to his former vanity. To whom much is forgiven, they love much. This is a fountain of evangelical repentance. As a traitor condemned to die, receiving a pardon, would wonderfully break his heart to think he should be so villainous to so gracious a prince, so it is with a Christian that beholds God's mercy to him.

Christians, after their conversion, desire to see their sins to the utmost, with all the circumstances that make them hateful—such as the object, nature, person, time, and so on in which they were done. They do this so that they may be the more humbled by them.

If it is not so—and it may be otherwise, for God is a free agent and is not tied to any proportion of sorrow—then such troubles as these usually seize on them:

1. First, they are often afflicted with this notion: that their conversion is not thorough and sound, and so they do not perform the duties of godliness with heartiness and cheerfulness.

2. Second, they are many times haunted with listlessness and coldness in their progress in Christianity.

3. Third, they are visited with some cross or other, which sticks by them—to make them lay a greater load upon sin.

4. Fourth, they are more subject to be overtaken with their besetting sin, because they have sorrowed for it no more; for the less it is sorrowed over—the more it ensnares men.

5. Fifth, some of them have been assaulted upon their death-bed with sorrowful and strong temptations. Not that men should think this is always the reason of it, for God has aims in all His works known only to Himself; but I have known some have so been troubled, and this may be in great mercy to make a weak conversion more strong.

Lest any Christian should be troubled at it, note that in true contrition there must be sorrow of heart because of sin. There must be a dislike of it in the will; there must be a strong reasoning in the mind out of the Word of God against sin—this is the sinew of repentance. There must be a resolution and striving and watching against sin, like Job, who made a covenant with his eyes. There must be a grieving that he is not excelling in all these, and here he must make up what he lacks in the former.

These are in some measure present in all Christians. Some are more eminent in one part, some in another—as Joseph had little sorrow, but a strong resolution, because he had so strong a temptation and withstood it; he had strong reasons beyond nature to resist sin, and resolve against it. So that it is not so much the measure as the truth of every part that is required. But if they are not excelling in great sinners, they are to mourn for the lack of them.

# ROBERT BOLTON

## Heart Surgery

God is provoked with sin. Sin is the only object of God's infinite hatred. His love is diversified to Himself, His Son, the angels, the creatures; but His hatred is confined only to sin. What infinite of infinities of hatred you have on your soul, with all your sins, when each sin has the infinite hatred of God upon it!

Each sin is against the majesty of that awesome Lord of heaven and earth, who can turn all things into hell; nay, He can turn heaven and hell into nothing by His sheer word. Now, against this God you sin, and what are you but dust and ashes and all that is nothing! And what is your life but a span, a bubble, a dream, a shadow of a dream? And shall such a pitiable thing as yourself—offend such an awesome God?

Every sin strikes at the glory of God's pure eye! Sin is that which killed His Son! The least sin could not be pardoned, except by Christ's carrying His heart blood to His Father and offering it for sin.

Each sin is an offense to all His mercies. This aggravated the sin upon Eli (1 Samuel 2:29) and of David (2 Samuel 12:8–9). Mercy is the most eminent attribute of God, and therefore the sin against it is the greater. What therefore are our sins in the time of the gospel?

Consider how you are hurt by it, for each sin ruins your soul, which is better than the world. Each sin, though it brings ever so much pleasure in the committing, leaves a threefold sting:

1. **A Natural sting.** After worldly pleasure comes melancholy, and properly, either because it lasted no longer or they had no more delight in it, and so on. Just as all waters end in the salty sea—so all worldly joys are swallowed up in sorrow's bottomless gulf.

2. **A Temporal sting.** There is labor in getting, care in keeping, and sorrow in parting with worldly goods!

3. **An Immortal sting.** God will call you to judgment for it. Each sin robs you of abundance of comfort. What a vast difference do we see in conquering sin and being conquered by sin. As, for instance, in Joseph and David: the one raised after his conquest to much honor; the other, scarcely enjoyed one good day after he was conquered—but walked heavily in the bitterness of his soul all his days.

Your own conscience will accuse you one day for every sin, though now it seems hidden to you; and your conscience is more than a thousand witnesses. Therefore you will certainly be overthrown. For the sins which perhaps you live in now and count but of no consequence—many poor souls are at this instant burning in hell for! What misery and hurt, then, awaits you for the same!

# CHRISTOPHER LOVE

## Wrath and Mercy

**Question:** How can it stand with God's mercy that He should, in His eternal counsels, appoint any of His creatures to be objects of His wrath when it is said that He beheld all the works of His hands, and behold they were all very good? How can it consist with the mercy of God to damn those creatures that He has made—nay, to appoint them to be objects of His wrath even before He made them?

**Answer:** It may very well stand with God's mercy to appoint His creatures to wrath. God has an absolute sovereignty over all His creatures to do with them as He pleases. "May not I do with mine own what I will? And who can say unto Me, 'What do you do?'" And, "Such a power as the potter hath of the same lump of clay, to make one vessel to honor, and another to dishonor" (Romans 9:21). Such a power has God over all the sons and daughters of men. He has an absolute sovereignty over all His creatures to do with them what seems good in His own eyes. And who are you, O man, to reply against God?

There is a great deal of reason why God should destroy and damn all the creatures that He has made. First, because when God made man, He made him holy and upright, perfect and able to do His will in all things. He was able both to do the will of God and also to continue in that estate wherein God made him, and so

247

to be everlastingly happy. It is true, had God infused any vicious qualities into man, it would be something. But God's hand was free from any such thing.

God at first made man upright, but he has since sought out many inventions (Ecclesiastes 7:29). Adam was in a state of perfection, but only under a possibility of falling if he chose. And since God foresaw that man would fall, there was great reason why every man should be damned because every man did fall. So the angels were at first made perfect, yet mutable, and because they fell the Lord condemned every one of them and saved none. But He does not deal so with us. He spared none of the fallen angels, but yet He does save some of us. And therefore He has shown greater mercy to you, the sinful sons and daughters of Adam, than He did to the fallen angels because all angels that fell were damned; but man fell, too, and yet the Lord rescues a remnant who are not appointed to wrath, but to obtain salvation through Jesus Christ.

The Lord shows more mercy in the saving and appointing of one man to life and salvation than He would have done rigor of justice if He had condemned all the men in the world. I shall make it appear to you because God was not bound to save any; therefore, if He does, it is an act of grace and mercy. Give me leave to illustrate it to you by this comparison. Suppose a company of malefactors were all condemned to die. Now if a prince should come in among them and choose out one of them, he would show more mercy in saving that one than he would have shown rigor if he had hanged them all, because every one of them deserved it.

Thus it is with us: we have all transgressed and violated God's law, and thereby lay under the guilt of condemnation. And, being all condemned persons, it is more mercy in God to save but one of us than it would be rigor if He should have saved none.

# CHRISTOPHER LOVE

## Two Queries About Hell

**Question:** Why must there be a hell?

**Answer:** First, because of the filthy nature of sin. Sin is against an infinite God, and the offense being infinite, the punishment must be infinite also. But the punishment cannot be infinite upon earth because you stay here but a while and your bodies rot in the grave. Therefore, of necessity, there must be a hell that keeps the bodies and souls of the wicked so that they may receive proportional punishment to the sins they committed here upon the earth.

Second, because otherwise the justice of God could never be satisfied for the sins of wicked men done here upon earth. And the reason is, first, because Christ would not satisfy and suffer God's wrath for wicked men; therefore they must bear it themselves. Second, upon earth they cannot satisfy God's wrath. Why? Because sin is an infinite offense, and so their punishment can be but finite, lasting for a time. Therefore, all their sufferings here cannot satisfy God's wrath due to them for their sins. Therefore, of necessity, there must be a hell to keep men for all eternity so that, by everlasting torments, God's justice may be satisfied, which otherwise it could not be (2 Thessalonians 1:6).

Third, it appears there must be a hell by those horrors and terrors of conscience that are in wicked men when they are dying.

Many a man in his health will tush at hell; he will scorn the fire and scoff at the flames. Many a man, while he is in health, never thinks of hell; but he can drink one day, swear another day, play the adulterer the third day, and sin every day, and the thoughts of hell never trouble him. But now bring this man to his sickbed and what horrors and fears seize upon his soul!

Tell me, what would you say on that day? What would you then give for Christ? What would you then give for a pardon that you might not be damned?

# STEPHEN CHARNOCK

Discourse on the Cleansing Virtue of Christ's Blood

No freedom from the guilt of sin is to be expected from mere mercy. The figure of this was notable in the legal economy. The mercy-seat was not to be approached by the high priest without blood. Christ Himself, typified by the high priest, expects no mercy for any of His followers but by the merit of His blood. What reason have any, then, to expect remission upon the account of mere compassion, without pleading His blood?

Mercy is brought to us only by the smoke of this sacrifice. The very title of justification implies not only mercy, but justice—and more justice than mercy; for justification is not upon a bare petition, but a propitiation. To be pardoned indeed implies mercy. Pardon is an act of favor whereby the criminal is graced and gratified, but to be justified is to be discharged in a legal way, or by way of compensation. A man may be pardoned as a supplicant but not pronounced righteous upon the merits of his cause. He that employs mercy, acknowledges guilt, but insists not upon a righteousness.

Justification or pardon is not the act of God as Creator, for then it had been mere mercy; nor as a lawgiver, according to the terms of the first covenant, for then no man after his revolted state could be justified. It is the act of God as judge, according to the laws of redemption—and that in a way of righteousness and justice (2 Timothy 4:8). God is not to be sought for this concern, but in Christ; nor mere mercy implored without the Redeemer's merit, because God does not forgive our sins or reconcile our persons to Himself but for the propitiating blood of His Son. To expect pardon only upon the account of mercy is to honor one attribute with the denial of the other. Though God be merciful, yet He is just; His mercy is made known in remission, His justice manifested in justification.

Forget not the great demonstration of His justice when you come to plead for mercy. Plead both in the blood of Christ because God is merciful to none out of Christ. He is merciful to none but to whom He is just—merciful to them in regard of themselves and their own demerits; just and righteous to them in regard of the blood and merit of His Son.

# STEPHEN CHARNOCK

## Discourse on the Cleansing Virtue of Christ's Blood

The blood of Christ does not perfectly cleanse us here from sin, in regards to the stirrings of it. The old serpent will be sometimes stinging us and sometimes foiling us. The righteous soul will be vexed with corruptions within it, as well as the abominations of others without it. The Canaanite is in the land, and therefore the virtue of the blood of Christ is expressed in our power of wrestling, not yet in the glory of a triumph. It does not here perfectly free us from the remainders of sin so that we may be still sensible that we are fallen creatures and have every day fresh notices and experiments of its powerful virtue; and that His love might meet with daily valuations in a daily sense of our misery.

But this blood shall perfect what it has begun, and the troubled sea of corruption that sends forth mire and dirt shall be totally removed. Then shall the soul be as pure as unstained wool, as spotless as the dew from the womb of the morning; no wrinkles upon the face, no bubbling up of corruption in the soul. The blood of Christ shall still the waves, expel the filth, and crown the soul with an everlasting victory (Hebrews 12:23–24).

But the blood of Christ perfectly cleanses us from sin here in regards to condemnation and punishment. Thus it blots it out of the book of God's justice; it is no more to be remembered in a way of legal and judicial sentence against the sinner. Though the nature of sin does not cease to be sinful, yet the power of sin ceases to

253

be condemning. The sentence of the law is revoked, the right to condemn is removed, and sin is not imputed to them.

Where the crime is not imputed, the punishment ought not to be inflicted. It is inconsistent with the righteousness of God to be an appeased, and yet a revenging, judge. When the cause of His anger is removed, the effects of His anger are extinguished. Where there is a cleansing from the guilt, there necessarily follows a removal of the punishment. What is the debt we owe upon sin? Is it not the debt of punishment, which is righteously exacted for the fault committed? When the blood of Christ therefore purifies any from their guilt, it rescues them from the punishment due to that guilt.

Herein does the pardon of sin properly consist: in a remission of punishment. The crime cannot be remitted, but only in regard of punishment merited by it. If God should punish a man that is sprinkled with the blood of Christ and pleaded for by the blood of Christ, it would be contrary both to His justice and mercy—to His justice because He has accepted the satisfaction made by Christ, who paid the debt and acquitted the criminal when He bore his sin in His own body upon the tree. It would be contrary to His mercy because it would be cruelty to adjudge a person to punishment who is legally discharged and put into the state of an innocent person by the imputation of the righteousness of the Redeemer.

Though the acts of sin are formally the same that they were, yet the state of a cleansed sinner is not legally the same that it was; for being free from the charge of the law, he is no longer obnoxious to the severity of the law. "There is no condemnation to them that are in Christ" (Romans 8:1).

# CHRISTOPHER LOVE

## The Mortification of Sin

Let mortification be attended to inward and secret sins, as well as to outward and scandalous sins. Not only the lusts of the flesh, but those of the mind are to be mortified; not only the deeds of the body, but the thoughts of the heart and corruptions in the inward man are to be subdued. You are to extend mortification to the subduing of vicious affection, as well as base actions.

In Colossians 3:5 the apostle writes, "Mortify, therefore, your members which are upon the earth, fornication, uncleanness," and so on. Maybe you think that these two are one. No, fornication is sin in action; uncleanness is sinning in affections and thought. The apostle bids them mortify fornication, that is, uncleanness in action; but he does not stop there. He tells them they must subdue their sinful affections and inclinations to those sins. You must mortify the very first motions and secret propensities to any sin in your hearts.

More, let mortification be especially directed to strike at those sins that act your master—sins that are most prevalent and predominant in your heart, that yet you have most prayed against and are least able to resist, that strongly assault you and most easily beset you and are masters over you. Thus David, in Psalm 18:23, says, "I have kept myself from mine iniquity," that is, from my special sins, my constitutional sins, my bosom iniquities.

I might give you the same advice that the King of Syria gave his captains in 2 Chronicles 18:30: "Fight neither with small nor great, but only with the King of Israel." So I say to you, fight not so much against any sin as against your beloved, darling, constitutional sins that most easily beset you and prevail over you.

# OCTAVIUS WINSLOW

## Morning Thoughts

"When He, the Spirit of truth, has come, He will guide you into all truth" (John 16:13).

New and enlarged views of the Holy Spirit mark a regenerate mind. Having received the Holy Spirit as a quickener, he feels the need of Him now as a teacher, a sanctifier, a comforter, and a sealer. As a teacher, discovering to him more of the hidden evil of the heart, more knowledge of God—of His word, and of His Son. As a sanctifier, carrying forward the work of grace in the soul, impressing more deeply on the heart the Divine image, and bringing every thought and feeling and word into sweet, holy, and filial obedience to the law of Jesus. As a comforter, leading him in the hour of his deep trial to Christ; comforting, by unfolding the sympathy and tenderness of Jesus, and the exceeding preciousness and peculiar fitness of the many promises with which the word of truth abounds for the consolation of the Lord's afflicted. As a sealer, impressing upon his heart the sense of pardon, acceptance, and adoption; and entering himself as the "earnest of the inheritance, until the redemption of the purchased possession."

Oh! What exalted views does he now have of the blessed and eternal Spirit—of His personal glory, His work, His offices, His influences, His love, tenderness, and faithfulness! The ear is open to the softest whisper of His voice; the heart expands to the gentlest impression of His sealing, sanctifying influence. Remembering that

257

He is "a temple of the Holy Spirit," he desires so to walk lowly, softly, watchfully, and prayerfully. Avoiding everything that would "grieve the Spirit," resigning every known sin that would dishonor and cause Him to withdraw, the one single aim of his life is to walk so as to please God, that "God in all things may be glorified."

# JOHN FLAVEL

## The Mystery of Providence

There is an eminent favor Providence bestows on the saints that has not yet been considered, and indeed is too little minded by us. That is the aid and assistance Providence gives the people of God in the great work of mortification.

Mortification of our sinful affections and passions is one half of our sanctification: "dead indeed unto sin, but alive unto God" (Romans 6:11). This is the great evidence of our interest in Christ. It is our safety in the hour of temptation. The corruptions in the world are through lust, but our instrumental fitness for service depends much upon Providence (John 15:2; 2 Timothy 2:20–21). How great a service to our souls therefore must that be, by which this blessed work is carried on in them!

Now there are two means or instruments employed in this work of mortification: the Spirit, who effects it internally (Romans 8:13), and Providence, which assists it externally. The Spirit indeed is the principal agent upon whose operation the success of this work depends, and all the providences in the world can never effect it without Him. But there are secondary and subordinate means, which, by the blessing of the Spirit upon them, have a great part in the work.

The most wise God orders the dispensations of Providence in a blessed subordination to the work of His Spirit. There is a sweet harmony between them in their distinct workings. They all meet in that one blessed issue to which God has, by the counsel of His will, directed them (Romans 8:28; Ephesians 1:11). Hence it is that the Spirit is said to be in, and to order the motions of, the wheels of Providence; so they move together by consent.

# WILLIAM AMES

## Sanctification

Sanctification is the real change in man from the sordidness of sin to the purity of God's image. "You were taught, with regard to your former way of life, to put off your old self, which is being corrupted by its deceitful desires; to be made new in the attitude of your minds; and to put on the new self, created to be like God in true righteousness and holiness" (Ephesians 4:21–24).

Just as in justification a believer is properly freed from the guilt of sin and has life given him (the title to which is, as it were, settled in adoption), so in sanctification the same believer is freed from the sordidness and stain of sin, and the purity of God's image is restored to him.

Sanctification is not to be understood here as a separation from ordinary use or consecration to some special use—although this meaning is often present in Scripture, sometimes referring to outward and sometimes to inward or effectual separation. If this meaning is taken, sanctification may relate to calling or that first rebirth in which faith is communicated as a principle of new life. A common confusion of regeneration and sanctification hereby arises. The term is rather to be understood as that change in a believer in which he has righteousness and indwelling holiness imparted to him (2 Thessalonians 2:13–14). . . .

The starting point of sanctification is the filthiness, corruption, or stain of sin (2 Corinthians 7:1). Its end is the purity of God's image—said to be fashioned or created once more in knowledge, righteousness, and holiness (Ephesians 4:24)—or conformity to the law of God (James 1:25), newness of life (Romans 6:4), the new creation (2 Corinthians 5:17), and the divine nature (2 Peter 1:4).

# MATTHEW HENRY

## Discourse on Meekness and Quietness of Spirit

Meekness is the silent submission of the soul to the Word of God; the understanding bowed to every divine truth, and the will to every divine precept—and both without murmuring or disputing.

The Word is then an "engrafted word" when it is received with meekness; that is, with a sincere willingness to be taught and a desire to learn. Meekness is a grace that cleaves the stock and holds it open so that the Word, as a shoot, may be grafted in. It breaks up the fallow ground and makes it fit to receive the seed; it captivates the high thoughts and lays the soul like white paper under God's pen.

When the dayspring takes hold of the ends of the earth, it is said to be turned as clay under a seal (Job 38:12–14). Meekness, in like manner, does dispose the soul to admit the rays of divine light, which before it rebelled against. It opens the heart, as Lydia's was opened, and sets us down with Mary at the feet of Christ—the learner's place and posture.

The promise of teaching is made to the meek because they are disposed to learn: "the meek He will teach His way." The Word of God is gospel indeed, "good tidings to the meek"; they will entertain it and bid it welcome. The "poor in spirit" are evangelized, and Wisdom's alms are given to those that with meekness wait daily at her gates, and like beggars wait at the posts of her doors (Proverbs 8:34).

The language of this meekness is that of the child Samuel: "Speak, Lord, for your servant hears." And like that of Joshua who, when he was in that high post of honor, giving command to Israel and bidding defiance to all their enemies—his breast filled with great and bold thoughts—yet, upon the intimation of a message from heaven, submits himself to it: "What says my Lord unto his servant?" And that of Paul—and it was the first breath of the new man—who said: "Lord, what will You have me to do?" And that of Cornelius: "And now we are all here present before God, to hear all things that are commanded you of God."

To receive the Word with meekness is to be delivered into it as into a mould; this seems to be Paul's metaphor in Romans 6:17—that "form of doctrine which was delivered you." Meekness softens the wax that it may receive the impression of the seal, whether it be for doctrine or reproof, for correction or instruction in righteousness. It opens the ear to discipline, silences objections, and suppresses the risings of the carnal mind against the Word; consenting to the law that it is good and esteeming all the precepts concerning all things to be right, even when they give the greatest check to flesh and blood.

# MATTHEW HENRY

## Discourse on Meekness and Quietness of Spirit

Quietness of spirit is the evenness, the composure, and the rest of the soul that speaks both the nature and the excellence of the grace of meekness.

The greatest comfort and happiness of man is sometimes set forth by quietness. That peace of conscience which Christ has left for a legacy to His disciples, that present sabbatism of the soul which is an earnest of the rest that remains for the people of God, is called "quietness and assurance forever." It is promised as the effect of righteousness. So graciously has God been pleased to entwine interests with us, as to enjoin the same thing as a duty which he proposes and promises as a privilege.

Justly may we say that we serve a good Master whose "yoke is easy." It is not only easy, but sweet and gracious, so the Word signifies; not only tolerable, but amiable and acceptable. Wisdom's ways are not only pleasant, but pleasantness itself, and all her paths are peace.

It is the character of the Lord's people, both in respect to holiness and happiness, that, however they be branded as the troublers of Israel, they are "the quiet in the land." If every saint be made a spiritual prince, having a dignity above others and a dominion over himself, surely he is like Seraiah, "a quiet prince." It is a reign with Christ, the transcendent Solomon, under the influence of whose golden scepter there is "abundance of peace as long as the moon endures"; yes, and longer, for "of the increase of His government and peace there shall be no end."

Quietness is recommended as a grace which we should be endued with, and a duty which we should practice. In the midst of all the affronts and injuries that are or can be offered us, we must keep our spirits sedate and undisturbed, and we must evidence by a calm and even and regular behavior that they are so. This is quietness.

Our Savior has pronounced the blessing of adoption upon the peacemakers (Matthew 5:9); those that are for peace, as David professes himself to be, in opposition to those that delight in war (Psalm 120:7). Now, if charity be for peace-making, surely this charity begins at home and is for making peace there in the first place. Peace in our own souls is some conformity to the example of the God of peace, who, though He does not always give peace on this earth, yet evermore "makes peace in His own high places." Some think this is the primary intention of that peace-making on which Christ commands the blessing: it is to have strong and hearty affections to peace, to be peaceably-minded.

In a word, quietness of spirit is the soul's stillness and silence from intending provocation to any, or resenting provocation from any with whom we have to do.

# THOMAS HOOKER

## The Christian's Two Chief Lessons

Godly sorrow is known by the companions of it—or as I call them, the effects of it (2 Corinthians 7:11)—including the following:

1. **Carefulness:** that is, an earnest thinking of ourselves joined with diligence in the means whereby we may avoid the sin we mourn for.

2. **Clearing of ourselves,** which is an endeavor to approve ourselves in the dislike of what we mourn for by the contrary deed done. "Behold, the half of my goods I give to the poor" (Luke 19:8).

3. **Indignation,** whereby a man is angry with himself, loathes himself, is even weary of himself.

4. **Fear,** which is an awful regard whereby we are afraid both of the sin and of all the occasions for it, with respect to God's displeasure (Proverbs 28:14).

5. **A vehement desire** whereby we are so affected that we do not more strongly long for anything than to be preserved from that evil by which we have fallen, and also to do the contrary good. "My heart breaks for the fervent desires that it has to Your commandments" (Psalm 119:20).

6. **Zeal,** when upon the consideration of how we have dishonored God by our sin, we are so much the more desirous of His glory by all well doing. This is apparent by Paul, who was so much the more zealous in the propagation of the gospel than he had been serious in persecuting it.

7. **Revenge,** when a man shows his displeasure against sin by punishing the instruments and occasions of it (Acts 19:19).

Godly sorrow may be discerned by this train of graces wherewith it is accompanied—these that worldly sorrow lacks at least in the truth of them (though it may have some shadows).

But what is the use of such an understanding of godly sorrow? That we do not content ourselves to have sorrow for sin, but labor to find out whether it be a godly sorrow or not. By these marks we may grow to some resolution to discover to ourselves, and that we be not mistaken in some legal frights or worldly griefs instead of godly sorrow, which is a special part of repentance.

Examine what sets our sorrow to work—whether it be the terrible nature of God's judgments or the experience of His fatherly mercies. Consider of what continuance your sorrow is, whether of a fleeing nature or more permanent, such as dwells with us and does not only lodge with us for a night. Look whether your sorrow be indifferent, and see what you find to be your best cordials for comfort—whether God's Word or by natural means.

But most of all, advisedly consider whether your sorrow is attended with the forenamed carefulness, clearing of yourself, indignation, fear, vehement desires, zeal, and revenge. Accordingly you may be comforted in your mourning or discouraged in respect of your estate.

# RICHARD SIBBES

## Divine Meditations

If God's mercy might be overcome with our sins, we should overcome it every day. It must be rich mercy that can fully and forever satisfy the soul, and therefore the apostle never speaks of it without the extensions of love, the height and depth. We lack words; we lack thoughts to form any idea of it. We should therefore labor through grace to frame and raise our souls to rich and large conceptions and apprehensions of mercy that is sovereign and divine.

God is rich in mercy, not only to our souls but in providing all things we stand in need of. He keeps us from evil and so He is called a Buckler. He gives us all good things and so He is called a Sun. He keeps us now in a good condition, and will advance us still higher, even so far as our nature shall be capable in the heavenly world.

No sin is so great but the satisfaction of Christ and His mercies are greater; it is beyond comparison. Fathers and mothers in tenderest affections are but beams and trains to lead us upwards to the infinite mercy of God in Christ.

He that seeks us before we sought Him, will He refuse us when we seek after Him? Let no man therefore despair or even be discouraged; if there be in you the height and depth, and length and breadth of sin, there is also much more the height and depth and length and breadth of mercy in God. And though we have played the harlot with many lovers, yet let us return again. For His thoughts are not as ours, and His mercies are the mercies of a reconciled God.

# WILLIAM AMES

## Baptism

Baptism is the sacrament of initiation or regeneration. Although it seals the whole covenant of grace to all believers, when it is specially made our own it represents and confirms our very ingrafting into Christ. See Romans 6:3, 5: "All of us who were baptized into Christ Jesus . . . have been united with Him in a death like His. . . ."

From the time of our first ingrafting into Christ by faith, a relationship of justification and adoption is entered into. As the sacrament of that ingrafting, baptism stands for the remission of sins (Mark 1:4). And it stands, also, for adoption in that we are consecrated by it to the Father, Son, and Holy Spirit, whose names are pronounced over the baptized.

And because holiness always comes from Christ into whom we are ingrafted, to all the faithful, baptism is also the seal of sanctification. "He saved us through the washing of rebirth and renewal by the Holy Spirit" (Titus 3:5).

And since glorification cannot be separated from true holiness, it is at the same time the seal of eternal glory, "so that, having been justified by His grace, we might become heirs having the hope of eternal life" (Titus 3:7). Romans 6:8 adds: "Now if we died with Christ, we believe that we will also live with Him."

Because those benefits are sealed by initiation in baptism, it should be noted, first, that baptism is only to be administered once.

There is only one beginning of spiritual life by rebirth as there is but one beginning of natural life by birth. Second, baptism ought to be administered to all those in the covenant of grace, because it is the first sealing of the covenant now first entered into.

# THOMAS BROOKS

## A Word in Season to Suffering Saints

Look upon death as that which is best. "Better is the day of death, than the day of one's birth" (Ecclesiastes 7:1). "I desire to depart and be with Christ, which is better by far" (Philippians 1:23). The Greek is very significant—"far, far the better!" A saint's dying day is the daybreak of eternal glory! In respect of pleasure, peace, safety, company and glory—a believer's dying day is his best day.

Look upon death as a remedy, as a cure. Death will perfectly cure you of all bodily and spiritual diseases at once: the infirm body and the defiled soul, the aching head and the unbelieving heart. Death will cure you of all your ailments, aches, diseases, and distempers. In Queen Mary's day, there was a lame Christian and a blind Christian—both burned at one stake. The lame man, after he was chained, casting away his crutch, bade the blind man to be of good cheer; "For death," says he, "will cure us both; you of your blindness, and me of my lameness!"

As death will cure all your bodily diseases, so it will cure all your soul distempers, also. Death is not the death of the man, but the death of his sin! Death will at once free you fully, perfectly, and perpetually from all sin; yes, from all possibility of ever sinning! Sin was the midwife which brought death into the world—and death shall be the grave to bury sin.

Why, then, should a Christian be afraid to die, unwilling to die—seeing that death gives him an eternal separation . . . from infirmities and weaknesses, from all aches and pains, from griefs and gripings, from distempers and diseases, both of body and soul? When Samson died, the Philistines died together with him. Just so, when a saint dies, his sins die with him. Death came in by sin, and sin goes out by death! Death kills sin which bred it.

Look upon death as a rest, a full rest. A believer's dying day is his resting day . . . from sin, from sorrow, from afflictions, from temptations, from desertions, from dissensions, from vexations, from oppositions, from persecutions. This world was never made to be the saints' rest. Arise and depart, for this is not your resting place, because it is polluted! (Micah 2:10).

Death brings the saints . . . to a full rest, to a pleasant rest, to a matchless rest, and to an eternal rest!

# JONATHAN EDWARDS

## From the Sermon "Praise, One of the Chief Employments of Heaven"

The saints in heaven are employed. They are not idle; they have there much to do. They have a work before them that will fill up eternity.

We are not to suppose that the saints will have nothing to do when they have finished their course and done the works appointed them here in this world and are got to their journey's end, to their Father's house. It is true that saints, when they get to heaven, rest from their labors and their works follow them. Heaven is not a place of labor and travail, but a place of rest. "There remains a rest for the people of God" (Hebrews 4:9). And heaven is a place of the reward of labor.

But the rest of heaven does not consist in idleness and a cessation of all action, but only a cessation from all the trouble and toil and tediousness of action. The most perfect rest is consistent with being continually employed. So it is in heaven. Though the saints are exceedingly full of action, yet their activity is perfectly free from all labor, or weariness, or unpleasantness. They shall rest from their work—that is, from all work of labor and self-denial, grief, care, and watchfulness. But they will not cease from action.

The saints in glory are represented as employed in serving God, as well as the saints on earth, though it be without any difficulty or opposition. "And there shall be no more curse: but the throne of God and of the Lamb shall be in it; and His servants shall serve Him" (Revelation 22:3). Yes, we are told, that they shall serve God day and night—that is, continually or without ceasing (Revelation 7:15). In this world, saints labor in the wearisome heat of the sun; but there, though they shall still serve God, yet shall the sun not light on them, nor any heat.

In one sense, the saints and angels in heaven do not rest day or night. That is, they never cease from their blessed employment. Perfection of happiness does not consist in idleness; on the contrary, it very much consists in action. The angels are blessed spirits, and yet they are exceedingly active in serving God. God Himself enjoys infinite happiness and perfect bliss, and yet He is not inactive, but is Himself in His own nature a perfect act. He is continually at work bringing to pass His own purposes and ends.

That principle of holiness that is in its perfection in the saints in heaven is a most active principle; so that though they enjoy perfect rest, yet they are a great deal more active than they were when in this world. In this world they were exceedingly dull, and heavy, and inactive—but now they are a flame of fire. The saints in heaven are not merely passive in their happiness. They do not merely enjoy God passively, but in an active manner. They are not only acted upon by God, but they mutually act towards Him. And in this action and re-action consists the heavenly happiness.

# LIFE IN THE KINGDOM OF GOD

"He who communes with God is always at home."

—*The Treasury of David*

# JOSEPH ALLEINE

## An Alarm to the Unconverted

Conversion turns the bent of the *affections*. These all run in a new channel. The Jordan is now driven back, and the water runs upwards against its natural course. Christ is his hope. This is his prize. Here his eye is; here his heart. He is content to cast all overboard, as the merchant in the storm about to perish—so he may but keep this jewel.

The first of his desires is not after gold—but grace. He hungers for it; he seeks it as silver; he digs for it as for hidden treasure. He had rather be gracious than great. He had rather be the holiest man on earth than the most learned, the most famous, the most prosperous. While carnal, he said, "Oh if I were but in great esteem, rolling in wealth and swimming in pleasure; if my debts were paid, and I and mine provided for, then I would be a happy man." But now the tune is changed. "Oh!" says the convert, "if I had but my corruptions subdued, if I had such a measure of grace and fellowship with God, though I were poor and despised—I would not care, I would account myself a blessed man."

Reader, is this the language of your soul?

His *joys* are changed. He rejoices in the way of God's testimonies as much as in all riches. He delights in the law of the Lord, in which he once had little savor. He has no such joy as in the thoughts of Christ, the enjoyment of His company, the prosperity of His people.

His *cares* are quite altered. He was once set for the world, and any scrap of spare time was enough for his soul. Now his cry is, "What must I do to be saved?" (Acts 16:30). His great concern is how to secure his soul. Oh, how he would bless you, if you could but put him out of doubt concerning this!

His *fears* are not so much of suffering—as of sinning. Once he was afraid of nothing so much as the loss of his estate or reputation; nothing sounded so terrible to him as pain, or poverty, or disgrace. Now these are little to him in comparison with God's dishonor or displeasure. How warily does he walk, lest he should tread upon a snare! He looks in front and behind; he has his eye upon his heart and is often casting it over his shoulder, lest he should be overtaken with sin. It kills his heart to think of losing God's favor; this he dreads as his only undoing. No thought pains him so much as to think of parting with Christ.

His *love* runs in a new course. "My Love was crucified," says Ignatius—that is, my Christ. "This is my beloved," says the spouse (Song of Solomon 5:16). How often does Augustine pour his love upon Christ! He can find no words sweet enough:

> Let me see You, O Light of my eyes. Come, O Joy of my spirit; Let me behold You, O Gladness of my heart. Let me love You, O Life of my soul. Appear unto me, O my great delight, my sweet comfort, O my God, my life, and the whole glory of my soul. Let me find You, O Desire of my heart; let me hold You, O Love of my soul. Let me embrace You, O Heavenly Bridegroom. Let me possess You.

His *sorrows* have now a new vent (2 Corinthians 7:9–10). The view of his sins, the sight of Christ crucified—all of which could scarcely stir him before, now how much do they affect his heart!

His *hatred* boils, his anger burns against sin. He has no patience with himself; he calls himself fool, and beast, and thinks any name too good for himself when his indignation is stirred up against sin (Psalm 73:22; Proverbs 30:2). He could once wallow in it with much pleasure; now he loathes the thought of returning to it as much as of licking up the filthiest vomit!

# STEPHEN CHARNOCK

## Discourse on the Word, the Instrument
## of Regeneration

Attend upon the Word of God submissively. It is not the hearer, but the humble hearer, who shall find the power of the Word working in him—just as it is not the speaking of a prayer, but the wrestling and struggling of the heart with God in prayer, that receives a gracious answer. The humble are the fittest subjects for grace—those that lie upon the ground with their mouth close to the pipe.

Resign yourselves to the Word. Struggle not against the battery it makes, nor the wind that blows; receive every stroke until you see the frame of a new creature. Let a silence be imposed upon the flesh, and let self be bowed down to the dust, while Christ the great prophet speaks. Acknowledge God as a free agent and submit to His sovereign pleasure. A truly humble bow to God will prevail more than all the saucy expostulations of proud flesh.

In hearing the Word, pick not here a part and there a part, as suits your humor, but consider what really is God's will—and submit to it. "A humble soul," says Kempis, "by the grace of God understands more the reasons of eternal truth in a trice than a man who has studied many years in the schools, because he has the operations of them in his heart."

Receive the Word of God with faith. I do not mean the faith that is a part of the new creature, but rather an assent. There is a rational belief that it is the Word of truth, which is in many men

282

that have no justifying faith. Actuate this. Believing the word to be the Word of God is the first step to receiving advantage by it. No man will ever comply with that which he believes not to be true, or believes himself not concerned in. There can never be a full compliance with Christ, in order to experience a new birth, if there is not first an assent to the Word. If you do not believe with Naaman that the waters of Jordan are appointed by God for this end, and not those of Abana and Pharpar, you will never be rid of the spiritual death, no more than he would have been of his leprosy.

# WILLIAM PERKINS

## The Art of Prophesying

Application is the skill by which the doctrine which has been properly drawn from Scripture is handled in ways which are appropriate to the circumstances of the place and time and to the people in the congregation. This is the biblical approach to exposition: "'I will feed My flock, and I will make them lie down,' says the Lord God. 'I will seek what was lost and bring back what was driven away, bind up the broken and strengthen what was sick'" (Ezekiel 34:15–16).

The basic principle in application is to know whether the passage is a statement of the law or of the gospel. For when the Word is preached, the law and the gospel operate differently. The law exposes the disease of sin, and as a side-effect stimulates and stirs it up—but it provides no remedy for it. However, the gospel not only teaches us what is to be done, it also has the power of the Holy Spirit joined to it. When we are regenerated by Him we receive the strength we need both to believe the gospel and to do what it commands. The law is, therefore, first in the order of teaching; then comes the gospel.

A statement of the law indicates the need for perfect inherent righteousness, of eternal life given through the works of the law, of the sins which are contrary to the law and of the curse that is due them. "For as many as are of the works of the law are under the curse; for it is written, 'Cursed is everyone who does not continue in all things which are written in the book of the law, to do them.'

But that no-one is justified by the law in the sight of God is evident, for the just shall live by faith" (Galatians 3:10–11). "Brood of vipers! Who warned you to flee from the wrath to come. . . . And even now the axe is laid to the root of the trees. Therefore every tree which does not bear good fruit is cut down and thrown into the fire" (Matthew 3:7, 10). By contrast, a statement of the gospel speaks of Christ and His benefits, and of faith being fruitful in good works. For example, "For God so loved the world that He gave His only begotten Son, that whoever believes in Him should not perish but have everlasting life" (John 3:16).

For this reason many statements which seem to belong to the law are, in the light of Christ, to be understood not legally but as qualified by the gospel. "Blessed are those who hear the word of God and keep it!" (Luke 11:28). "For this commandment which I command you today is not too mysterious for you, nor is it far off. . . . But the word is very near you, in your mouth and in your heart, that you may do it" (Deuteronomy 30:11, 14). This same sentence which is legal in character in Moses is evangelical in character in Paul (Romans 10:8). "He who has My commandments and keeps them, it is he who loves Me. And he who loves Me will be loved by My Father. . . . If anyone loves Me, he will keep My word; and My Father will love him, and We will come to him and make Our home with him" (John 14:21, 23).

# WILLIAM PERKINS

## The Art of Prophesying

There are seven ways in which application of the Scriptures should be made, in keeping with seven different spiritual conditions:

1. *Those who are unbelievers and are both ignorant and unteachable.* These must first of all be prepared to receive the doctrine of the Word. This preparation should be partly by discussing or reasoning with them, in order to become aware of their attitude and disposition, and partly by reproving any obvious sin, so that their consciences may be aroused and touched with fear and they may become teachable (Acts 9:3–5; 16:27–31; 17:17; 17:22–24).

   If there is no positive response to such teaching, then it should be explained in a more detailed and comprehensive way. But if they remain unteachable and there is no real hope of winning them, they should simply be left.

2. *Those who are teachable, but ignorant.* We should instruct such people by means of a catechism (Luke 1:4; Acts 18:25–26). This is a brief explanation of the foundational teaching of the Christian faith given in the form of questions and answers. This helps both the understanding and the memory. The content of a catechism, therefore, should be the fundamentals

of the Christian faith—a summary of its basic principles (Hebrews 5:12).

3. *There are those who have knowledge, but have never been humbled.* Here we need to see the foundation of repentance stirred up in what Paul calls godly sorrow (2 Corinthians 7:8–10). Godly sorrow is grief for sin simply because it is sin. To stir up this affection, the ministry of the law is necessary. This may give birth to a real sense of contrition in the heart, or to terror in the conscience. Although this is not wholesome and profitable on its own, it provides a necessary remedy for subduing sinful stubbornness, and for preparing the mind to become teachable.

4. *Those who have already been humbled.* Here we must carefully consider whether the humbling that has already taken place is complete and sound, or only just begun and still light or superficial. It is important that people do not receive comfort sooner than is appropriate. If they do they may later become hardened in the same way iron which has been cast into the furnace becomes exceptionally hard when it is cold.

5. *Those who already believe.* We must teach them the gospel: the biblical teaching on justification, sanctification, and perseverance. We must teach them the law, but as it applies to those who are no longer under its curse, so that they may be taught how to bear the fruit of a new obedience in keeping with their repentance. Although someone who is righteous and holy in the sight of God should not be threatened with the curse of the law, the opposition of the law to their remaining sin should still be stressed.

6. *Those who have fallen back.* Some may have partly departed from the state of grace, either in faith or in lifestyle. Failure in faith is either in the knowledge of the doctrine of the gospel or in apprehending Christ. Failure in knowledge involves declining into error, whether in a secondary or fundamental doctrine. Failure in lifestyle takes place when a Christian commits actual sin, as in the case of Noah's drunkenness, David's adultery, Peter's denial, and similar examples. The strength and disposition of indwelling grace may be lost for a time in terms of both the sense and the experience of the power of it. The law must be expounded along with the gospel to those who have thus fallen. Every new act of sin requires a new act of faith and repentance (Isaiah 1:4, 16, 18).

7. *Churches with both believers and unbelievers.* This is the typical situation in our congregations. Any doctrine may be expounded to them, either from the law or from the gospel, so long as its biblical limitations and circumscriptions are observed (John 7:37–38). This was what the prophets did in their sermons when they announced judgment and destruction on the wicked, and promised deliverance in the Messiah to those who repented.

But what if someone in the congregation despairs, when the rest are hardened? What should be done? The answer is: those who are hardened must be made to hear the law circumscribed within the limits of the persons and the sins in view. But the afflicted conscience must be helped to hear the voice of the gospel applied especially to it.

# JOHN BUNYAN

## From the Sermon "The Barren Fig Tree"

"A certain man had a fig tree planted in his vineyard, and he came seeking fruit on it and found none. Then he said to the keeper of his vineyard, 'Look, for three years I have come seeking fruit on this fig tree and find none. Cut it down; why does it use up the ground?' But he answered and said to him, 'Sir, let it alone this year also, until I dig around it and fertilize it. And if it bears fruit, well. But if not, after that you can cut it down.'"

When a man has got a profession and is crowded into the church and house of God, the question is not, "Has he life?" The question is not, "Has he right principles?" The question is: "Has he fruit?"

"He came seeking fruit on it." It matters not who brought you in here—whether God or the devil—or your own vainglorious heart. But do you have fruit? Do you bring forth fruit unto God? It says in 2 Timothy 2:19: "Everyone who confesses the name of the Lord must turn away from wickedness." He does not say, "And let every one that has grace," or, "Let those that have the Spirit of God." Rather: "Everyone who confesses the name of the Lord must turn away from wickedness."

What do men meddle with religion for? Why do they call themselves by the name of the Lord Jesus, if they have not the grace of God, if they have not the Spirit of Christ? God, therefore, expects fruit. What do they do in the vineyard? Let them work, or get them out; the vineyard must have laborers in it. "Son, go

289

*work* today in my vineyard" (Matthew 21:28). Wherefore, a lack of grace and a lack of Spirit will not keep God from seeking fruit. He requires that which He seems to have. Every man in the vineyard and house of God promises himself, professes to others, and would have all men take it for granted that a heavenly principle is in him. Why then should not God seek fruit?

As for them, therefore, that will retain the name of Christians, fearing God, and yet make no conscience of bringing forth fruit to Him—He says to such, "Away!" Barren fig tree, do you hear? God expects fruit, God calls for fruit, yes, God will shortly come seeking fruit on this barren fig tree. Barren fig tree, either bear fruit or go out of the vineyard; and yet then your case will be unspeakably damnable. Yes, let me add, if you shall neither bear fruit nor depart, God will take His name out of your mouth (Jeremiah 44:26). He will have fruit. And I say further, if you will do neither, yet God in justice and righteousness will still come for fruit. And it will be in vain for you to count this austerity. He will reap where He has not sowed, and gather where He has not strewn (Matthew 25:24–26).

Barren fig tree, do you hear?

# THOMAS WATSON

## The Beatitudes

"Blessed are those who mourn" (Matthew 5:4). It is a sign that the Sun of Righteousness has risen upon us when our frozen hearts thaw and melt for sin. Weeping for sin is a sign of the new birth. As soon as the child is born—it weeps. Mourning shows a "heart of flesh" (Ezekiel 36:26). A stone will not melt. When the heart is in a melting frame, it is a sign the heart of stone is taken away.

"Let your tears flow like a river. Give yourselves no rest from weeping day or night" (Lamentations 2:18). Tears for sin are blessed tears. Tears poison our corruptions. Salt-water kills worms. Just so, the brinish water of repenting tears will help to kill that worm of sin which would gnaw the conscience.

Mourning also fences us against the devil's temptations. Temptations are called "fiery darts" (Ephesians 6:16), because indeed they set the soul on fire. Temptations enrage anger and inflame lust. Now the waters of holy mourning quench these fiery darts! Wet gunpowder will not easily catch fire. Just so, when the heart is wetted and moistened with sorrow, it will not so easily catch the fire of temptation.

Penitential tears are precious. Tears dropping from a mournful, penitent eye are like water dropping from the roses—very sweet and precious to God. A fountain in the garden makes it pleasant. That heart is most delightful to God that has a fountain of sorrow running in it. "Mary stood at Christ's feet weeping" (Luke 7:38).

291

Her tears were more fragrant than her ointment. The incense, when it is broken, smells sweetest. When the heart is broken for sin, then our services give forth their sweetest perfume.

Surely, God delights much in tears—else He would not keep a bottle for them. "You keep track of all my sorrows. You have collected all my tears in Your bottle. You have recorded each one in Your book" (Psalm 56:8). Tears are powerful orators for God's mercy. Tears melt the heart of God. When a man comes weeping in prayer and smites on his breast, saying, "God be merciful to me a sinner!"—this melts God's heart towards him. Tears, though they are silent, yet have a voice: "The Lord has heard the voice of my weeping" (Psalm 6:8). Tears in the child's eye sometimes move the angry father to spare the child. Penitential tears melt God's heart and bind His hand. Tears have a mighty influence upon God.

Repentant tears are sweet. Mourning is the way to solid joy. A Christian thinks himself sometimes in the suburbs of heaven when he can weep. Sugar when it melts is sweetest. When a Christian melts in tears, now he has the sweetest joy. When the daughter of Pharaoh descended into the river—she found a babe there among the reeds. Just so, when we descend into the river of repenting tears, we find the babe Jesus there, who shall wipe away all tears from our eyes.

Tears water our graces and make them flourish. Where the springs of sorrow run—there the heart bears a fruitful crop. The tender-eyed Christian usually brings forth more of the fruit of the Spirit. A weeping eye is the water-pot to water our graces! If there is so much profit and benefit in gospel-sorrow, then let every Christian wash his face every morning in the laver of tears.

Our mourning for sin here will prevent mourning in hell. Hell is a place of weeping (Matthew 8:12). The damned mingle their drink with weeping. God is said to have His bottle for our tears. Those who will not shed a bottle-full of tears now shall hereafter shed rivers of tears. "Woe to you who laugh now—for you shall mourn and weep" (Luke 6:25).

There is but one way to blessedness, and that is through the valley of tears. If you do not go this way, you will miss Paradise. "I tell you, unless you repent, you shall all likewise perish" (Luke 13:3). There is only one way leading to heaven, and that is a tear dropping from the eye of faith. A man may have a disease in his body, which twenty medicines will heal. But only the medicine of repentance will heal the mortal disease of sin.

Think what a sinner you have been. You have filled God's book with your debts—and what need you have to fill His bottle with your tears! He who weeps here is a blessed mourner. He who weeps in hell is a cursed mourner. If God's bottle is not filled with tears—His vial will be filled with wrath!

Repentant tears are but finite. It is but a short time that we shall weep. After a few showers fall from our eyes, we shall have a perpetual sunshine. "God shall wipe away all tears" (Revelation 7:17). When sin shall cease—tears shall cease! "Weeping may endure for a night, but joy comes in the morning" (Psalm 30:5).

# JOHN FLAVEL

## Fountain of Life Opened Up

If Christ did not sit down to rest in heaven until He had finished His work on earth, then it is in vain for us to think of rest until we have finished our work, as Christ also did His.

How willing are we to find rest here! To dream of that which Christ never found in this world, nor any ever found before us. Think not of resting until you have finished working and finished sinning. Your life and your labors must end together. "Blessed are the dead that die in the Lord, for they rest from their labors" (Revelation 14:13).

Here you must have the sweat, and there the sweet. It is too much to have two heavens. Here you must be content to dwell in the tents of Cedar; hereafter you shall be within the curtains of Solomon. Heaven is the place of which it may be truly said, "There the weary be at rest." Oh, think not of sitting down on this side heaven.

There are four things will keep the saints from sitting down on earth to rest: grace, corruption, devils, and wicked men.

First, grace will not suffer you to rest here. Its tendencies are beyond this world. It will be looking and longing for the blessed hope. A gracious person takes himself for a pilgrim, seeking a better country, and is always suspicious of danger in every place and state. It is still beating up the sluggish heart with such language as this: "Arise, depart, this is not your rest, for it is polluted" (Micah

2:10). Its further tendencies and continual jealousies will keep you from sitting still for long in this world.

Second, your corruptions will keep you from rest here. They will continually exercise your spirits and keep you upon your watch. Saints have their hands filled with work by their own hearts every day—sometimes to prevent sin, and sometimes to lament it. And always to watch and fear, to mortify and kill it. Sin will not long suffer you to be quiet.

Third, there is a busy devil to keep you from rest. He will find you work enough with his temptations and suggestions, and unless you can sleep quietly in his arms as the wicked do, there is no rest to be expected. "Your adversary, the devil, goes about as a roaring lion, seeking whom he may devour" (1 Peter 5:8).

Fourth, nor will his servants and instruments let you be quiet on this side [of] heaven. Their very name speaks their turbulent disposition. "My soul is among lions, and I lie even among them that are set on fire, even the sons of men, whose teeth are spears and arrows" (Psalm 57:4).

Well then, be content to enter into your rest as Christ did into His. He sweat, then sat, and so must you.

# RICHARD SIBBES

## Divine Meditations

Partial obedience is not obedience at all. To single out easy things
that do not oppose our lusts, which are not against our reputation, therein some will do more than they need; but our obedience
must be universal to all God's commandments, and that because
He commands it. Empty relationships are nothing; if we profess
ourselves God's servants and do not honor Him by our obedience,
we take but an empty title. Let us seek grace to make our professed
relationship good, at least in our affections, that we may be able to
say, I desire to fear Thy Name; yea with my spirit within me will
I seek Thee early (Isaiah 26:8–9).

All the contention between the flesh and the Spirit lies in this,
whether God shall have His will or we have ours. Now God's will
is straight but ours is crooked, and therefore if God will have us
offer up our Isaac we must submit to Him, and even acquiesce in
the whole will of God. The more (through grace) emptied of self,
the more free and happy we shall be by being more subject to God,
for in what measure we part with anything for Him we shall receive
even in this world an hundredfold in joy and peace.

Sincerity is the perfection of Christians. Let not Satan therefore
abuse us. We do all things when we endeavor to do all things and
purpose to do all things and are grieved when we cannot do better;
then in some measure we do all things.

There are many that will give some way to divine truths, but they have a reservation of some sin. When Herodias is once touched, John Baptist must lose his head. Such truths as come near, make transgressors fret because their consciences tell them they will not yield obedience to all. Some sin has got the dominion over their affections, but conscience says, "I warn thee against this sin," and then that hatred which should be turned upon the sin is turned upon the Word and the minister. Some vermin when they are driven to a stand will fly in a man's face, so these men, when they see they must yield, grow malicious, so that what they will not follow, that they will reproach. Therefore it should be our care at all times to yield obedience according to what we know of the divine will.

# THOMAS GOUGE

## A Word to Sinners and a Word to Saints

Observe this truth: that true faith may be exceedingly weak. The words of Christ, "You of little faith," with which He often upbraided His disciples, are an evident proof of this truth. So is that expression of the poor man who cried unto Christ, "Lord, I believe; help my unbelief." The former word, *believe,* shows the truth of his faith. But the latter word, *unbelief,* shows the weakness of his faith, which was so weak that he calls it unbelief.

Are you conscious of the weakness of your own faith? Be thankful to God for that measure and degree that you have, though it be but as a grain of mustard seed in quantity. For the least dram of true faith is of greater value than mountains of gold and silver.

But do not be content with a small measure of faith, for contentedness with a weak faith is an argument of no faith. Besides, the greater and stronger your faith is, the greater and stronger will be your comfort and consolation. For the stronger your faith is, the clearer will your apprehension be of your interest in Christ and of the pardon of your sins, in and through the merits of His death and passion; the more virtue and strength will you draw from Christ for the mortifying of your lusts, and for the quickening of your graces. Yes, with a greater cheerfulness will you go on in your Christian course.

Therefore labor and strive after a greater measure and degree of faith. Labor to grow from faith to faith, from one degree of faith unto another, until you attain the highest degree thereof—even to a full assurance. To this end be earnest with God in prayer for the increase of your faith. For every grace depends upon Him not only for birth, but also for growth and increase.

# CHRISTOPHER LOVE

## Weak Measures of Grace in Christians

God not only takes notice of, but also tenderly cherishes and graciously rewards the smallest beginnings and weakest measures of grace which He works in the hearts of His own people. I might produce a cloud of testimonies to confirm this point. Our Savior Christ said that He will not "break the bruised reed, nor quench the smoking flax" (Matthew 12:20). Observe, the bruised reed shall not be broken; not the light and flaming torch, but the smoking flax shall not be quenched. Smoking flax, where there is but little fire and much smoke of infirmity, yet Christ will not quench it. He will cherish it.

Solomon speaks of the fig tree putting forth her green figs, and the vine with her tender grapes giving a good smell. That is, the little measure and weak beginnings of grace in young converts please the Lord Jesus Christ, and are as a sweet smell in His nostrils. Again, Christ said, "Let us see if the vine flourish, whether the tender grapes appear, and the pomegranate bud forth" (Song of Solomon 7:12). The green buds are regarded by Christ as well as the ripe and grown fruit. . . .

Be not then discouraged, you who discern in yourselves but small measures of grace; look on your wants and imperfections so as to grow in grace, and not to be content with any measure. But look not on the small beginnings in grace as discouragement to you. When you see a great oak in a field, you may say this great tree was once but a small acorn. Those Christians who now are but small sprigs may hereafter be tall cedars. Say to your soul, "Though I am but weak, yet I shall be strong."

Grace, where it is true, will be growing; the smoking flax may be a burning and shining lamp in God's candlestick. And therefore, as you may not be content with the greatest measure of grace, so neither be discouraged with the least measure of grace. A grain of mustard seed may grow a great tree.

Content not yourselves with small measures of grace. A little of the world will not content you. In the womb a foot contents us, three feet in the cradle, and seven feet in the grave. But between the cradle and the grave, a whole world will not content us; and shall a little grace content us?

# WILLIAM GURNALL

## The Christian in Complete Armor

Out of all men, the Christian needs courage and resolution. Indeed, there is nothing that he does as a Christian, or can do, that is not an act of valor. A cowardly spirit is beneath the lowest duty of a Christian. "Be strong and very courageous, that you may"—What? Stand in battle against those warlike nations? No, but that you may "observe to do according to all the law, which Moses my servant commanded you" (Joshua 1:7). It requires more prowess and greatness of spirit to obey God faithfully than to command an army of men; more to be a Christian than a captain.

What seems less valiant than for a Christian to pray? Yet this cannot be performed aright without a princely spirit, as Jacob is said to have behaved when he did but pray; for which he came out of the field as God's banneret. Indeed, if you call that prayer which a carnal person performs, nothing is more poor and dastard-like. Such a one is as great a stranger to this enterprise as the craven soldier to the exploits of a valiant chieftain.

The Christian in prayer comes up close to God, with a humble boldness of faith, and takes hold of Him, wrestles with Him—yes, will not let Him go without a blessing. And all this in the face of his own sins and divine justice, which let fly upon Him from the fiery mouth of the law! While the other's boldness in prayer is but the child, either of ignorance in his mind, or hardness in his heart; not feeling his sins, and not knowing his danger, he rushes upon duty with a blind confidence, which soon quails when conscience awakes and gives him the alarm that his sins are upon him, as the Philistines on Samson. Alas, then in a fright the poor-spirited wretch throws down his weapon, flies from the presence of God with guilty Adam, and dares not look Him in the face.

There is no duty in the Christian's whole course of walking with God, or acting for God, that is not lined with many difficulties that shoot like enemies through the hedges at him while he is marching towards heaven, so that he is put to dispute every inch of ground as he goes. They are only a few noble-spirited souls who dare take heaven by force; only a few that are fit for this calling.

# COTTON MATHER

## From the Sermon "Satisfaction in God"

Our continual *apprehension* of God may produce our continual *satisfaction* in God, under all His dispensations. Whatever enjoyments are by God conferred upon us, where lies the relish, where the sweetness of them? Truly, we may come to relish our enjoyments only so far as we have something of God in them. It was required in Psalm 37:4, "Delight in the Lord." Yes, and what if we should have no delight but the Lord? Let us ponder with ourselves over our enjoyments: "In these enjoyments I see God, and by these enjoyments I serve God!"

And now, let all our delight in, and all our value and fondness for our enjoyments, be only, or mainly, upon such a divine score as this. As far as any of our enjoyments lead us unto God, so far let us relish it, affect it, embrace it, and rejoice in it. "O taste, and feed upon God in all;" and ask for nothing, no, not for life itself, any further than as it may help us in our seeing and our serving of our God.

And then, whatever afflictions do lay fetters upon us, let us not only remember that we are concerned with God therein, but let our concernment with God procure a very profound submission in our souls. Be able to say with him [David] in Psalm 39:9, "I open not my mouth, because You did it." In all our afflictions, let us remark the justice of that God before whom, "why should a living man complain for the punishment of his sin?" The wisdom of that

God "whose judgments are right"; the goodness of that God who "punishes us less than our iniquities do deserve." Let us behave ourselves as having to do with none but God in our afflictions. And let our afflictions make us more conformable unto God—which conformity being effected, let us then say, "It is good for me that I have been afflicted."

Sirs, what was this but a pitch of holiness, almost angelical! Oh! Mount up, as with the wings of eagles, of angels. Be not a sorry, puny, mechanick sort of Christians any longer; but reach forth unto these things that are thus before you.

# THOMAS MANTON

## From the Sermon "The Scripture Sufficient Without Unwritten Traditions"

Our duty is to stand fast in the faith of Christ and profession of godliness, whatever temptations we have to the contrary. "Stand fast" is a military term, and it alludes to a soldier's keeping his ground. The phrase is opposed to two things: a cowardly flight and a treacherous revolt.

A cowardly flight implies our being overcome in the evil day by the many afflictions that befall us for the truth's sake. "Wherefore take to you the whole armor of God, that you may be able to withstand in the evil day, that after you have done all things ye may stand" (Ephesians 6:13). Their temptation was the many troubles and persecutions that befell them, called there the evil day. Their defense lay in the whole armor of God, which is there made of six pieces: the girdle of truth or sincerity, which is a strength to us as a girdle to the loins; the breastplate of righteousness, or a holy inclination and desire to perform our duty to God in all things; the shield of faith, or a steadfast adhering to the truths of the gospel, whether delivered in a way of command, promise, or threatening; the helmet of hope, or a certain and desirous expectation of the promised glory; the shoe of the preparation of the gospel of peace, which is a readiness to endure all encounters for Christ's sake, who has made our peace with God; and the sword of the Spirit, which is the Word of God.

Now, if we take this armor and use it in our conflicts, what does it serve for? To withstand and stand; the first is the act of a soldier, the second is the posture of a conqueror. Here is withstanding until the field is won, and then standing when the day of evil is over. Here we make our way to heaven by conflict and conquest, and hereafter we triumph.

A treacherous revolt implies yielding to the enemy by complying with those things that are against the interests of Christ and His kingdom, and doing so for our advantage. "Demas has forsaken us, and loved the present world" (2 Timothy 4:10).

Backsliders in heart are the worst sort of apostates; those who lose their affection to God, their delight in His ways, and their esteem of His glorious recompenses—all for a little pleasure, profit, or pomp of living. They "sell the birthright for one morsel of meat" (Hebrews 12:15–16). Some fail in their understandings, but most miscarry by the perverse inclination of their wills; they are carnal, worldly hypocrites that never thoroughly mortified the fleshly mind. They prize things as they are commodious to the flesh, and will save them from sufferings.

The bias of such men's hearts does easily prevail against the light of their understandings.

# JONATHAN EDWARDS

## A Treatise Concerning Religious Affections

All gracious affections have a tendency to promote this Christian tenderness of heart. Not only godly sorrow, but even a gracious joy does this. "Serve the Lord with fear, and rejoice with trembling" (Psalm 2:11). The same is true of a gracious hope: "Behold, the eye of the Lord is upon them that fear Him; upon them that hope in His mercy" (Psalm 33:18). Yes, the most confident and assured hope—hope that is truly gracious—has this tendency.

The higher a holy hope is raised, the more there is of this Christian tenderness. The banishing of servile fear by a holy assurance is attended with a proportionate increase of a reverential fear. The diminishing of the fear of God's displeasure in future punishment is attended with a proportional increase of fear of His displeasure itself; a diminished fear of hell with an increase of the fear of sin. The vanishing of jealousies concerning the person's state is attended with a proportional increase of jealousy of his heart, in a distrust of its strength, wisdom, stability, faithfulness, and so on.

The less apt a man is to be afraid of natural evil—having his heart fixed, trusting in God, and so not afraid of evil tidings—the more apt is he to be alarmed with the appearance of moral evil, or the evil of sin. As he has more holy boldness, so he has less of self-confidence, or a forward assuming boldness, and more modesty. As he is more sure than others of deliverance from hell, so he has a greater sense of its desert. He is less apt than others to be shaken in faith; but more apt to be moved with solemn warnings, with God's frowns, and with the calamities of others. He has the firmest comfort but the softest heart. He is richer than others but poorest of all in spirit. He is the tallest and strongest saint, but the least and tenderest child among them.

# WILLIAM GURNALL

## The Christian in Complete Armor

There is a reason why there are so many professors and so few Christians; so many that run and so few that obtain; so many who go into the field against Satan, and so few who come out conquerors. This is because all have a desire to be happy, but few have courage and resolution to grapple with the difficulties that meet them in the way to their happiness. All Israel came joyfully out of Egypt under Moses' conduct, yes, and a mixed multitude with them. But when their bellies were pinched with a little hunger and the greedy desires of a present Canaan deferred, instead of peace and plenty, war and penury, they, like white-livered soldiers, are ready to fly from their colors and make a dishonorable retreat into Egypt.

Thus the greatest part of those who profess the gospel, when they come to push the pike—to be tried what they will do—deny to endure for Christ and instead grow sick of their enterprise. Alas! Their hearts fail them; they are like the waters of Bethlehem. But if they must dispute their passage with so many enemies, they will even content themselves with their own cistern, and leave heaven to others who will venture more for it.

Oh, how many part with Christ at this cross-way! Like Orpah, they go a furlong or two with Christ, while He goes to take them off from their worldly hopes and bids them prepare for hardship—and then they fairly kiss and leave Him, loath indeed to lose heaven, but more loath to buy it at so dear a rate. Like some green heads that childishly make choice at some sweet trade, such as is the confectioner's, from a liquorish tooth they have to the junkets it affords, but when meeting with the sour sauce of labor and toil that goes with them, they give in and are weary of their service.

So the sweet bait of religion has drawn many to nibble at it, and so it has left many who are offended with the hard service it calls to. It requires another spirit than the world can give or receive to follow Christ fully.

# THOMAS MANTON

## A Treatise on the Life of Faith

We never act nobly in anything until we live the life of faith. There is a twofold life: the animal life, and the spiritual or divine life. "The natural man receives not the things of the Spirit of God" (1 Corinthians 2:14). The human soul accommodates itself to the interests and concerns of the body; but the divine life is animated by heavenly things, and is carried out to look after more noble things than back and belly concernments.

We never live comfortably until we live by faith. While we are guided by sense, we are tossed to and fro, according to the variety of accidents in the world. But a believer in the greatest straits does not only make a poor and sorry shift to live, but has a comfortable means of subsistence. "The just shall live by his faith" (Habakkuk 2:4). For while he dwells under the shadow of imputed righteousness to cover all his defects and sins, and to hide him from death and wrath, and while he can draw virtue from Christ to enable him to do every good word and work, and while he has the power of God to make use of for his inward and outward support, and the hopes of glory to comfort him when this life is ended—what should hinder his rejoicing even in the hardest dispensations?

Even more: the life of faith is glory begun. First we live by faith, and then by sight (2 Corinthians 5:7). Faith now serves instead of sight and fruition. As it says in Hebrews: "Faith is the substance of things hoped for, and the evidence of things not seen" (11:1). The life of glory is inconsistent with any misery; but the life of faith makes us to rest as quietly upon God and His gracious promise as if there were no misery, where it has any efficacy and vigor, so as no allurements or terrors can turn us aside; we follow our Lord in all conditions with delight and cheerfulness. The expectation cannot affect us as the enjoyment, but in some measure it does. "We rejoice in hope of the glory of God; and not only so, but we glory in tribulation also" (Romans 5:2–3). We are contemptible in the world, but we hope for a glorious estate, and so we can forego those transitory contentments which worldlings so much magnify. This quiets and comforts God's children, even in the meanest condition.

# THOMAS BROOKS

## The Unsearchable Riches of Christ

Every man naturally would have his name immortal, if it were possible. Now there is no way in the world to have your names immortal like this: of growing rich in grace. A man who is spiritually rich shall live, and his name shall live when he is dead. In Nehemiah 7:2 it is said of Hananiah that "he was a faithful man, and feared God above many." His name lives, though his body for many hundred years has been turned to dust.

So in Acts 7:55, "Stephen was a man full of the Holy Spirit." Though Stephen was stoned, yet his name lives—his memorial is precious among the saints to this very day. . . . So it is in Psalm 112:6, 10: "The righteous shall be had in everlasting remembrance—but the name of the wicked shall rot." The great man's name, and the rich man's name, shall rot, says he. But "the name of the righteous shall be had in everlasting remembrance."

The Persians used to write their kings' names in golden letters; so the Lord writes the names of souls rich in grace in golden characters. Their names are always heirs to their lives. Believe it, there is no such way in the world to have immortal names like this: of growing rich in grace. One man thinks to make his name immortal by making himself great; another by heaping up silver and gold as the dust of the earth or the stones of the street; and another by doing some strange exploits. But for all this the Lord will make good His word: "the name of the wicked shall rot." If

God is God, the names of the wicked must rot; but "the righteous shall be had in everlasting remembrance;" they leave their names behind for a blessing (Isaiah 65:15).

It is sad to consider what many poor, carnal creatures have done and suffered to make their names immortal. The Romans' desire of praise and a name made them bountiful of their purses and prodigal of their lives. Erostratus set the temple of Diana on fire on that night that Alexander was born, only that he might be talked of when he was dead. Calvin observes that Servetus in Geneva, in the year 1555, gave all his goods to the poor and his body to be burned—and all for a name, for a little glory among men.

But these poor creatures have all missed the mark. There is no way, Christians, to have your names immortal like this: of growing rich in grace. Neither Satan nor the world shall ever be able to bury such men's names who are rich in grace; their names shall rise in glory here, as well as their bodies hereafter.

# JOSEPH ALLEINE

## The Gospel in a Map

I am your inheritance, which no line can measure, no arithmetic can value, and no surveyor can describe. Lift up your eyes now to the ancient mountains, to the utmost bounds of the everlasting hills; all that you can see is yours. But your short sight cannot perceive half of what I give you. And when you see and know most, you are no less than infinitely short of the discovery of your own riches (Job 26:14).

Yes, further, I will be yours in all My personal relationships: I am the everlasting Father, and I will be a Father to you (John 20:17). I take you for My sons and daughters (2 Corinthians 6:18). Behold, I receive you not as servants, but as sons to abide in My house forever (John 8:35–36). Whatever love or care children may look for from their father, that you may expect from Me (Matthew 6:31–32), and so much more since I am wiser, greater, and better than any earthly parents. If earthly fathers will give good things to their children, much more will I give to you (Luke 11:13). If such cannot forget their children, much less will I forget you (Isaiah 49:15). What would My children have? Your Father's heart, His house, His care, His ear, His bread, and His rod? These shall all be yours.

You shall have My fatherly affection. My heart I share among you. My tenderest loves I bestow upon you (1 John 3:1; Jeremiah 31:3; Isaiah 54:8).

You shall have My fatherly compassion. As a father pities his children, so will I pity you (Psalm 103:13–14). I will consider your frame, and not be extreme to mark what is done amiss by you, but will cover all with the mantle of My excusing love (Psalm 78:39).

You shall have My fatherly instruction. I will cause you to hear the sweet voice behind you, saying, "This is the way" (Isaiah 30:21). I will be tender to your weaknesses and inculcate My admonitions, line upon line, and will feed you with milk when you cannot digest stronger food (Isaiah 28:9–10; 1 Corinthians 3:2). I will instruct you and guide you with My eyes (Psalm 32:8).

You shall have My fatherly protection. In My fear is strong confidence, and My children shall have a place of refuge (Proverbs 14:26). My name shall be your strong tower, to which you may at all times fly and be safe (Proverbs 18:10). To your stronghold, you prisoners of hope (Zechariah 9:12). I am an open refuge, a near and inviolable refuge for you (Psalm 48:3; Deuteronomy 4:7; John 10:29).

You shall have My fatherly provision. Do not be afraid of need; in your Father's house there is bread enough (Psalm 34:9; Luke 15:17). I will care for your bodies. Do not worry about what you shall eat, drink, or put on. Let it suffice you that your heavenly Father knows that you have need of all things (Matthew 6:25–34; Luke 12:22–32). I will provide for your souls: food for them, mansions for them, and portions for them (John 6:30–59; Lamentations 3:22–23).

Behold, I have spread the table of My gospel for you, with privileges and comforts that no man can take from you (Isaiah 25:6; Matthew 22:4; Proverbs 9:2). I have set before you the bread of life, the tree of life, and the water of life (John 6:48; Revelation 2:7; 22:17).

Eat, O friends; drink abundantly, O beloved!

# JEREMIAH BURROUGHS

## The Rare Jewel of Christian Contentment

Exercise much faith; that is the way for contentedness. After you have done with all the considerations that reason may suggest to you, if you find that these do not do it, oh—then call for the grace of faith. A man may go very far with the use of reason alone to help him to contentment, but when reason is at a nonplus, then set faith at work.

Exercise faith not only in the promise that all shall work together for good to them that fear God, but likewise exercise faith in God Himself—as well as in His Word and in the attributes of God. It was a saying of Socrates, a heathen: "Since God is so careful for you, what need you be careful for anything yourselves?"

Oh, Christian, if you have any faith, think this way in the time of extremity: that this is the time God calls for the exercise of faith. What can you do with your faith, if you cannot quiet the discontent in your heart? . . . What do you get by being a believer, a Christian? What can you do by your faith? I can do this: I can in all states cast my care upon God, cast my burden upon God, and commit my way to God in peace. Faith can do this.

Therefore, when reason can go no higher, let faith get on the shoulders of reason and say, "I see land though reason cannot see it; I see good that will come out of all this evil." Exercise faith by often resigning yourself to God, by giving yourself up to God and His ways. The more you surrender up yourself to God in a believing way, the more quiet and peace you will have.

# WILLIAM BATES

## From the Sermon "How Men Are Said to Be the Sons of God"

The love of God has its rise from the consideration of His amiable excellencies, which render Him infinitely worthy of the highest affection; and from the blessed benefits of creation, preservation, redemption, and glorification—which we may expect from His pure goodness and mercy. This is the most clear and essential character of a child of God, and most peculiarly distinguishes him from unrenewed men, however accomplished by civil virtues.

Now the internal exercise of love to God—in the valuation of His favor as that which is better than life, in earnest desires of communion with Him, in ravishing joy in the testimonies and assurance of His love, in mourning for what is displeasing to Him—is in the secret of the soul; but with this there is inseparably joined a true and visible declaration of our love in obedience to Him. And this is the love of God, the most real and undeceitful expression of it: "that we keep His commandments" (1 John 3:21–22).

Therefore the following are true regarding the obedience that springs from love:

1. *The obedience of love is uniform and universal, for the two principal and necessary effects of love are an ardent desire to please God and an equal care not to displease Him in anything.* Now the law of God is the signification of His sovereign and

holy will, and the doing of it is very pleasing to Him, both upon the account of the subjection of the creature to His authority and conformity to His purity. Indeed, He declares that obedience is better than the most costly sacrifice. There is an absolute peremptory repugnance between love to Him and the despising of His commands—and so it follows that love inclines the soul to obey all God's precepts, not only those of easy observation, but even the most difficult and distasteful to the carnal appetites. . . . Love regards the whole law in all its injunctions and prohibitions; not merely to please ourselves, that we may not feel the stings of an accusing conscience, but also to please the lawgiver.

2. *The obedience of love is accurate, and this is a natural consequence of the former.* The divine law is a rule not only for our outward conversation, but of our thoughts and affections—all the interior workings of the soul—that are open before God. Thus it requires religious service not only in the external performance, but those reverent holy affections, those pure aims, wherein the life and beauty, the spirit and true value of divine worship consists. Thus it commands the duties of equity, charity and sobriety, all civil and natural duties for divine ends, to "please and glorify God" (Hebrews 13:16). Such obedience forbids all kinds and degrees of sin; not only gross acts, but also the inward lustings that have a tendency to them. . . .

3. *The obedience of love is chosen and pleasant.* "This is the love of God, that we keep His commandments, and His commandments are not grievous" (1 John 5:3). Those that are strangers to this heavenly affection imagine that a solicitous, diligent respect to all God's precepts is a melancholy task.

But in reality it is delightful to the saints, for obedience is the continual exercise of love to God, the paradise of holy souls. The mortification of the carnal appetites and the restraint from such objects as powerfully insinuate and engage carnal hearts is with a freer complacency to a saint than a sensual fruition of them. The sharpest sufferings for religion are allayed, nay sweetened, to a saint from the love of God that is then most sincerely, strongly, and purely acted. The apostle more rejoiced in sharp tribulation for Christ's sake than in divine revelation.

4. *The love of God produces persevering obedience.* Servile compliance is inconstant. A slave hates the duties he performs and loves the sins he dares not commit; therefore as soon as he is released from his chain and his fear, his obedience ceases. But a son is perfectly pleased with his Father's will, and the tenor of his life is correspondent to it. He that is pressed by fear to serve in an army will desert his colors the first opportunity; but a volunteer that for the love of valor, and of his country, lists himself will continue in the service. . . . Such is the love of God planted in the breast of a Christian.

# COTTON MATHER

## The Duties of Children to Their Parents

This is plain: those parents who are blessed with dutiful children do with an inexpressible agony wish all sorts of blessings to their children. If it were in their power to confer blessings upon their children; Oh, how much would they do for them! Now because it is in the power of God alone to confer blessings upon us, these parents go to God for their children, and they say with good old Jacob, "God bless the lads!"

I assure you, such benedictions from obliged parents have a more than ordinary authority and efficacy in them. For one's parents to go before God and plead: "Ah, Lord, such a child of mine has loved me and served me and helped me; and his good carriage to me has been such that even upon that account I have reason to wish him all the good in the world. I therefore bring that child unto You, and I pray You to bless him with all blessings of goodness."

To be thus blessed by one's parents, oh my children, is a thing of more value than if a rich inheritance were to be received from them.

This is very certain: there is no point of religion more certainly and commonly rewarded with blessings in this world than that of rendering unto parents the dues that pertain to them. A signal prosperity, even in this world, uses to attend those children who are very obedient or serviceable to their parents. Those Reckabites that obey the commandment of their Father, thus said the Lord of Hosts, "They shall stand before me forever."

There are children who have, with unspeakable pleasure, supported their aged parents in their necessities. They have said unto their necessitous parents, like Joseph, "Come down to me; you shall be near to me!" I believe there are some at this very time, in this very place, who can say that from the time they did for their parents as they have done, God has signally smiled upon them.

Friend, that aged father or mother in your house is not only the glory of your house, but a better and a richer thing than a mine of silver there. Children, be blessings to your parents, and be assured that those parents will be greater blessings to you than you can be to them. They will be so as long as they live. Yes, and more than so—after your parents are dead and gone, the effects of their prayers will yet live. All the prayers which those gratified parents put up for you will be still answering, after they are dead, as long as you yourselves do live.

# SAMUEL RUTHERFORD

## Fourteen Communion Sermons

"Wherefore, seeing we also are compassed about with so great a cloud of witnesses, let us lay aside every weight, and the sin which does so easily beset us, and let us run with patience the race that is set before us" (Hebrews 12:1).

We see the way to heaven is now a high market gate, and paved by hundreds and thousands who have gone before us; and we should follow after. Are you wanting a settled house and dwelling in the world? Then set forward, look for a city above. "Indeed," says Abraham, "I shall be witness of that, that you shall receive the recompense of reward." Will you rather suffer affliction with the people of God than enjoy the pleasures of sin for a season? Moses says, "I shall be witness then, that you shall win home safe and sound." In that way you may see a whole cloud of them as witnesses to lead you through the wilderness.

Where can you go, or what can befall you in your journey to glory, but in which the Lord's saints have gone before you? Are you alone and seeking God amongst many who live as they desire? So was Noah a walker with God, when all flesh had corrupted their ways. Let it be true you who have had all taken from you goods, children, and health. So was Job handled! The saints have set up steps and way-marks at every turn in your way, and they cry, "Ride about." And howbeit now, many fools think to win through at the nearest, yet they win not, but stick there.

The saints' going before in the way is a great benefit to us; their falls, and the ill steps that cumbered them, you must beware of. You must hold off adultery, for David stuck in that mire. Hold off drunkenness, for Noah and Lot wet their feet in that tub. Beware of mocking and persecuting the saints, for Paul's ship had almost sunk in that quicksand. See these dead carcasses lying on the road: Judas, Demas, Hymeneus, and Philetus broke their necks by attempting to go to Canaan and falling off again.

Make this use of holy men's lives, here condemned, who followed the devil but were recovered again. Beware of those temptations and sins which so easily beset them. Here is a cloud of witnesses; the world and the fashions thereof, they did not follow. Romans 12:2: "Be not conformed to this world," and the guises thereof; . . . yet you can justify yourselves in the daily transgression of this divine prohibition.

Wherefore is vanity in marriages and banquets? "It is the fashion," say they. Proud Scotland! Poor Scotland! Near cut out to your skin; it is worm-eaten. Wherefore is such vanity in apparel? So that women are become indecent, and men like monsters. Men are taking whole baronies of land on their backs? "It's the fashion," say they. Oh! Proud and poor Scotland. Men are cut out to their skin, and women want not vanity enough, but are not cut to the bone. And wherefore comes swearing, and drinking, see you not? No otherwise than from the fashion. "It is the fashion," say they.

But if you will follow such a cloud of fashionable witnesses, let me conclude you will go to hell also; for I can assure you that is the fashion. You may keep that excuse until the Day of Judgment. And when God asks what you have done, and wherefore you did so, you can say, "Lord, for nothing but the fashion," and see how you will win off.

# WILLIAM AMES

## Contentment

The virtue of contentment is the acquiescence of the mind in the lot God has given (1 Timothy 6:6; Hebrews 13:5; Philippians 4:11).

This contentment is ordered in the tenth commandment as appears from the words themselves. It is not at all proper to refer this precept to the inward and original purity of righteousness, which is the fountain of all obedience. Such purity is not commanded in any one commandment but in all. And the precept no more belongs to the second table where it is situated than to the first.

Of all the virtues contained in the second table, however, none is more internal or intimate to vital righteousness than contentment. By it we are, as it were, led by the hand to contemplate and seek righteousness. And so righteousness in its purity is fitly handled here.

Joy for the prosperity of our neighbor, as if it were our own, is part of contentment (Romans 12:15). In contentment and joy are found the height and perfection of all love towards our neighbor. Hence contentment is in a way the perfection of godliness and of a godly man. "But godliness with contentment is great gain" (1 Timothy 6:6).

Therefore, the last commandment stands at the end of an order which proceeds from the less to the more perfect and from the better known to the less known. For this is our most perfect duty and yet least known to us by nature: that whatever we conceive or will should be joined with the good of our neighbor.

Although by its nature this is first among duties to our neighbor as the foundation of all the others, it is commanded in the last place because it is the last to come into being for corrupted man.

# JEREMIAH BURROUGHS

## The Rare Jewel of Christian Contentment

Contentment is a sweet, inward heart-thing. It is a work of the Spirit indoors.

It is not only that we do not seek to help ourselves by outward violence, or that we forbear from discontented and murmuring expressions with perverse words and bearing against God and others. But it is the inward submission of the heart. "Truly, my soul waits upon God" (Psalm 62:1) and "My soul, wait only upon God" (Psalm 62:5). Not only must the tongue hold its peace; the soul must be silent.

Many may sit silently, refraining from discontented expressions, yet inwardly they are bursting with discontent. This shows a complicated disorder and great perversity in their hearts. And notwithstanding their outward silence, God hears the peevish, fretful language of their souls. A shoe may be smooth and neat outside, while inside it pinches the flesh. Outwardly there may be great calmness and stillness, yet within amazing confusion, bitterness, disturbance and vexation.

Some people are so weak that they cannot restrain the unrest of their spirits, but in words and behavior they reveal what woeful disturbances there are within. Their spirits are like the raging sea, casting forth nothing but mire and dirt, and are troublesome not only to themselves but also to all with whom they live. Others, however, are able to restrain such disorders of heart, as Judas did when he betrayed Christ with a kiss, but even so they boil inwardly and eat away like a canker. So David speaks of some whose words are sweeter than honey and butter, and yet have war in their hearts. . . .

If the attainment of true contentment were as easy as keeping quiet outwardly, it would not need much learning. It might be had with less strength and skill than an apostle possessed—yes, less than an ordinary Christian has or may have. Therefore, there is certainly more to it than can be attained by common gifts and the ordinary power of reason, which often bridle nature. Contentment is a business of the heart.

# RICHARD BAXTER

## The Practical Works of Richard Baxter

Understand in general of what moment and concern it is that the tongue be well governed and used. For they that think words are inconsiderable will use them inconsiderately. The conceit that words are of small moment (as some say of thoughts, that they are free) causes men to use their tongues as if they were free, saying, "Our lips are our own: who is lord over us?" (Psalm 12:4).

The tongue of man is his glory, the sins and duties by which expressively he excels the brutes. And a wonderful work of God it is that a man's tongue should be able to articulate such an exceeding number of words, for God has not given man so admirable a faculty for vanity and sin. The nobler and more excellent it is, the more to be regarded—and the greater is the fault of them that do abuse it.

Hilary compares such abusers to an ill barber that cuts a man's face, and so deforms him, when his work was to have made him more neat and comely. So it is the office of the tongue to be excellently serviceable to the good of others, and to be the glory of mankind. The shame therefore of its faults is all the more inexcusable.

The tongue is made to be the index or expresser of the mind; therefore, if the mind be regardable, the tongue is regardable. And if the mind be not regardable, the man is not regardable. For our Lord tells us that the tree is known by its fruit; an evil tree brings forth evil fruits, and "out of the abundance of the heart the mouth speaks" (Luke 6:45). Indeed, Aristotle says that "such as a man is, such are his speeches, such his works, and such his life."

Therefore by vain or sinful words you tell men the vanity and corruption of your minds.

# JOHN FLAVEL

## Method of Grace in the Gospel Redemption

I will not be tiresome, but will conclude all in a few requests to you (and to God for you both). That which I request of you is as follows:

1. That you will search and try your own hearts by these truths, especially now, when so great trials are likely to be made of every man's root and foundation in religion. Be certain that your first work, which Bellarmine calls "the first error of Protestants," is to make sure of your interest in Christ. Everything is as its foundation is; a true diamond will endure the smartest stroke of the hammer, but a false one will fly.

2. That you be humble under all that dignity and honor, which God has put upon you; be clothed with humility. It was the glory of the primitive Christians that they did not speak but live great things—so humility will be the luster of your other excellencies. Estates and honors are but appendages and fine trappings, which add nothing of any real worth. Yet how are some vain minds puffed up with these things! But you have not so learned Christ.

3. That you steadily persevere in those good ways of God in which you have walked, and that you beware of heart- or life-apostasy. You expect happiness while God is in heaven,

and God expects holiness from you while you are on earth. It was an excellent truth that Tossanus recommended to his posterity in his last will and testament, learned from his own experience: "I beseech you, my dear children and kindred, that you never be ashamed of the truths of the gospel, either by reason of scandals in the church, or persecutions upon it. Truth may labor for a time, but it cannot be conquered, and I have often found God to be wonderfully present with them that walk before Him in truth—though for a time they may be oppressed with troubles."

4. Lastly, I request that you keep a strict and constant watch over your own hearts, lest they be ensnared by the tempting, charming, and dangerous snares attending a full and easy condition in the world. There are temptations suited to all conditions. Those that are poor and low in estate and reputation are tempted to cozen, cheat, lie, and flatter, and all to get up to the mount of riches and honors. But those that were born upon that mount, though they be more free from those temptations, yet lie exposed to others no less dangerous. Therefore we find, "Not many mighty, not many noble are called" (1 Corinthians 1:26). Many great and stately ships, which spread much sail and draw much water, perish in the storms—even when small barks creep along the shore under the wind and get safe into their port. Never aim at a higher station in this world than that you are in. Some have wished in their dying hour that they had been lower, but no wise man ever wished himself at the top at honor while at the brink of eternity.

I will conclude all with this hearty wish for you: that as God has set you in a capacity of much service for Him in your generation, so your hearts may be enlarged for God accordingly, and that you may be very instrumental for His glory on earth and may go safe, but late, to heaven. That the blessings of heaven may be multiplied upon you . . . and your hopeful springing branches; and that you may live to see your children's children and peace upon Israel.

# OCTAVIUS WINSLOW

## Evening Thoughts

All love to God in the soul is the result of His love to us. It is begotten in the heart by His Spirit: He took the first step and made the first advance. "He first loved us" (1 John 4:19). Oh heart-melting truth! The love of God to us when yet we were sinners, who can unfold it? What mortal tongue can describe it? Before we had any being, and when we were enemies, He sent His Son to die for us; and when we were far off by wicked works He sent His Spirit to bring us to Him in the cloudy and dark day. All His dealings with us since then—His patience, restoring mercies, tender, loving, faithful care, yes, the very strokes of His rod—have but unfolded the depths of His love towards His people; this is the love we desire you to be filled with. "The Lord direct your hearts into the love of God" (2 Thessalonians 3:5).

Draw largely from this river; why should you deny yourselves? There is enough love in God to overflow the hearts of all His saints through all eternity. Why not be filled? "The Lord direct your hearts into the love of God;" stand not upon the brink of the fountain, linger not upon the margin of this river. Enter into it; plunge into it; it is for you—poor, worthless, unworthy, vile, as you feel yourself to be, this river of love is yet for you! Seek to be filled with it, that you may know the love of Christ, which passes knowledge, and that your heart, in return, may ascend in a flame of love to God.

Body of Divinity

Live so that, at the last day of judgment, you may be sure to be acquitted and have the glorious privileges with which the saints shall be crowned. How is that? If you would stand acquitted at the day of judgment, then:

1. *Labor to get into Christ.* "That I may be found in Him" (Philippians 3:9). Faith implants us into Christ, it engarrisons us in Him, and then "there is no condemnation." There is no standing before Christ except by being in Christ.

2. *Labor for humility, which is a kind of self-annihilation.* "Though I am nothing." Christian, have you great abilities? Can you cover them with the veil of humility, as Moses, when his face shone and he put a veil over it? If you are humble, you shall be acquitted at the day of judgment. "He shall save the humble person" (Job 22:29). A humble man judges himself for his sins, and Christ will acquit those who judge themselves.

3. *If you would stand acquitted at the last day, keep a clear conscience.* Do not load yourself with guilt, and furnish your judge with matter against you. "The Lord," says Paul, "has appointed a day in which He will judge the world" (Acts

17:31). How would Paul fit himself for that day? "Herein do I exercise myself, to have always a conscience void of offense toward God and toward men."

Be careful of the first and second table; be holy and just. Have hearts without false aims, and hands without false weights. Keep conscience as clear as your eye, that no dust of sin fall into it. Those who sin against conscience will be shy of their judge; as such as take in prohibited goods cannot endure to see the searchers that are appointed to open their packs. Christian, your pack will be opened at the last day—I mean, your conscience (and Christ is the searcher), to see what sins, what prohibited goods, you have taken in. And then He proceeds to judgment. Oh! Be sure to keep a good conscience, which is the best way to stand with boldness at the day of judgment. The voice of conscience is the voice of God. If conscience, upon just grounds, acquits us, God will acquit us. "If our heart condemns us not, then have we confidence toward God" (1 John 3:21).

4. *If you would stand acquitted at the last day, trade with your talents for God's glory.* Lay out yourselves for Him; honor Him with your substance; relieve Christ's members, that you may be acquitted. He who had five talents traded with them, and made them five talents more. "His Lord said unto him, Well done, good and faithful servant!" (Matthew 25:21).

5. *If you would stand acquitted at the day of judgment, get a sincere love to the saints.* Love is the truest touchstone of sincerity. To love grace for grace shows the spirit of God to be in a man. Does conscience witness for you? Are you perfumed with this sweet spice of love? Do you delight

most in those in whom the image of God shines? Do you reverence their graces? Do you bear with their infirmities? A blessed evidence that you shall be acquitted in the day of judgment. "We know that we have passed from death to life, because we love the brethren" (1 John 3:14).

# CHRISTOPHER LOVE

## From His Last Letter to His Wife

My most gracious Beloved,

I am now going from a prison to a palace. I have finished my work and am now going to receive my wages. I am going to heaven, where are two of my children, and leaving you on earth, where there are three of my babes. These two above need not my care, but the three below need yours. It comforts me to think that two of my children are in the bosom of Abraham, and three of them will be in the arms and care of such a tender and godly mother. God has many mercies in store for you, and the prayer of a dying husband for you will not be lost. To my shame, I never prayed for you at liberty as I have done in prison.

I can write much, but I have few practical counsels to leave with you:

1. Keep under a sound, orthodox, soul-searching ministry. Oh! There are many deceivers gone out into the world, but Christ's sheep know His voice, and a stranger they will not follow. Attend any minister that teaches the way of God in truth.

2. Bring up your children in the knowledge and admonition of the Lord. The mother ought to be a teacher in the father's absence (Proverbs 31:1).

3. Pray in your family daily, that yours may be in the number of the families who call upon God.

4. Labor for a meek and quiet spirit, which in the sight of God is of great price (1 Peter 3:4).

5. Pore not on the comforts you want, but upon the mercies you have. Look rather at God's ending in afflicting than to the measure and degree of your affliction.

6. Labor to clear up your evidence for heaven when God takes from you the comfort of earth, so that as your sufferings do abound, your consolation in Christ may abound much more. If ever I had confidence touching the grace of another, I have confidence of grace in you.

7. When you find your heart secure, presumptuous, and proud, then pore upon corruption more than grace: then look upon your grace without infirmities.

8. Study the covenant of grace, and the merits of Christ, and be troubled if you can; you are interested in such a covenant that accepts purposes for performances, desires for deeds, sincerity for perfection, the righteousness of another (that of Jesus Christ), as it were your own alone. Oh! My love! Rest in the love of God, the bosom of Christ.

9. Swallow up your will in the will of God. It is a bitter cup we are to drink, but it is the cup of our Father which has been put into our hands. Oh! Say you so, when I go to the Tower-Hill, "The will of the Lord be done!"

10. Rejoice in my joy. To mourn for me inordinately argues that you either envy or suspect my happiness. The joy of the Lord is my strength. Oh! Let it be yours also! Dear wife, farewell: I will call you wife no more. I shall see your face no more. Yet I am not much troubled, for now I am going to meet the Bridegroom, the Lord Jesus, to whom I shall be eternally married.

Farewell dear love, and again I say farewell. The Lord Jesus be with your spirit, the Maker of heaven and earth be a husband to you; and the Father of the Lord Jesus Christ be a father to your children—so prays your dying, your most affectionate friend till death, on the day of my glorification.

8

# OBSTACLES AND ADVERSARIES

"When we sail in Christ's company, we may not make sure of fair weather, for great storms may toss the vessel which carries the Lord Himself, and we must not expect to find the sea less boisterous around our little boat."

—*Morning and Evening*

# THOMAS BROOKS

A String of Pearls

This life is full of trials, full of troubles, and full of changes. Sin within, and Satan and the world without, will keep a Christian from rest until he comes to rest in the bosom of Christ. The life of a Christian is a race, and what rest have those who are still running their race? The life of a Christian is a warfare, and what rest have those who are still engaged in a constant warfare? The life of a Christian is the life of a pilgrim, and what rest has a pilgrim who is still traveling from place to place?

The fears, the snares, the cares, the changes which attend believers in this world are such that will keep them from taking up their rest here. A Christian hears that word always sounding in his ears: "Arise, for this is not your resting place, because it is polluted" (Micah 2:10). A man may as well expect to find heaven in hell as expect to find rest in this world! Rest is a jewel very desirable on earth, but we shall not wear it in our bosoms until we come to heaven.

Man's sorrows begin when his days begin, and his sorrows are multiplied as his days are multiplied. His whole life is but one continued grief: labor wears him, care tears him, fears toss him, losses vex him, dangers trouble him, crosses disquiet him, and nothing pleases him.

The rest reserved in heaven for believers is a universal rest—a rest from all sin; a rest from all sorrow; a rest from all afflictions;

a rest from all temptations; a rest from all oppression; a rest from all vexations; a rest from all labor and pains; a rest from all trouble and travail; a rest from all aches, weaknesses, and diseases.

"Blessed are those who die in the Lord from now on. Yes, says the Spirit, they are blessed indeed, for they will rest from all their toils and trials" (Revelation 14:13).

The end is called a new and divine creature. First, because it is not produced by those principles that are in us by nature, as is characteristic of all the arts pursued with industry and discipline; rather, it comes out of the new principle of life communicated by God to us in our calling. Second, because our natural disposition is of a completely different kind from what it was before. Third, because it takes for its model the highest perfection found in God Himself.

There are two degrees of sanctification on earth. One occurs in this life that is generally called an Infancy (1 Corinthians 13:11–12; Ephesians 4:14; 1 Peter 2:2). The variety found in this life is so great that some who are sanctified, when compared with others and even with themselves at different times, may rightly be called Infants and others Adults during their life here (Hebrews 5:13–14).

# WILLIAM PERKINS

## The Order of Salvation and Damnation

After original sin in Adam's posterity, actual transgression takes place. It is either inward or outward.

Inward is of the mind, will, and affections. The actual sin of the mind is the evil thought or intent thereof, which is contrary to God's Law. Examples of evil thoughts God (the only knower of the heart) has in diverse places set down in His Word: Psalm 10:4; Psalm 14:1; Luke 18:11; 1 Corinthians 2:14; Revelation 18:7; and more. Many carnal men pretend their good meaning, but when God opens their eyes, they shall see their rebellious thoughts rising in their minds as sparks out of a chimney.

The actual sin of both will and affection is every wicked motion, inclination, and desire. Galatians 5:17: "For the flesh lusts against the Spirit, and the Spirit against the flesh: and these are contrary the one to the other: so that you cannot do the things that you would."

An actual outward sin is that, to the committing whereof, the members of the body do together with the faculties of the soul concur. Such sins as these are infinite. Psalm 40:12: "For innumerable evils have compassed me about: mine iniquities have taken hold upon me, so that I am not able to look up; they are more than the hairs of mine head: therefore my heart fails me."

Actual sin is of omission or commission. Again, both these are in the words or deeds. In the sin of commission, observe the degrees in committing sin and the difference of sins committed.

347

The degrees are in number four: "But every man is tempted when he is drawn away of his own lust, and enticed. Then when lust hath conceived, it brings forth sin: and sin, when it is finished, brings forth death" (James 1:14–15).

The first degree is temptation, whereby man is allured to sin. Satan does this by offering to the mind that which is evil. Acts 5:3: "But Peter said, 'Ananias, why has Satan filled your heart to lie to the Holy Ghost, and to keep back part of the price of the land?'"

Temptation has two parts: abstraction and inescation. Abstraction is the first cogitation of committing sin, whereby the mind is withdrawn from God's service (to which it should be always ready pressed). Inescation is that whereby an evil thought conceived, and for a time retained in the mind by delighting the will and affections—as it were, laying bait for them to draw them to consent.

The second degree is conception, which is nothing else but a consent and resolution to commit sin. Psalm 7:14: "Behold, he travails with iniquity, and has conceived mischief, and brought forth falsehood."

The third degree is the birth of sin, namely the committing of sin, by the assistance both of the faculties of the soul and the powers of the body.

The fourth degree is perfection, when sin being custom perfect, and as it were, ripe, the sinner reaps death—that is, damnation.

# JOHN FLAVEL

## On Keeping the Heart

When Providence frowns upon you and blasts your outward comforts, then look to your heart; keep it with all diligence from repining against God or fainting under His hand. For troubles, though sanctified, are troubles still.

Jonah was a good man, and yet how fretful was his heart under affliction! Job was the mirror of patience, yet how was his heart discomposed by trouble! You will find it hard to get a composed spirit under great afflictions. Oh, the hurries and tumults which they occasion even in the best hearts. Let me show you, then, how a Christian under great afflictions may keep his heart from repining or desponding under the hand of God. . . .

One method for keeping the heart from sinking under afflictions is to call to mind that your own Father has the ordering of those afflictions. Not a creature moves hand or tongue against you but by His permission. Suppose the cup is bitter, yet it is the cup which your Father has given you; can you suspect poison in it? Foolish man, put home the case to your own heart. Can you give anything to your child that would ruin him? No! You would as soon hurt yourself as him. "If you then, being evil, know how to give good gifts to your children," how much more does God. The very consideration of His nature as a God of love, pity, and tender mercies—or of His relation to you as a father, husband, and friend—would be security enough if He had not spoken a word to quiet you in this case. And yet you have His word, too, by the prophet Jeremiah: "I will do you no hurt." You lie too near His heart for Him to hurt you; nothing grieves Him more than your groundless and unworthy suspicions of His designs. Would it not grieve a faithful, tender-hearted physician, when he had studied the case of his patient and prepared the most excellent medicines to save his life, to hear him cry out, "Oh, he has undone me; he has poisoned me!" because it pains him in the operation?

God respects you as much in a low condition as in a high condition; therefore it need not so much trouble you to be made low. No, He manifests more of His love, grace, and tenderness in the time of affliction than in the time of prosperity. As God did not at first choose you because you were high, He will not now forsake you because you are low.

Men may look shy upon you and alter their respects as your condition is altered. When Providence has blasted your estate, your summer-friends may grow strange, fearing you may be troublesome to them. But will God do so? No. No. "I will never leave you nor forsake you," says He. If adversity and poverty could bar you from access to God, it would indeed be a deplorable condition; but you may go to Him as freely as ever. Poor David, when stripped of all earthly comforts, could encourage himself in the Lord his God; why cannot you? Suppose your husband or son had lost everything at sea and came to you in rags; could you deny the relation or refuse to entertain him? If you would not, much less will God. Why then are you so troubled? Though your condition is changed, your Father's love is not changed.

# THOMAS GOODWIN

## The Wisdom of Patience

"If any of you lacks wisdom, let him ask of God, who gives to all liberally and without reproach, and it will be given to him" (James 1:5).

Let us pray, therefore, with all vehemency for ourselves, that this glorious power may come upon us and strengthen our inward man—and that this strength may provide us with "all might," as the apostle writes in Ephesians 3:16. The product of such might within us is the effect of that power in God as the cause.

That might you had in such or such a trial will not serve to strengthen you against the next trial that shall come; you must still have a new and special might for every new trial. Your dependence, therefore, is great upon God for this perfect work of patience, and yet your encouragements are great. For as it must be that, if God will please to strengthen us under any great temptations, that He should put forth no less than this "glorious power"; so we have heard how, from our apostle, God has promised He will give it, and give it freely and liberally, to them that make it their main, constant, earnest business to ask for it. Therefore, His grace, if applied to, is engaged to put this power forth.

It cannot but be a great support to a weak heart that finds itself so remote and distant from such a work of patience, and weak also in comparison of finding such an inward might, that it should have ground and cause to think and to believe that God's glorious power

351

is engaged most freely to be abundantly and readily put forth, if continued to be sought. Why, this, says the weak heart, will do it—namely, this glorious power. And I have found by some trials already that the strong God and a weak heart will be too hard for anything; yes, for the whole world.

Therefore, when you think your present trials have come upon you far greater than you can bear, think of the glorious power of God that is at hand to help you. It is a great word, that: "His glorious power." A greater attribute could not have been named or found out for our comfort. And it is a word of virtue, force, and power to hearten to or against anything whatever.

It is true your present trial may be, and is, above that inward strength which has served to act your graces in your ordinary walkings with God, holily and sincerely. A child may by its ordinary strength be able to walk up and down a room, chairs supporting it, without any other extraordinary help; but if it is to go up a pair of stairs, the strength that enabled it to do these lesser performances will not be sufficient. He must be carried and held up in the arms of one who is strong and mighty.

And so it is here. That other part of our Christian obedience . . . requires indeed God's power, for by it we are kept unto salvation all along. But when it comes to patience and long-suffering, and all patience, and when such a trial comes as will try all patience in you—then it is that the writer makes mention of that glorious power, and not before. Therefore the promise is that, in such a case, the Spirit of glory shall rest upon us, not only the Spirit of grace (1 Peter 4:14).

Therefore relieve and comfort yourselves with these things, and especially with this: that as your trials abound, so this glorious power of God will also abound towards you for your support. Amen.

# THOMAS GOUGE

## The Principles of the Christian Religion

From what did our first parents fall? It was from that blessed and happy estate wherein they were created. For, whereas they were created after the image of God in true knowledge, holiness, and righteousness, by their fall the image of God was defaced in them, and they became corrupted and polluted in all the faculties of their souls.

From this fall, after the temptations of Satan, let us learn not to be too bold and confident in our own strength. Have such tall cedars fallen? How then shall such poor, weak shrubs as we think to stand firm and immoveable? Adam, though he was endowed with a great measure of knowledge—yes, with power to abide in his state of innocence, having no inclination to evil—yet he was no sooner tempted than he yielded and was overcome, to the ruin of himself and all his posterity. What danger is there, then, of our falling in the day of temptation, when Satan is as malicious against mankind as ever and is now by experience grown much more cunning to deceive?

In order to better prevent the temptations of Satan, and to preserving yourself from being overcome by them, observe these directions:

- **Labor to be thoroughly sensible of your own weakness and impotency to withstand his temptations.** The truth is that the best of us are weak and of no strength; yes, confidence in our own strength is the forerunner of a fall, as you may see in Peter who, when he was most confident of his own strength, then was nearest to a fall.

- **"Be strong in the Lord, and in the power of His might."** This direction to keep us safe from Satan's assaults is given us by the apostle in Ephesians 6:10.

- **Let it be your daily prayer to God that you may not enter into temptation**; and when you are entered into it, that He would not suffer you to be overcome by it. It is only the power of God that keeps us from the temptations of Satan, and prayer is the means sanctified by God for obtaining it.

- **Exercise and actuate your faith in Jesus Christ**, believing He is both able and willing to strengthen you under all your trials and temptations, and to deliver you out of the same in the most seasonable time when it shall make most for His glory and your comfort. Oh, therefore, all you who complain of the temptations of Satan, go unto Christ for help and strength; go to Him whose arms are ever open to receive all poor tempted souls, and whose heart is likewise open and willing to yield unto you all needful succor and seasonable deliverance. Cast yourselves on Him for power, whereby you will engage His strength for you.

- **Take heed that you do not give entertainment to the suggestions of Satan**; do not revolve them in your mind by meditating on them. For, if so, you are in danger of being ensnared by them. Therefore speedily reject them with indignation. It was Eve's hearkening unto Satan's suggestions that was the cause of her fall.

- If you have given too hearty welcome unto the temptations

of Satan, so that they have gained a kind of consent, **yet put forth your utmost endeavors to restrain the external sinful action.** Though the devil has kindled a fire in your bosom, let not the sparks fly abroad. Close up the furnace and the fire will go out.

# JOHN BUNYAN

## An Exposition of the First Chapters of Genesis

"Now the serpent was more cunning than any beast of the field which the Lord God had made. And he said to the woman, 'Has God indeed said, "You shall not eat of every tree of the garden?"'" (Genesis 3:1). In these words we have an entrance of the first great spiritual conflict that was fought between the devil and flesh. And it is worth the observing how the enemy attempted, engaged, and overcame the world (2 Corinthians 11:3).

First, he tempts by means. He appears not in his own shape and hue, but assumes the body of one of the creatures, the body of the serpent, and so begins the combat. And from hence it is that in after ages he is spoken of under the name of that creature, "The dragon, that old serpent which is the devil, and Satan" (Revelation 20:2). Because as the Holy Ghost would have us beware of the devil, so of the means and engines which he uses; for where one is overcome by his own fearful appearance, ten thousand are overcome by the means and engines that he uses.

"The serpent was more cunning." The devil, in his attempts after our destruction, makes use of the most suitable means. The serpent was more cunning, therefore the cunning of the devil was least of all discerned. Had he made use of some of the most foolish of the creatures, Adam had luckily started back, for he knew the nature of all the creatures and gave them names accordingly; wherefore the serpent, Adam knew, was subtle; therefore Satan used him to catch this goodly creature. Hereby the devil least appeared; and least appearing, the temptation soonest took the tinder. . . .

This is he that undertook our first parents. But how did he undertake them? He labors to make them question the simplicity of the Word of God, bearing Adam's wife in hand, that there must be some meaning that palliates the text. "Has God indeed said, 'You shall not eat of every tree of the garden'?"

Therefore learn that so long as we retain the simplicity of the Word, we have Satan at the end of the staff. For unless we give way to a doubt about the truth and simplicity of it, he gets no ground upon us.

# JONATHAN EDWARDS

## Discourse on the Devil

Seeing that the devil is so cunning and subtle, it may seem a paradox why he will endeavor to frustrate the designs of an Omniscient Being, or to pretend to controvert Him who is omnipotent, seeing that God turns everything he does to the greater and more illustrious advancement of His own honor. And we see the devil has experienced this, since for so long a time all his deep-laid contrivances have at last come out to his own overthrow, and the work has been directly contrary to his design.

To this I say that, although the devil be exceeding crafty and subtle, yet he is one of the greatest fools and blockheads in the world—as the subtlest of wicked men are. Sin is of such a nature that it strangely infatuates and stultifies the mind. Men deliberately choose eternal torments rather than miss their pleasure of a few days; and to esteem a little silver and gold above eternal happiness makes men choose a few minutes' pleasure, though eternal misery be joined with it. This is what the most cunning of men do.

Sin has the same effect on the devils to make them act like fools, and so much the more as it is greater in them than in others. The devil acts here according to his deliberate judgment, being driven on to his own inexpressible torment by the fury of sin, malice, revenge, and pride. He is so entirely under the government of malice that, although he never attempted anything against God in which he was disappointed, yet he cannot bear to be quiet and refrain from exercising himself with all his might and subtlety against the increase of holiness.

# SAMUEL RUTHERFORD

## The Trial and Triumph of Faith

Many believe they are free of the devil. "I thank God," said one, "that I know not Satan, nor any of his works: I have peace. Satan did never tear me, nor cause me to fall to the earth, nor does he torment me."

But this is a fearful condition: it is an argument of a false peace. When the strong man is within, the house is in peace. Not to be tempted of the devil is the greatest temptation out of hell; and if there be any choice of devils, a raging and a roaring devil is better than the calm and sleeping devil. When the devil is within, he sleeps and is silent, and the house or soul he is in is silent, and there is a covenant with death and hell (Isaiah 28:15).

Now, hell keeps true to a natural man for a time; cessation of arms between the soul and Satan is security for a time, but it is not peace. The devil's war is better than the devil's peace. Carnal hypocrisy is a dumb and silent thing, but it is terrible to be carried to hell without any noise of feet. The wheels of Satan's chariot are oiled with carnal rest, and they go without rattling and noise. The devil carries few to hell with shouting and crying. Be suspect of dumb holiness: when the dog is kept out of doors, he howls to be in again. The covenant of Satan to Eve ("sin and you shall not die") stands with all men by nature, till Jesus Christ breaks peace between us and Satan.

Contraries meeting, such as hot and dry fire, and cold and

moist water, they conflict one with another; and where Satan finds a sanctified heart, he tempts with much importunity; as at one time, Christ found three mighty temptations, and he departed from Him only for a little time (Luke 4:13). Where there is most of God and of Christ, there, there are strong injections and firebrands cast in at the windows, so as some persons of much faith have been tempted to doubt, "Is there a Deity that rules all; and where is He? We see Him not." Another is often assaulted with this, "Is there a heaven for saints? Is there a hell for devils and wicked men? We never spoke with a messenger come from any of these two countries." A third is troubled with this, "Such a business I have expedient, whether God will or not."

The flower of the soul, the high lamp of the light of the mind, is frequently darkened with foggy and misty spirits coming up from the bottomless pit, and darkening any beams and irradiations of light that come from the Sun of Righteousness. Faith is more assaulted than any other grace: Satan shakes other graces, but faith is winnowed between heaven and earth (Luke 22:31–32).

Satan's first arrow shot at Christ labored to put a terrible "if" upon His light: "If You be the Son of God." It is as much as, if God be God, if the Son of God be the Son of God. It is not the evidence and certainty of fundamentals, nor the strength of grace, that privileges souls from Satan's shafts. Strength of saving light puts the saints often under the gunshot of Satan, that he may find a shot at them.

There is only law-surety against temptations up in heaven, when you are over score and out of time within eternity's lists. Never till then.

# STEPHEN CHARNOCK

## Discourse on the Power of God

Meditate on this power of God, and press it often upon your minds. We reason many things of God that we do not practically suck the comfort from because we lack deep thoughts of them and frequent inspection into them. We believe God to be true, yet distrust Him; we acknowledge Him powerful, yet we fear the motion of every straw. Many truths, though assented to in our understandings, are kept under covers by corrupt affections; they have not their due influence because they are not brought forth into the open air of our souls by meditation.

If we will but search our hearts, we shall find it is the power of God we often doubt.

When the heart of Ahaz and his subjects trembled at the combination of the Syrian and Israelite kings against him, for lack of a confidence in the power of God, God sends His prophet with commission to work a miraculous sign at his own choice in order to rear up his fainting heart. And when the king refused to ask for a sign out of diffidence to that almighty Power, the prophet complains of it as an affront to his Master (Isaiah 7:12–13). Moses, so great a friend of God, was overtaken with this kind of unbelief after all the experiences of God's miraculous acts in Egypt; the answer God gives him manifests this to be at the core: "Is the Lord's hand waxed short?" (Numbers 11:23).

For lack of thoughts carried out into practice of this, we are many times turned from our known duty by the blast of a creature—as though man had more power to dismay us than God has to support us in His commanded way. The belief of God's power is one of the first steps to all religion; without settled thoughts of it, we cannot pray lively and believingly to obtain the mercies we need, or to avert the evils we fear. We should not love God unless we are persuaded He has a power to bless us, nor fear Him unless we are persuaded of His power to punish us. The frequent thoughts of this would render our faith more stable and our hopes more steadfast; it would make us more feeble to sin and more careful to obey. . . .

Is it harder for God to make a virgin conceive a Son by the power of His Spirit than to make a world? Why does He reveal Himself so often under the title of Almighty, and press it upon us, but that we should press it upon ourselves? Shall we be forgetful of that which everything about us, everything within us, is a mark of? How did we come by the power of seeing and hearing, and this act of understanding and will, except by this Power framing us, this Power assisting us?

It is true that the thunder of His power cannot be understood, no more than any other perfection of His nature can be understood; but shall we, therefore, seldom think of it? The sea cannot be fathomed, yet the merchant does not excuse himself from sailing upon the surface of it. We cannot glorify God without due consideration of this attribute.

Those that have strong temptations in their course and over-pressing corruptions in their hearts have need to think of God's power out of their own interest, since nothing but this can relieve them. Those that have experienced the working of it in their new creation are obliged to think of it out of gratitude. It was this mighty power over Himself that gave rise to all that pardoning grace already conferred, or hereafter expected; without it our souls would have been consumed, the world overturned. Without it we could not expect a happy heaven, but would lay yelling in an eternal hell—yes, had not the power of His mercy exceeded that of His justice, and His infinite power executed what His infinite wisdom had contrived for our redemption.

# JOHN FLAVEL

## On Keeping the Heart

"Keep your heart with all diligence; for out of it are the issues of life" (Proverbs 4:23).

The heart of man is his worst part before it is regenerated and the best afterward; it is the seat of principles and the fountain of actions. The eye of God is, and the eye of the Christian ought to be, principally fixed upon it.

The greatest difficulty in conversion is to win the heart to God; and the greatest difficulty after conversion is to keep the heart with God. Here lies the very force and stress of religion; here is that which makes the way to life a narrow way, and the gate of heaven a strait gate. . . .

What the philosopher says of water is properly applicable to hearts—it is hard to keep them both within any bounds. God has set limits to them, yet how frequently do they transgress not only the bounds of grace and religion, but even of reason and common honesty? This is that which affords the Christian matter of labor and watchfulness to his dying day.

It is not the cleaning of the hand that makes the Christian—for many a hypocrite can show as fair a hand as he—but the purifying, watching, and right ordering of the heart. This is the thing that provokes so many sad complaints and costs so many deep groans and tears. It was the pride of Hezekiah's heart that made him lie in the dust, mourning before the Lord. It was the fear of hypocrisy's invading the heart that made David cry, "Let my heart be sound in Your statutes, that I be not ashamed." It was the sad experience he had of the divisions and distractions of his own heart in the service of God that made him pour out the prayer, "Unite my heart to fear Your name."

# JOHN BUNYAN

## Grace Abounding to the Chief of Sinners

Of all tears, they are the best that are made by the blood of Christ; and of all joy, that is the sweetest that is mixed with mourning over Christ. Oh! It is a goodly thing to be on our knees, with Christ in our arms, before God. I hope I know something of these things.

I find to this day seven abominations in my heart: (1) Inclinings to unbelief. (2) Suddenly to forget the love and mercy that Christ has manifested. (3) A leaning to the works of the law. (4) Wanderings and coldness in prayer. (5) To forget to watch for what I pray for. (6) Apt to murmur because I have no more, and yet ready to abuse what I have. (7) I can do none of those things which God commands me, but my corruptions will thrust in themselves—"When I would do good, evil is present with me."

These things I continually see and feel, and am afflicted and oppressed with; yet the wisdom of God does order them for my good. (1) They make me abhor myself. (2) They keep me from trusting my heart. (3) They convince me of the insufficiency of all inherent righteousness. (4) They show me the necessity of fleeing to Jesus. (5) They press me to pray unto God. (6) They show me the need I have to watch and be sober. (7) And provoke me to look to God, through Christ, to help me, and carry me through this world. Amen.

# JEREMIAH BURROUGHS

## Gospel Fear

It may be a use of a great deal of encouragement to all the ministers of God to preach to people. It may be that sometimes even they are discouraged, and think to themselves: Lord, how hard are the hearts of men, and how difficult it is to work upon the hearts of men! I have labored with all my might. I have studied and sought to invent all the arguments I possibly could—the most moving arguments that I could possibly imagine. When I have been in my study, I have told myself, "Surely if the Lord is pleased to bless these truths that I am to deliver, they will work upon the hearts of people."

And when it comes to the preaching of that sermon, perhaps the minister finds that they are not at all stirred one whit. "Why, Lord, what shall I do then? I cannot think ever to speak things that are more powerful than those that I have spoken, and those have done no good. Therefore I am afraid I shall never do good."

Oh, no, do not say so and do not think so. The Lord is pleased sometimes to show us our vanity this way, and to rebuke us. Many times the Lord will not go along with the ministry of the Word when it comes with the greatest power and the strongest arguments and, yet, at another time, the Lord will be pleased to bless a word that you only speak in passing. It may do more than all the others. There is scarcely any one faithful minister in the world who observes the work of God upon his ministry who does not find this to be true.

Yet this is no argument why a minister should not labor with all his might and come with the strongest arguments. He is bound to do his duty. Aye, be not discouraged. He may afterwards prevail, and God, I say, may bless many things that come from Him. Therefore I would exhort those who are to speak to such an audience with the words of Ecclesiastes 11:6: "In the morning sow your seed, and in the evening withhold not your hand; for you know not whether shall prosper, either this or that, or whether they both shall be alike good."

Therefore, let ministers go on and sow their seed and preach still. That which they have spoken (perhaps they have been delivering arguments that they thought would have moved the heart of a devil) has been opening the miserable condition of men and opening the riches of Jesus Christ. Well, there must be no discouragement; go on and sow your seed in the morning, and in the evening withhold not your hand. Go on and preach again and again, and let the Word of God be presented before the hearts of the people. Though it has not wrought at one time, yet it may work at another time.

Yes, though you should grow weaker and weaker, yet for all that the Lord may do good to you even when you are at your weakest. In 2 Timothy 2:25 the apostle says to Timothy, "In meekness instructing those that oppose themselves, if God will give them repentance." Perhaps this day a truth may be handed from God to a soul—maybe this text, maybe that text—and so the soul may be brought in.

# RICHARD SIBBES

## The Bruised Reed

Suffering brings discouragements because of our impatience. "Alas!" we lament, "I shall never get through such a trial." But if God brings us into the trial, He will be with us in the trial, and at length bring us out, more refined. We shall lose nothing but dross (Zechariah 13:9). From our own strength we cannot bear the least trouble, but by the Spirit's assistance we can bear the greatest. The Spirit will add His shoulders to help us to bear our infirmities. The Lord will give His hand to heave us up (Psalm 37:24).

"You have heard of the patience of Job," says James (5:11). We have heard of his impatience, too, but it pleased God mercifully to overlook that. It yields us comfort also in desolate conditions, such as contagious sicknesses and the like, in which we are more immediately under God's hand, that then Christ has a throne of mercy at our bedside and numbers our tears and our groans. And, to come to the matter we are now about, the sacrament was ordained not for angels, but for men; and not for perfect men, but for weak men; and not for Christ, who is truth itself, to bind Him, but because we are ready, by reason of our guilty and unbelieving hearts, to call truth itself into question.

Therefore it was not enough for His goodness to leave us many precious promises, but He gives us confirming tokens to strengthen us. And even if we are not so prepared as we should be, yet let us pray as Hezekiah did: "The good Lord pardon everyone

369

that prepares his heart to seek God, the Lord God of his fathers, though he be not cleansed according to the purification of the sanctuary" (2 Chronicles 30:18–19). Then we come comfortably to this holy sacrament, and with much fruit. This should carry us through all duties with such cheerfulness that, if we hate our corruptions and strive against them, they shall not be counted ours. "It is no more I that do it," says Paul, "but sin that dwells in me" (Romans 7:17). . . .

Where, then, do these discouragements come from? Not from the Father, for He has bound Himself in covenant to pity us as a father pities his children (Psalm 103:13) and to accept as a father our weak endeavors. And what is lacking in the strength of duty, He gives us leave to take up in His gracious indulgence. In this way we shall honor that grace in which He delights as much as in more perfect performances.

Also, not from Christ, for He by office will not quench the smoking flax. We see how Christ bestows the best fruits of His love on persons who are mean in condition, weak in abilities, and offensive for infirmities—nay, for grosser falls. And this He does, first, because it pleases Him to confound the pride of the flesh, which usually measures God's love by some outward excellency. And secondly, in this way He delights to show the freedom of His grace and confirm His royal prerogative that "he that glories" must "glory in the Lord" (1 Corinthians 1:31).

In the eleventh chapter of Hebrews, among that cloud of witnesses, we see Rahab, Gideon, and Samson ranked with Abraham, the father of the faithful (Hebrews 11:31–32). Our blessed Savior, as He was the image of His Father, so in this He was of the same mind, glorifying His Father for revealing the mystery of the gospel to simple men, neglecting those that carried the chief reputation of wisdom in the world (Matthew 11:25–26).

Neither do discouragements come from the Spirit. He helps

our infirmities, and by office is a comforter (Romans 8:26; John 14:16). If He convinces of sin, and so humbles us, it is that He may make way for His office of comforting us. Discouragements, then, must come from ourselves and from Satan, who labors to fasten on us a loathing of duty.

# THOMAS GOODWIN

## From the Sermon "The Vanity of Thoughts"

The vanity and sinfulness of the mind appears in a loathness to enter into holy thoughts—to begin to set itself to think of God and the things belonging unto our peace. Many people are as loath to such thoughts as schoolboys are to their books, not wanting to busy their minds about their lessons because their heads being full of play. In the same way are our minds loath to enter into serious considerations—into sad, solemn thoughts of God or death.

Men are as loath to think of death as thieves of the execution; or to think of God as thieves are of their judge. Even more to go over their own actions in a review of them and read the blurred writing of their hearts, and to commune with them at night in the end of the day (as David did). Men are as loath to do this as schoolboys are to parse their lesson and the false Latins they have made. "Depart from us," they say unto God, for "we desire not the knowledge of Your ways" (Job 21:14). They would not think of Him, or know Him, by their good wills. And therefore our minds, like a bad stomach, are nauseated with the very scent of good things, and soon cast them up again. "They like not to retain the knowledge of God" (Romans 1:28).

Let us go and try to wind up our souls to holy meditations—to think of what we have heard, or what we have done, or what is our duty to do—and we shall find our minds, like the pegs of an instrument, slip between our finger, as we are winding them up, and to fall down suddenly again before we are aware of it. Yes, you shall find that men labor to shun what may occasion such thoughts, even as they go out of their way when they see they must meet with someone they are loath to speak with.

Yes, men dare not be alone for fear that such thoughts should return upon them. The best shall find gladness for an excuse by other occasions to knock off their thoughts from what is good; whereas in thinking of vain earthly things, we think the time passes too fast, clocks strike too soon, and hours pass away before we are aware of it.

# WILLIAM GOUGE

## Commentary on Hebrews

For preventing or redressing covetousness, the following rules are to be observed:

1. **The judgment must rightly be informed in two points:** 1) In the nature of true happiness, and 2) In the vanity and deceitfulness of riches. Many learned men lack this point of understanding.

   It is the blindness of a man's mind that makes him place a kind of happiness in the things of this world, whereby he is brought even to coat upon them. If therefore we shall be rightly instructed that happiness consists in matters of another kind than this world affords, and that the things of this world are so vain that they can afford no solid comfort to a man (especially in spiritual distress), and so uncertain as they may suddenly be taken away from men, or men from them—surely their immoderate desire of riches could not be but much allayed.

2. **The will and heart of man must follow the judgment well informed, and must raise themselves up to that sphere where true happiness rests.** "Set our affection on things above, not on things on the earth" (Colossians 3:2). This will keep the heart from coating on things below, for

"where your treasure is, there will your heart be also" (Matthew 6:21). A beast which is feeding in fair and fresh pasture will not stray into a bare and barren heath; much less will an understanding man, one who finds the sweetness of spiritual and heavenly blessings, feed upon earthly trash. This made Paul account all outward things but dung because his heart had tasted of the sweetness of Christ (Philippians 3:8).

3. **A man's confidence must be placed on God and His providence.** God's providence is an overflowing and ever-flowing fountain. The richest treasures of men may be exhausted; God's cannot be. Be therefore fully resolved of this, that God will provide. This casting of our care on God's providence is much pressed in Scripture, as in 1 Peter 5:7 and Matthew 6:25–26. By experience we see how children depend on their parents' providence. Should not we much more depend on our heavenly Father? This resting upon God's providence is the more to be pressed in this case because nothing makes men more to misplace their confidence than riches.

4. **Our appetite or desire for riches must be moderate.** You must have the mind of him who prayed, "Give me neither poverty nor riches; feed me with food convenient for me" (Proverbs 30:8). Be content, therefore, with that portion God gives you, and be persuaded it is best for you. This is the lesson Paul had learned well (Philippians 4:11). Contentedness and covetousness are directly opposite, as light and darkness.

5. **We must pray against covetousness**, like he who said, "Incline my heart unto your testimonies, and not to

covetousness" (Psalm 119:36). We ought rather to pray to God against covetousness because it is a hereditary disease, and in that respect the more hardly cured. Remember that it was one of Christ's greatest miracles to cure one that was born blind (John 9:32).

# WILLIAM GURNALL

## The Christian in Complete Armor

**Question.** Why does God, when He has made a promise, make His people wait so long?

**Answer.** I shall answer this question by asking another: why does God make any promise at all to His creatures? This may be well asked, considering how free God was from owing any such kindness to His creatures. Only by the mere good pleasure of His will has He put Himself into bonds and made Himself, by a promise, a debtor to His elect.

This proves the former question to be saucy and over-bold—as if some great rich man should make a poor beggar that is a stranger to him his heir, and when he tells him this, the beggar should ask, "But why must I wait so long for it?" Truly, any time is too soon for him to receive a mercy from God that thinks God's time in sending it too late. This hasty spirit is as grievous to God as His waiting could be to us. It is no wonder God takes it so heinously, if we consider the bitter root that bears it.

First, such a root proceeds from a selfishness of spirit, whereby we prefer our own contentment and satisfaction before the glory of God. This does not become a gracious soul. Our comfort flows in by the performance of the promise, but the revenue of God's honor is paid to Him by our humble waiting on Him in the interval between the promise and the performance, and it is the main reason why He forbears the paying of it hastily. Jacob served seven years for Rachel, and God sure may better make us wait before the promise is given in to our embraces by the full accomplishment of it. "For you have need of patience, that, after you have done the will of God, you might receive the promise" (Hebrews 10:36).

It is very fit that the master should dine before the man. And if he would not like a servant that would think much to stay so long from his meal as is required at his hands for waiting at his master's table, how much more must God dislike the rudeness of our impatient spirits—we that would be set at our meal and have our turn served in the comfort of the promise before God has the honor of our waiting on Him!

Second, this root proceeds from deep ingratitude; and this is a sin odious to God and man. "They soon forgot His works; they waited not for His counsel" (Psalm 106:13). God was not back-handed with His people. It was not so long since He had given them an experiment of His power and truth. He had but newly lent them His hand, and led them dry-shod through a sea, with which they seemed to be much confirmed in their faith (and enlarged in their acknowledgments) when they came safe to shore: "then they believed His words; they sang His praise" (Psalm 106:12).

One would have thought that God's credit now would have gone for a great sum with them ever after. But it proved not so. They dared not trust God with so much as their bill of fare—what they would eat and drink; therefore it is said, "they waited not for His counsel, but lusted exceedingly in the wilderness." That is, they prevented the wisdom and providence of God, which would have provided well for them if they could but have stayed to see how God would have spread their table for them. And why all this haste? "They forgot His works." They had lost the thankful sense of what was past, and therefore could not wait for what was to come.

# THOMAS MANTON

## From the Sermon "The Man of Sin, the Son of Perdition"

The gospel kingdom is a kingdom of light, life, and love. Opposite to light is ignorance and error. Opposite to life is a religion that consists of shows, dead rites, and empty ceremonies. Opposite to love is uncharitableness, malice, and especially hatred of the power of godliness.

Now, where these prevail eminently, there is an opposite kingdom set up to the kingdom of Christ; certainly a falling off from His kingdom. That is to say, where error is taught in opposition to light, where ignorance is counted the mother of devotion, and where people are restrained from the means of knowledge, as if the height of Christian faith and obedience did consist in an implicit believing what the church believes—and where, instead of life, men place their whole religion in superficial rites and ceremonies, and some trifling acts of seeming devotion and exterior mortifications. Instead of love to God and souls, all things are sacrificed to private ambition and forcing consciences with the highest penalties and persecutions to submit to their corruptions. In that place there is a manifest subversion of the interests of Christ's kingdom.

In short, God's witnesses were "slain in that city which spiritually is called Sodom and Egypt, and where our Lord was crucified" (Revelation 11:8). That city which answers to Sodom for impurity, to Egypt for idolatry, and to Jerusalem for persecution of the saints—there may you find the great apostasy. . . .

Sometimes grievous judgments come in this world for the corruptions of religion; but in the world to come, dreadful is the end of apostates. "For if after they have escaped the pollutions of the world through the knowledge of the Lord and Saviour Jesus Christ, they are again entangled therein and overcome, the latter end is worse with them than the beginning; for it had been better for them not to have known the way of righteousness than, after they had known it, to turn from the holy commandment delivered unto them" (2 Peter 2:20–21).

# THOMAS WATSON

## The Godly Man's Picture Drawn
## With a Scripture Pencil

Here is a sharp rebuke to such as are "glittering dross" Christians, who only make a show of godliness—like Michal, who put "an image in the bed" and so deceived Saul's messengers (1 Samuel 19:16). These our Saviour calls "whited sepulchers" (Matthew 23:27). Their beauty is all paint! How many are painted only with the vermilion of a profession, whose seeming luster dazzles the eyes of beholders, but within there is nothing but putrefaction.

Hypocrites are like the swan, which has white feathers but a black skin; or like the lily, which has a fair color but a bad scent. "You have a name that you live, and are dead" (Revelation 3:1). These the apostle Jude compares to "clouds without water" (Jude 12). They claim to be full of the Spirit, but they are empty clouds; their goodness is but a religious cheat. . . .

**Question:** When is a man under the dominion and power of hypocrisy?

**Answer:** There are two signs of its predominance: 1) A squint eye, when one serves God for sinister ends. 2) A good eye, when there is some sin dear to a man, which he cannot part with. These two are as clear signs of a hypocrite as any I know.

Oh, let us take David's candle and lantern, and search for this leaven, and burn it before the Lord. Christian, if you mourn for hypocrisy, yet find this sin so potent that you cannot get the mastery of it, go to Christ. Beg of Him that He would exercise His kingly office in your soul; that He would subdue this sin and put it under the yoke. Beg of Christ to exercise His spiritual surgery upon you. Desire Him to lance your heart and cut out the rotten flesh, and that He would apply the medicine of His blood to heal you of your hypocrisy. Say that prayer of David often: "Let my heart be sound in Your statutes" (Psalm 119:80).

Lord, let me be anything rather than a hypocrite. Two hearts will exclude one from heaven.

# OCTAVIUS WINSLOW

## Words of Divine Comfort

"Yet return again to Me, says the Lord" (Jeremiah 3:1). Could there be a more touching "Thus says the Lord" than this? The voice of Jesus, as it echoed over the mountains and along the valleys of our unregenerate distance from God, seeking and finding and bringing us home, was inexpressibly sweet and irresistibly gracious. But, to hear that same voice—after our many wanderings, our repeated relapses, our sad backslidings—still seeking, still inviting, still imploring us to return, though we had "played the harlot with many lovers," oh, there is music in that voice such as the heavenly minstrelsy must bend their ear to catch.

My soul, you are "bent upon backsliding, even as a backsliding heifer" (Hosea 4:16). Your heart is as a broken bow, treacherous to the arrow fixed upon the string and ready for its flight. Your purposes of good formed, but thwarted; resolutions of amendment made, but broken; plans of usefulness laid, but frustrated; prayers for grace offered, but forgotten; desires and aspirations after God sent up, but, through a deceitful and wicked heart, dissolving into air. Oh! How many and aggravated have your backslidings from God been—backslidings in heart, backslidings in deed, secret wanderings, open wanderings. You have "left your first love," have "forgotten your resting-place." And, straying from the cross, have gone back to walk no more with Jesus.

But, has the Lord, by some gentle movement of His grace, or by some solemn event of His providence, aroused, overtaken, arrested you? Has He set a hedge around your path, that you could not find your lovers, bringing you to reflection, to penitence, to prayer? Then, listen, O my soul, to the gracious words of your first husband: "Yet return again to Me, says the Lord."

Spiritual restoration implies a spiritual re-conversion. In this sense we are to interpret our Lord's words to His fallen apostle Peter: "When you are converted, strengthen your brethren" (Luke 22:32). That is, when you are restored, recovered, turned back again, employ your restored grace—the experience you have derived and the lessons you have learned by your fall and recovery—in strengthening your weak brethren, in warning and exhorting, in restoring and comforting those who have been alike tempted, and have alike fallen.

There is something very expressive, tender, and touching in the word "again." "Yet return again." It sounds like the forgiveness of seventy times seven. Lord! I have wandered from You times without number, "Yet return again." Lord! I have so often sinned and repented, "Yet return again." Lord! You have received and forgiven me more than seventy times seven, "Yet return again." Lord! I come confessing the same sins, deploring the same backslidings, acknowledging the same self-will and base ingratitude—"Yet return again to Me, says the Lord." Then, Lord! I come with weeping, and mourning, and confession, since Your tenderness, grace, and changeless love, and outstretched hand bid me.

"Return to Me." My soul, rest not until you rest in Jesus. Let nothing come between your returning heart and your advancing, loving, forgiving Father. There is no true return of a backsliding believer but that which takes him past his repentance, past his tears, past his confessions, past his amendments, past his minister, and brings him at once close to Christ. There is no healing of the hurt, no binding up of the wound, no cleansing, no peace, no comfort, no joy, but as the soul comes to the blood, and nestles once more within the very heart of Jesus. "Return unto Me!"

# AUTHOR BIOGRAPHIES

### Joseph Alleine (1634–1668)

A Puritan nonconformist pastor in England, Alleine authored several books—most notably *An Alarm to Unconverted Sinners*. He was expelled from the Church of England after the 1662 Act of Uniformity and thereafter was primarily a traveling preacher (with some connection to John Wesley).

### William Ames (1576–1633)

Ames was an English theologian and philosopher who also spent much time in the Netherlands. He authored several books and, later in life, became embroiled in the growing controversy between Calvinists and Arminians.

### William Bates (1625–1699)

The Cambridge-educated Bates had a hand in negotiations that led to the restoration of Charles II, which won him subsequent favor with the crown. Known as the "politest" of the nonconformist ministers, he wrote several books and eventually pastored a Presbyterian church in Hackney.

### Richard Baxter (1615–1691)

Baxter gained great influence as a speaker and author amid English political and theological upheaval. As a public voice before and after the monarchy's restoration, he earned both important connections and troubling adversaries. His later life was marred by persecution; he spent several stints in prison.

### Robert Bolton (1572–1631)

Noted as a scholar, author, and preacher, Bolton was an influential figure in the Church of England throughout his lifetime. He also had five children, four of them daughters. His best-known book is *General Directions for a Comfortable Walking with God.*

### Thomas Brooks (1608–1680)

After several years as a naval chaplain, Brooks was licensed as a pastor and ministered at the Church of St. Thomas the Apostle in London. He was a prodigious author, most notably of various treatises, and like many Puritans he fell under persecution after the 1662 Act of Uniformity.

### John Bunyan (1628–1688)

John Bunyan, an English preacher and author, was incarcerated more than twelve years for his refusal to stop preaching and to attend an Anglican parish. It was during this time that he wrote *The Pilgrim's Progress,* which would become one of the most popular and beloved books of all time.

### Jeremiah Burroughs (1600–1646)

An apprentice of Thomas Hooker, Burroughs became a popular preacher and leading Puritan in London until his death after falling from a horse. A prolific author, he invested much in attempting to forge reconciliation and peace during the intense theological and ideological debates of his time.

### Stephen Charnock (1628–1680)

A graduate of Cambridge, Charnock rose to become the chaplain of

Henry Cromwell, governor of Ireland. Displaced from his position after the restoration of Charles II, he returned to England and served the remainder of his life as a pastor at Crosby Hall in London.

## John Cotton (1585–1652)

The grandfather of Cotton Mather, John Cotton was a leading Puritan minister and professor who often drew hostile attention from the Church of England. Eventually he sailed to America with several other ministers, settled in the Massachusetts Bay Colony, and wrote a catechism called *Milk for Babes*, believed to be the first children's book written by an American.

## Jonathan Edwards (1703–1758)

Born in Connecticut, Jonathan Edwards is recognized as one of America's most important theologians. He also was a renowned revivalist, a missionary to Native Americans, and the author of several famous sermons—most notably "Sinners in the Hands of an Angry God."

## John Flavel (1628–1691)

Ejected from the pulpit for noncomformity with the Church of England, Flavel was well suited as an outlaw preacher, often leading secret meetings and baptisms. Freed to preach publicly after the Glorious Revolution, he spent the final years of his life ministering in his adopted town of Dartmouth.

## Thomas Goodwin (1600–1680)

Nicknamed "The Elder" by his Puritan counterparts, Goodwin served as chaplain to Oliver Cromwell and as president of Magdalen College at Oxford. Settling in London after the restoration of Charles II, he spent his remaining years writing and ministering at Fetter Lane Independent Church.

## Thomas Gouge (1605–1681)

The son of William Gouge, Thomas quickly established himself as a respected nonconformist minister in his own right. He was also extremely generous, choosing to give away more than two-thirds of his annual income to charity.

## William Gouge (1575–1653)

Gouge regularly attended the Westminster Assembly, and in 1644 he was made chairman of the committee chosen to draft the Westminster Confession. A noted author, he spent time in prison after publishing a book called *Calling of the Jews,* which displeased King James I.

## William Gurnall (1617–1679)

Author of *The Christian in Complete Armor,* which remains popular today, Gurnall saw the book go through at least six printings in his lifetime. Unlike many contemporaries, he signed a declaration in support of the 1662 Act of Uniformity.

## Matthew Henry (1662–1714)

A Puritan author, Henry was denied degrees from both Oxford and Cambridge due to his nonconformist beliefs. He made good use of his alternate studies, however, and went on to write one of the most famous biblical commentaries ever recorded.

## Thomas Hooker (1586–1647)

Hooker was a popular and powerful preacher in Chelmsford when he began to experience persecution from the Bishop of London. Eventually forced to flee, he wound up in America—first in Boston, then leading others to found a new community in Hartford, Connecticut.

## Christopher Love (1618–1651)

A prolific author and popular preacher, Love was one of the

Westminster Assembly's youngest members. He was arrested by Cromwell's forces, suspected of raising money for the king's restoration, and denied the charges but was beheaded on Tower Hill, London, at just thirty-three.

### Thomas Manton (1620–1677)
Manton was a highly esteemed author as well as a Puritan clergyman. After the death of Oliver Cromwell, he participated in the Savoy Conference, which resulted in the restoration of Charles II. Like so many others of his day, he was ejected from his post—he'd served at Covent Gardens—because of the Act of Uniformity, and his difficult final years included time in prison.

### Cotton Mather (1663–1728)
Probably the most celebrated of the New England Puritans, Mather spent his life in Boston and entered Harvard at age twelve. He was involved with the Salem Witch Trials; all told he published more than four hundred works.

### William Perkins (1558–1602)
Known as the principal architect of the Puritan movement, Perkins was a noted preacher and lecturer at Great Saint Andrew's Church in Cambridge. He also served as dean of Christ College and was a fellow there for more than a decade. His writings, popular then, have remained influential.

### Samuel Rutherford (1600–1661)
Rutherford was a Scottish minister and professor who became embroiled in episcopal and political controversies. He was a beloved pastor, preacher, and author, but his defense of Calvinism and arguments for limiting the divine right of kings resulted in several instances of persecution.

### Richard Sibbes (1577–1635)

Sibbes was a respected theologian and early leader of the Puritan movement. Unlike some of his contemporaries, he was adept at avoiding intense controversies and maintaining peaceful relationships. He authored several books, including *The Bruised Reed.*

### Thomas Watson (1620–1686)

A kind of outlaw preacher, Watson was among the ministers imprisoned in 1651 for a plot to restore the monarchy during the rule of Oliver Cromwell. Upon his freedom, he became a prolific author and served as co-pastor with Stephen Charnock at Crosby Hall in Bishopsgate.

### Octavius Winslow (1808–1878)

Winslow, a contemporary of Charles Spurgeon, was a popular speaker who also ministered in America. The eighth surviving child of his parents (thus his name), he was a descendant of Edward Winslow, who sailed on the *Mayflower.* He preached at the Metropolitan Tabernacle's opening in 1861.

# EXCERPTS TAKEN FROM . . .

**Joseph Alleine**
*An Alarm to the Unconverted*
*A Sure Guide to Heaven*
*The Gospel in a Map*

**William Ames**
*Baptism*
*Contentment*
*Sanctification*
*The Manner of Worship*

**William Bates**
*From the Sermon "How Men Are Said to Be the Sons of God"*
*The Danger of Prosperity*
*The Great Duty of Resignation*

**Richard Baxter**
*A Call to the Unconverted to Turn and Live*
*The Practical Works of Richard Baxter*
*The Reformed Pastor*
*The Saint's Everlasting Rest*

**Robert Bolton**
*Heart Surgery*

**Thomas Brooks**
*Apples of Gold*
*A String of Pearls*
*A Word in Season to Suffering Saints*
*The Golden Key to Open Hidden Treasures*
*The Unsearchable Riches of Christ*

John Bunyan

*A Discourse Touching Prayer*
*An Exposition of the First Chapters of*
    *Genesis*
*From the Sermon "The Barren Fig Tree"*
*Grace Abounding to the Chief of Sinners*

Jeremiah Burroughs

*Christ Is All in All*
*Gospel Fear*
*The Incomparable Excellencies and Holi-*
    *ness of God*
*The Rare Jewel of Christian Contentment*

Stephen Charnock

*Discourse on the Cleansing Virtue of*
    *Christ's Blood*
*Discourse on the Power of God*
*Discourse on the Word, the Instrument of*
    *Regeneration*
*The Necessity of Regeneration*

John Cotton

*A Holy Fear of God and His Judgments*

Jonathan Edwards

*A Treatise Concerning Religious Affections*
*Discourse on Christian Knowledge*
*Discourse on Procrastination*
*Discourse on the Devil*
*Discourse on the Preciousness of Time*
*From the Sermon "Praise, One of the*
    *Chief Employments of Heaven"*
*From the Sermon "Sinners in the Hands*
    *of an Angry God"*
*From the Sermon "The Peace Which*
    *Christ Gives His True Followers"*

John Flavel

*Fountain of Life Opened Up*
*Method of Grace in the Gospel Redemption*
*On Keeping the Heart*
*Pneumatologia: A Treatise on the Soul of*
    *Man*
*The Mystery of Providence*

| | |
|---|---|
| Thomas Goodwin | *From the Sermon "The Vanity of Thoughts"* |
| | *The Riches of God's Love to His Elect* |
| | *The Wisdom of Patience* |
| Thomas Gouge | *A Word to Sinners and a Word to Saints* |
| | *Christian Directions* |
| | *The Christian Householder* |
| | *The Principles of the Christian Religion* |
| | *The Young Man's Guide Through the Wilderness of This World* |
| William Gouge | *Commentary on Hebrews* |
| William Gurnall | *The Christian in Complete Armor* |
| Matthew Henry | *A Method for Prayer* |
| | *A Scripture Catechism in the Method of the Assembly's* |
| | *Discourse on Meekness and Quietness of Spirit* |
| Thomas Hooker | *The Application of Redemption* |
| | *The Christian's Two Chief Lessons* |
| Christopher Love | *A True Map of Man's Miserable State by Nature* |
| | *From His Last Letter to His Wife* |
| | *The Mortification of Sin* |
| | *Two Queries About Hell* |
| | *Weak Measures of Grace in Christians* |
| | *When Is Prayer Heard?* |
| | *Wrath and Mercy* |
| Thomas Manton | *A Treatise on the Life of Faith* |
| | *A Treatise on Self-Denial* |
| | *From the Sermon "Be Not Soon Shaken in Mind"* |

From the Sermon "God's Word in Our
Hearts"
From the Sermon "The Man of Sin, the
Son of Perdition"
From the Sermon "The Scripture Suffi-
cient Without Unwritten Traditions"
Man and Sin

Cotton Mather

From the Sermon "Satisfaction in God"
The Diary of Cotton Mather
The Duties of Children to Their Parents
The Duties of Parents to Their Children
What Must I Do to Be Saved?

William Perkins

Cases of Conscience
The Art of Prophesying
The Order of Salvation and Damnation

Samuel Rutherford

Fourteen Communion Sermons
From a Letter to the Lady Cardoness
From a Letter to Lady Kenmure
From the Sermon "Crying Unto Jesus"
The Trial and Triumph of Faith

Richard Sibbes

Divine Meditations
The Bruised Reed
The Complete Works of Richard Sibbes

Thomas Watson

A Divine Cordial
Body of Divinity
The Beatitudes
The Doctrine of Repentance
The Godly Man's Picture Drawn With a
Scripture Pencil

Octavius Winslow

Evening Thoughts
Morning Thoughts

*None Like Christ*
*The Atonement*
*The Titles of Christ*
*Words of Divine Comfort*

# AUTHOR INDEX

**James Stuart Bell** is a Christian publishing veteran and the owner of Whitestone Communications, a literary development agency. He is the editor of many story collections including the CUP OF COMFORT, LIFE SAVORS, and EXTRAORDINARY ANSWERS TO PRAYER series and the coauthor of numerous books in THE COMPLETE IDIOT'S GUIDE series. He and his family live in West Chicago, Illinois.